TRANSFORMING RELATIONSHIPS FOR HIGH PERFORMANCE

The Power of Relational Coordination

JODY HOFFER GITTELL

STANFORD BUSINESS BOOKS

An Imprint of Stanford University Press
Stanford, California

Stanford University Press
Stanford, California

© 2016 by the Board of Trustees of the Leland Stanford Junior University. All
rights reserved.

No part of this book may be reproduced or transmitted in any form or by any
means, electronic or mechanical, including photocopying and recording, or in
any information storage or retrieval system without the prior written permission
of Stanford University Press.

Special discounts for bulk quantities of Stanford Business Books are available to
corporations, professional associations, and other organizations. For details and
discount information, contact the special sales department of Stanford University Press. Tel: (650) 736-1782, Fax: (650) 725-3457

Printed in the United States of America on acid-free, archival-quality paper

Library of Congress Cataloging-in-Publication Data

Names: Gittell, Jody Hoffer, author.
Title: Transforming relationships for high performance : the power of relational
    coordination / Jody Hoffer Gittell.
Description: Stanford, California : Stanford Business Books, an imprint of Stan-
    ford University Press, 2016. | Includes bibliographical references and index.
Identifiers: LCCN 2015050233 | ISBN 9780804787017 (cloth : alk. paper) | ISBN
    9780804797047 (electronic)
Subjects: LCSH: Organizational change. | Interpersonal relations. |
    Organizational behavior.
Classification: LCC HD58.8 .G575 2016 | DDC 658.4/06—dc23
LC record available at http://lccn.loc.gov/2015050233

Typeset by Newgen in 10.5/15 Minion

CONTENTS

PREFACE

As I began to observe organizational change in real time, I found many surprises. For example, I realized that something needs to happen for people to have different, more productive conversations, to be able to get past the barriers of "you're in this role and I'm in this role, and I can't say what I think," and open up that path of communication to create new relational dynamics. Another surprise was seeing people take the network measure of relational coordination that I had invented as a research tool and use it instead as a mirror to provide feedback and to notice "Oh, look, this isn't good communication between us and this other group. We thought it was, but it wasn't." It was as if they were using the measure as a boundary object, observing together what was going on, then giving themselves and each other permission to communicate and relate in different ways.

The cases presented in this book demonstrate the Relational Model of Organizational Change in action; they show that transformed relationships are at the heart of sustainable positive change. This model took shape in early 2011, when Ed Schein invited Amy Edmondson and me to regular meetings in his living room overlooking the Charles River and the Boston Museum of Science. Over the course of several months, he demonstrated what it means to create a relational space—a space in which it is safe to admit what you don't know and to learn from others—not so easily accomplished among academics, who tend to have a fair amount of ego! My major insight from these conversations was that organizational change does not start with the adoption of new structures, as my previous work had argued. Rather, it starts with participants changing their patterns of relationships just as they change the way they do the work. Structures cannot be overlooked—indeed, they are essential for supporting and sustaining those new patterns. But by themselves they cannot create those new patterns. Sustainable change is likely to require relational and work process interventions, accompanied by structural interventions. These conversations prompted me to observe change agents in action and helped me to notice new things.

In this book, you will meet change agents—such as Tony Suchman, Marjorie Godfrey, Curt Lindberg, Carsten Hornstrup, Diane Rawlins, Kim DeMacedo, and their colleagues and clients—who turned the Relational Model of Organizational Change into a living, breathing reality. You will see how theory meets reality and helps to transform it, and vice versa: how reality meets theory and helps to transform it. Our journey takes place amid tremendous performance pressures we are facing in our world today—pressures that require a relational response.

ACKNOWLEDGMENTS

Transforming Relationships for High Performance would not have been possible without the generosity and openness of many change agents in many organizations—especially Group Health, Varde Municipality, Dartmouth-Hitchcock, and Billings Clinic. There were others as well. In 2011, a series of influential individuals, most of whom I had not known before, approached me one by one with the idea that relational coordination could provide practical insights for organizational change. They included Tony Suchman of Relationship Centered Health Care; Dale Collins Vidal and Marjorie Godfrey of Dartmouth-Hitchcock; Ken Milne, Nancy Whitelaw, and Margaret Nish of Salus Global; Thomas Huber of Kaiser Permanente; Gene Beyt of Indiana University Health; Kathryn McDonald of Stanford Health Policy; and Deborah Ancona, John Carroll, and Edgar Schein of MIT Sloan School of Management.

I thank these individuals for inspiring me to establish the Relational Coordination Research Collaborative, an international network of scholars and practitioners headquartered in the Heller School of Brandeis University, and for serving in many cases as its original board members. I thank the colleagues who have staffed the Collaborative with me—Joanne Beswick, Megan Cunniff, Debbie DeWolfe, and Lynn Garvin—and those who have led the spin-off we created to better serve clients around the world—Saleema Moore, Michael Noce, and Stan Wallack of Relational Coordination Analytics.

As always, I thank my family for providing me with inspiration and support throughout the long process of researching and writing this book. In this book, more than my previous ones, they have contributed their insights as well. Ross Gittell provides a macroperspective through his work on building human capital and social capital for economic development. Our youngest, Grace Hoffer Gittell, provides a microperspective, with her reflections on creating change through personal example. Our oldest, Rose Hoffer Gittell, links micro and macro relational patterns through her study of neuroscience and macroeconomics. My parents, John and Shirley Hoffer, have role modeled relational coordination in their daily lives ever since I can remember. All of their perspectives have informed this book, particularly the concluding chapter.

Now I invite you to read on, to become inspired by the many change agents you will meet, and to inform your own journey of creating positive relational change.

TRANSFORMING RELATIONSHIPS

FOR HIGH PERFORMANCE

PART ONE   RELATIONSHIPS AND PERFORMANCE

We begin our journey in Part I by identifying the need for a relational response to the performance pressures we face in today's dynamic and uncertain world. When faced with these pressures, organizations often undermine quality to achieve efficiency, or undermine worker outcomes to achieve customer or shareholder outcomes. These are *low-road* approaches. However, evidence suggests that *high-road* approaches, which seek to achieve better outcomes for all parties, have been more successful in the manufacturing and service sectors. To take the high road requires a different approach—a fundamental transformation of relationships among co-workers, between workers and their customers, and between workers and their leaders.

I introduce the concept of *relational coordination* among co-workers, explaining how this process drives a wide range of performance outcomes, from quality and efficiency to worker and client engagement to learning and innovation. I show how these dynamics look when workers partner with their customers in a process called *relational coproduction*. Finally, I show how leaders support these dynamics using a process called *relational leadership*.

This section closes as I reveal how these three dynamics are supported—or undermined—by the organizational structures we rely on every day to get things done. The bottom line is that real change requires us not only to transform our organizational dynamics but also to redesign many of our existing support structures at work.

1 MEETING PERFORMANCE PRESSURES WITH A RELATIONAL RESPONSE

Organizations in virtually every industry are facing pressures to do more with less. Whether these pressures come from customers, supply chain partners, shareholders, policy makers, or regulators, organizations are compelled to provide better, higher quality outcomes, more rapidly and at lower costs. Although these performance pressures are now widespread, it was the manufacturing sector that faced them first, in the form of lower cost, higher quality competition from abroad. In response, manufacturers either moved operations overseas or invested domestically in smarter, more efficient methods of production through better coordination among frontline workers, their leaders, their supply partners, and their customers.[1]

More recently, the service sector has faced these same performance pressures, as competitive forces have loomed large in industries from airlines to banking to trucking, from food services to consulting, from engineering to legal services, and more. These industries have been forced to transform radically in many cases, choosing between low-road strategies that rely on the reduction of wages and working conditions, and high-road strategies that rely on investments in smarter, more efficient methods of delivery enabled by better coordination among key stakeholders.[2]

Now these performance pressures have finally penetrated the healthcare, education, and human services sectors, sectors that until recent years were somewhat protected from competition. Budgetary crises around the globe—with underlying causes that include aging populations, the growth of chronic illness, educational institutions struggling to meet changing demands, failing public infrastructures, and the natural environment under stress—have brought these performance pressures home to roost. Meanwhile, younger generations are seeking more balanced lives, with more satisfying work environments and fewer hours spent at work, so it is not likely that we will be able to solve these challenges simply by working harder and longer.

In this book, I argue that the intense performance pressures we are facing will require organizational transformations similar to those achieved earlier in the manufacturing and service sectors, but on a larger, more comprehensive scale.

CHOOSING THE HIGH ROAD

As always, when facing performance pressures, there are critical choices to be made—namely, will we pursue low-road strategies that rely primarily on the reduction of wages and the degradation of working conditions? Or will we instead pursue the high-road strategies that produce positive outcomes for a broader range of stakeholders?[3] These approaches have been called many names, including *mutual gains* and *high-road, win-win,* or *integrative solutions.*[4]

One thing is clear. High-road strategies are fundamentally relational, powered by high-quality connections across key stakeholders.[5] Why? High-road strategies require stakeholders to create new value and share it fairly. To do this, human capital is only half the story—it is through social capital that human capital is combined and leveraged for maximum impact.[6] Thus the primary focus in this book is on relational coordination: coordinating work through high-quality communication, supported by relationships of shared goals, shared knowledge, and mutual respect. High-road strategies are fundamentally relational because the worker skills and knowledge so central to these strategies need to be connected through relationships in order to create value. Without relationships, worker skills and knowledge are like disconnected icebergs of expertise floating in the sea.

RELATIONAL COORDINATION

Relational coordination is a powerful way to connect worker skills and knowledge to create value and make high-road or win-win solutions possible. Relational coordination is simply the patterns of communicating and relating through which workers integrate their tasks into a whole. In the early 1990s, I "discovered" relational coordination while conducting research on the flight departure process, as I later documented in *The Southwest Airlines Way*. Airlines carry out the flight departure process hundreds of times daily, in dozens of locations. The success or failure of the flight departure process can make or break an airline's efficiency and its reputation for reliability. Between the arrival of a plane and its next departure, a highly interdependent set of tasks is performed, in the face of uncertainty and time constraints, by workers in twelve distinct roles—pilots, flight attendants, mechanics, gate agents, ticketing agents, ramp agents, baggage transfer agents, aircraft cleaners, caterers, fuelers, freight agents, and operations agents, as illustrated in Figure 1.1.

As the airline industry became more competitive following deregulation in the late 1970s, coordinating this work process became one of the keys to competitive success. I found that efficiency and quality performance outcomes—

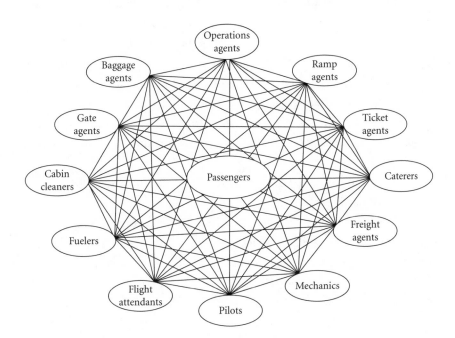

FIGURE 1.1   Flight departures: a coordination challenge
SOURCE: J. H. Gittell, *The Southwest Airlines Way: Using the Power of Relationships to Achieve High Performance* (New York: McGraw-Hill, 2003).

turnaround times, employee productivity, on-time performance, customer satisfaction, baggage handling—were all powerfully influenced by the strength or weakness of relational coordination among workers.[7] Since then, a wide range of quality and efficiency outcomes for relational coordination have been documented across many industries, as we will see in Chapter 2. The strength of relational coordination clearly matters for achieving performance under pressure.

BEYOND RELATIONAL COORDINATION

But the performance pressures we face today cannot be addressed by workers alone, even when they partner closely across functional, organizational, and sectoral boundaries. We also need to coordinate more closely with our customers. Customers are capable of doing important work, particularly with support from skilled workers. This is called coproduction, and we have seen evidence of this emerging trend in many industries. Consider the work that airline passengers now do without thinking twice, such as booking their own flights, and the work that banking and retail customers increasingly do, such as managing their own accounts and completing transactions without staff support, enabled by technology. Some of the most effective companies are turning work over to their customers, even connecting customers with each other to create value, whether by sharing information or creating communities of support, or both.[8]

When we fail to engage our customers and treat them instead as passive recipients of our expertise, we are missing an opportunity to create value and thus to respond to the very performance pressures we are facing. When we extend relationships of shared goals, shared knowledge, and mutual respect to include our customers, we are engaging in *relational coproduction*.

Relational coordination needs the full support of leaders as well—leaders who understand and respect the complexity of the work that their employees carry out every day. When I began to study flight departures, I interviewed Bob Baker, vice president of operations at American Airlines, who explained, "This is one of the most complex things we do every day, and most people here at headquarters don't realize that." Baker had risen to his leadership position having started as a ramp manager on the frontline. Many of his colleagues in top management at American lacked his deep understanding and respect for the work carried out on the ground. During CEO Robert Crandall's tenure, that lack of respect was often reciprocated, and the gulf between top management and frontline workers grew larger, leaving many mid-level managers stranded in between.

This scenario was in stark contrast to what I found at American Airlines' high-performing counterpart, Southwest Airlines, located next door in the same city of Dallas, Texas. At Southwest, leaders, including the CEO, tended to be highly attentive to the importance of frontline workers. A Southwest pilot explained:

> Herb Kelleher is not your average CEO. He really cares to let people know he cares . . . He sets the example of respect for everyone. All are important. Treat each other with the same respect as our customers. So people are happy . . . I can call [our CEO] today . . . He listens to everybody. He's unbelievable when it comes to personal etiquette. If you've got a problem, he cares.

The Southwest CEO was exhibiting *relational leadership*.

We will learn how all three relational dynamics—relational coordination, relational coproduction, and relational leadership—work together to drive high performance. And they are mutually supporting. Figure 1.2 shows that relational coordination among co-workers enables them to more effectively

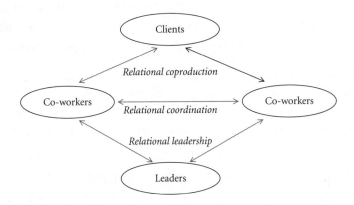

FIGURE 1.2   The three relational dynamics

engage in relational coproduction with the clients they serve. To do so, workers must be supported by leaders who practice relational leadership, developing reciprocal relationships of shared goals, shared knowledge, and mutual respect throughout the organization. While none of these three relational dynamics are rocket science, they run counter to the bureaucratic legacy we have inherited.

GETTING FROM HERE TO THERE: A RELATIONAL MODEL OF ORGANIZATIONAL CHANGE

Pressure for change comes when our task demands change in ways that require us to engage in new relationship patterns in order to coordinate our work. Pressure for change also comes when an industry becomes more competitive, making coordination more relevant to the success or survival of the organization. In industries facing disruptive change—for example, the auto industry in the 1980s, the airline industry in the 1990s, and the healthcare industry right now—both happen simultaneously. Changing task demands call for higher levels of relational coordination, and at the same time, increased competition makes relational coordination more critical for survival. As a clinical nurse specialist pointed out, "Miscommunication between the physician and the nurse is common because so many things are happening so quickly. But because patients are in and out so quickly [due to pressure from the payers], it's even more important to communicate well." At the same time, a physician at a nearby hospital reflected, "The communication line wasn't there. We thought it was, but it wasn't. We talk to nurses every day, but we aren't really communicating." Down the street, at a competing health system, a physician lamented:

> We're all being held with a gun to our heads, that if you continue doing things the way we did things, we are going to be a nonentity . . . You can't lose a million dollars a week and survive . . . And we're frustrated . . . We don't get the time with the patients that we once got . . . It's not a happy place for us. But if you don't make the changes, you're going to be doing catering.[9]

We need a model of change that helps us to understand how structures and relationships interact to support new ways of coordinating work in the face of changing task demands—and how they can be intentionally redesigned for this purpose. Some would argue that the high performance work systems model offered in *The Southwest Airlines Way* and *High Performance Healthcare* already meets this need. That model shows how organizational structures can either weaken or support relational coordination, thereby influencing performance outcomes, particularly when work is highly interdependent, uncertain, and time constrained.

But while that model was helpful for thinking about organization design, it was not helpful for understanding the process of change—how we get from here to there. As most of us know from personal experience, relationships emerge in ways that are not entirely predictable. Relationships among large numbers of people are therefore difficult to change in an intentional way, and even more difficult to *sustain* in an intentional way. How can we move beyond the bureaucratic legacy we have inherited to achieve a high-performing relational alternative and keep it flourishing over time?

Drawing on research across multiple disciplines and change efforts, this book proposes the Relational Model of Organizational Change, which combines three types of interventions. *Relational interventions* are needed to disrupt and transform existing relationship patterns. These relational interventions are best carried out along with *work process interventions*, using methods such as quality improvement or lean to ensure that the newly formed relationship patterns are embedded in the work itself, not disconnected from it. Finally, *structural interventions* are needed to support and sustain these new relationship patterns over time by embedding them in new roles, replacing the traditional bureaucratic structures that serve to undermine them. Together, these interventions support high levels of relational coordination, coproduction, and leadership. Although these three types of intervention are all relatively common, they are more often treated as alternatives to one another, rather than as complements. As a result, they are rarely combined in an intentional way to create and sustain positive change.

OBSTACLES TO TRANSFORMATION

People around the world have asked whether strong unions are positive or negative for relational coordination. In the United States in particular, many people have been enculturated to believe that unions have a negative impact, a bias I experienced firsthand when I was studying the airline industry. I learned quickly, however, that the highest performing airline in my study, Southwest Airlines, was also the most highly unionized. An additional study conducted by myself and colleagues, which looked across the industry over fifteen years, showed that unionization had a positive effect on productivity as well as on workers' earnings. But what had a greater impact on a firm's performance was the quality of the labor-management relationship, a relationship that varies between organizations and over time, and that requires thoughtful efforts to develop and sustain.[10]

Why is it so challenging to learn new ways to coordinate? In short, the new relationship patterns that are required often disrupt our sense of professional identity—even personal identity. This is particularly true when coordination is required between roles that in the past were not expected to coordinate. Our personal and professional identities are shaped primarily by our interactions with others, as visionary thinker Mary Parker Follett described in the 1920s and 1930s. Thus, when the need arises to coordinate more closely across boundaries with others who are different from ourselves, our identities are disrupted.[11] To make matters worse, the new relationship patterns may disrupt our existing, taken-for-granted, often invisible patterns of privilege and power. When new demands disrupt both identity and power, we can expect a painful period of adjustment for individuals, professions, occupations, organizations, and industries, with many defensive reactions and false starts.

Consider an organization whose fragmented relationships, reinforced by siloed bureaucratic structures, are no longer well suited to the demands of a task. The existing relationship patterns tend to self-replicate over time, reinforced by the existing structures, inhibiting the organization's ability to adapt to the new demands. For example, we may hire people for their individual expertise, with little regard for their ability to coordinate with colleagues, customers, and leaders. We may then train, measure, and reward them—and design their jobs, meetings, protocols, and information systems—in ways that further reinforce their fragmented patterns of interaction. This dynamic explains the difficulty that organizations have faced when attempting to transition from traditional bureaucracies to more cross-functional organizational forms.

In sum, I have seen five obstacles that organizations must confront when building relational coordination, coproduction, and leadership.

1. Workers who don't engage in teamwork with their colleagues in other functions or with their customers because it threatens their power or sense of identity

2. Clients who don't engage in teamwork with workers because it requires them to take greater accountability for outcomes, and to play a more active role

3. Leaders who don't support teamwork among their workers and don't collaborate with their workers because it threatens their power or sense of identity

4. Change agents who don't engage in teamwork with each other because it threatens their power or sense of identity

5. Organizational structures that reinforce all of these silos

The good news is that all of these can be overcome. In this book, we will learn from organizations that are struggling against these obstacles and succeeding in their efforts to overcome them.

THIS BOOK

In Chapter 2 we will explore relational coordination and its performance outcomes more deeply. In Chapter 3 we will extend relational coordination to incorporate customers and citizens into the dynamic, creating relational coproduction. In Chapter 4 we explore relational leadership, looking at the leadership approaches that are supportive of relational coordination and relational coproduction. In Chapter 5 we will come to understand how organizational structures can be redesigned to *support and sustain* relational coordination, coproduction, and leadership by embedding reciprocal relationships into the roles of participants, going beyond individual personalities and the question of "who likes whom."

In Part II, we get to the heart of the transformation challenge. We learn about the Relational Model of Organizational Change and why it is not sufficient to change how we relate to one another, and why it is not sufficient to redesign the old structures that reinforce counterproductive behaviors. Rather, we need to do both. We see this model in action as we follow the real-time journeys of four organizations and witness the challenges, setbacks, and triumphs they and their change agents are experiencing.

Distilling the lessons from these four stories, Part III offers a set of tools to implement effective change in your organization by carrying out the three basic types of intervention—relational interventions, work process interventions, and structural interventions—needed to transform relationships among co-workers, customers, and leaders.

One of the most influential lessons I have learned in this journey has come from the change agents I have met along the way. That lesson is simple— we need to practice relational coordination to achieve relational coordination. There are no shortcuts. Simply put, there can be no organizational transformation—or social transformation—without personal transformation. As Mahatma Gandhi said, "We must be the change we wish to see in the world." This simple lesson has profound implications for our personal as well as our professional lives, and for our families and friends, as well as our communities. In the concluding chapter, we return to this lesson and ask what it means for creating positive change in our personal lives, our organizations, and our society more broadly.

2 HOW RELATIONAL COORDINATION DRIVES HIGH PERFORMANCE

Although relational coordination seems idealistic, it is also extremely practical. Organizations need well-functioning relationships that cut across silos, enabling workers to get things done in a timely way without wasting effort or resources. Personal relationships alone cannot achieve this. We need relationships that are embedded into roles that allow people to coordinate effectively regardless of the individuals they are working with. Embedding relationships into roles is all the more essential when coordinating across an extended supply network that includes people who do not and cannot all know each other personally.

Relational coordination, the capacity for high-quality communicating and relating for the purpose of task integration, can help to meet this challenge. In this chapter we explore what relational coordination is and how it departs from traditional bureaucracy. We will also find out *how* and *why* relational coordination drives critical performance outcomes under conditions of task interdependence, uncertainty, and time constraints.

Relational coordination is straightforward. It is simply coordinating work through relationships of shared goals, shared knowledge, and mutual respect. Together, these relational dimensions foster communication that is sufficiently frequent, timely, accurate, and focused on problem solving rather than blaming. Knowing what others contribute to the overall process enables participants to communicate in a way that is conscious of who needs to know what, why, and with what degree of urgency. Shared goals increase participants' motivation to engage in high-quality communication and the likelihood that they will resort to problem-solving communication rather than

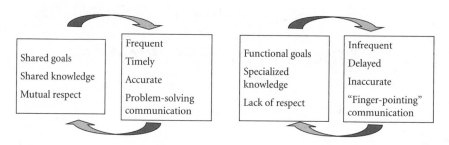

FIGURE 2.1   The seven dimensions of relational coordination

blaming when problems arise or new information emerges. Mutual respect increases the likelihood that participants will be receptive to input from their colleagues in other functions, irrespective of their relative status. Figure 2.1 shows the seven dimensions of relational coordination and how they reinforce one another.

As we learned in the last chapter, coordinating flight departures is challenging due to the wide array of functions involved and due to the rapid changes in operational parameters that cause information to become inaccurate, unavailable, or obsolete. Of the nine sites whose operations I studied, all aimed to get passengers to their destinations on time safely, with their bags, and satisfied with their experience, and to do so efficiently. This required coordination among the twelve key functions involved in flight departures and with airport personnel, air traffic control, and colleagues at the airports where passengers and cargo were coming from and going to. According to a frontline employee, "If everyone is trying to do their own thing, it's not going to work."

At each site, employees were well trained in the sense of knowing their own jobs well. But their capacity to coordinate with each other varied dramatically. At some sites, workers described coordination with colleagues in other functions as occurring through communication that was sufficiently frequent, timely, accurate, and focused on problem solving rather than blaming. In other sites, workers described communication that was insufficiently frequent, often delayed and inaccurate, and focused on blaming rather than problem solving when things went wrong. Workers described their own specific functional goals without reference to a broader set of shared goals, a reliance on their own specialized knowledge without the benefit of systems knowledge, and a perceived a lack of respect for their work from other groups.

When I measured these dimensions using a brief network survey that would become known as the Relational Coordination Survey (RC Survey), I found that these dimensions varied significantly across the sites I had studied. I also found that the communicating and relating dimensions were highly correlated with each other, reflecting the mutually reinforcing dynamics among them, so I created an index of what would become known as "relational coordination." When I added this index to a set of risk-adjusted equations, relational coordination turned out to be a highly significant predictor of the quality and efficiency outcomes that the airlines were trying to achieve every day. Figure 2.2 shows a graphical summary of the results, where the quality/efficiency performance index is an equally weighted average of risk-adjusted turnaround time at the gate, full-time employees per passenger enplaned, customer complaints per million passengers enplaned, lost bags per thousand passengers enplaned, and percentage of flights that arrived late.

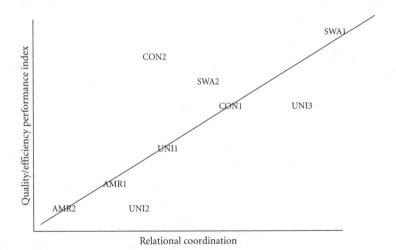

FIGURE 2.2   Relational coordination as a driver of flight departure performance
SOURCE: Adapted from J. H. Gittell, *High Performance Healthcare: Using the Power of Relationships to Achieve Quality, Efficiency and Resilience* (New York: McGraw-Hill, 2009).
NOTE: AMR, American Airlines; CON, Continental Airlines; SWA, Southwest Airlines; UNI, United Airlines.

BEYOND FLIGHT DEPARTURES: RELATIONAL
COORDINATION OF PATIENT CARE

Once I discovered relational coordination in flight departures, I began to see it in other contexts, even when I entered the hospital during the study to have my first baby. My nurses seemed to be coordinating quite well with each other. As multiple nurses came and went from my room, they carried out their tasks in a way that indicated awareness of and alignment with each other's tasks. I was impressed and asked if they had been working on coordination. "Oh, yes, we've been doing Total Quality Management and it's working really well," I was told. But when I asked where my doctor was, the response was, "Oh, we don't know. They don't tell us anything." As with the airlines, relational coordination ties *within* workgroups seemed to be stronger than the ones *between* workgroups.

Soon afterward, when my dissertation was complete and I had graduated from the Massachusetts Institute of Technology (MIT), I became a professor and designed a nine-hospital study of surgical patients to see whether relational coordination might be relevant beyond flight departures. I chose to focus on the care of patients who had undergone joint-replacement surgery because a fairly good predictive model already existed for their outcomes. I was fortunate to gain access to employee and patient data of the orthopedic surgery departments of nine hospitals with high volumes of joint-replacement patients—four in Boston, three in New York City, and two in Dallas. I learned quickly that the healthcare industry, like the airlines, faced growing pressure to achieve better-quality outcomes at lower costs. It was not clear how long hospitals could continue with business as usual, as payment reform had been repeatedly stalled and then reinvigorated. But it was evident that the existing high-cost, mediocre quality-of-care model needed to be transformed, and many of the people I met were worried about the prospects.

My initial interviews suggested that relational coordination might indeed play a role in patient care. Dr. Clem Sledge, long-time chief of orthopedics at the Brigham and Women's Hospital in Boston, explained, "The communication line just wasn't there. We thought it was, but it wasn't. We talk to nurses all the time, but we aren't really communicating." Across town, at the

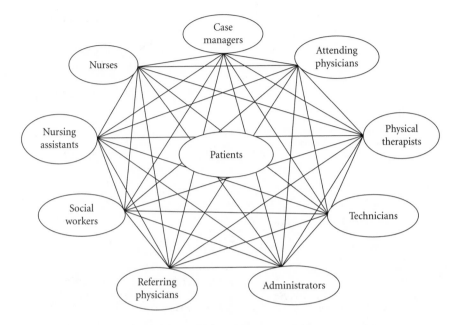

FIGURE 2.3   Patient care: a coordination challenge

SOURCE: J. H. Gittell, *High Performance Healthcare: Using the Power of Relationships to Achieve Quality, Efficiency and Resilience* (New York: McGraw-Hill, 2009).

Massachusetts General Hospital, a clinical nurse specialist elaborated, "Miscommunication between the physician and the nurse is common because so many things are happening so quickly. But because our patients are in and out so quickly, it's even more important to communicate well." The relational map shown in Figure 2.3 shows some of the key parties involved in coordinating patient care.

After an intense data collection effort involving nearly nine hundred patients and more than three hundred care providers, I found that the strength of relational coordination among surgeons, nurses, physical therapists, social workers, and case managers predicted shorter lengths of hospital stays, higher satisfaction; and better clinical outcomes for patients, measured in terms of reduced joint pain and increased functioning six weeks after surgery, controlling for patient characteristics. Figure 2.4 provides a graphical summary of the results, where the quality/efficiency performance index is an equally weighted

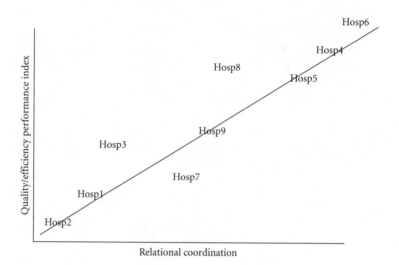

FIGURE 2.4   Relational coordination as a driver of patient care performance
SOURCE: Adapted from J. H. Gittell, *High Performance Healthcare: Using the Power of Relationships to Achieve Quality, Efficiency and Resilience* (New York: McGraw-Hill, 2009).

average of risk-adjusted length of stay, patient satisfaction, postoperative pain, and postoperative functioning.[1]

What was going on here? Why was coordination such a challenge among people who were well-trained and, for the most part, highly committed to their professional goal of providing excellent patient care? More recently, I had the opportunity to interview an obstetrical leader, Bill Mundle of Windsor Regional Health Center, who described how communication can break down over time:

> If you have the perception that every time you come and tell me something I discard it or don't pay attention to it, then, eventually, you're going to say, "What's the sense in talking to this doctor because he doesn't respect what I have to say?" And so, if you have, let's say an anesthesiologist, or an obstetrician, or a midwife, who tends to be a little bit less attentive or harder to get ahold of, if you just assume at the outset that I can never get ahold of so and so, then sometimes you don't follow through with the communication that you should. Like, you might not say, "Hey doc, I'm really worried about this baby and I need you to see it."

So even when it is safe to speak up, people may stop doing so over time if they feel that others are not listening. This is not just a doctor-nurse dynamic. Mundle explained:

> It's like, "Why waste my effort?" This can happen at all levels . . . Even as medical director of obstetrics, I can't make Dr. Jones come urgently, because I'm not in charge of the anesthesiology department. So all I can do is call Dr. Jones. I can write in the record, I asked the nurses to call Dr. Jones at 9:50. And I can write in the record: 9:55, paged Dr. Jones again. What you really need is the anesthesiologist but you can't make that happen.
>
> There's a process for addressing problems afterward, but there's no authority. And it's the same with the nurses as with me. They can't make me come and see the patient right now. They can call me, they can call me again, but there's nothing they can physically do. Same with me; if I say "we need to check her blood pressure every ten minutes," I can have the conversation and I can write it down, but I can't physically make the nurse do it.

Regardless of the industry we work in, these dynamics are all too familiar. One impediment to effective communication is a perceived lack of respect: if you are not listening to me, I feel disrespected and will stop communicating with you over time. Another is a lack of shared goals: if my goal is to complete my functional tasks, rather than to achieve a healthy birth, that decreases my chance of communicating well. Another is a lack of shared knowledge: if I do not understand your work, I may not understand how dependent you are on a timely response from me, or even what constitutes a timely response for you. Each participant operates in his or her own bubble, following directives from above without being adequately responsive to colleagues in other functions.

MOVING BEYOND OUR BUREAUCRATIC LEGACY

In traditional bureaucracy, whose legacy we have inherited, coordination is exercised primarily at the level of top management, which keeps frontline workers divided within their areas of expertise and unaware of the larger picture.[2] Mary Parker Follett recognized that in traditional bureaucratic organizations, the functional division of responsibility tends to overshadow the sense that each participant is responsible for the whole. Referring issues up the chain of command for resolution is not sufficient, she argued, because it ignores the process of reciprocal interrelating through which people come to understand, and to act effectively upon, the world around them. "When you have a purely up and down the line system of management . . . ," Follett writes, "you lose all the advantage of the first-hand contact, that backwards and forwards, that process of reciprocal modification."[3]

One of bureaucracy's fundamental flaws is its disruption of the intersubjective cognitive process through which participants gain an understanding of a situation and the ability to respond to it holistically.[4] Follett argued that effective coordination requires systems thinking, a sharing and integration of knowledge itself. She distinguished between treating coordination as an *additive total* and treating it as a *relational total*, meaning that relational coordination is not a process of adding up all the factors in a situation but, rather, a process of understanding their interpenetration or interdependence.

> My first principle, coordination as the reciprocal relating of all factors in a situation, shows us just what this process of coordination actually is, shows us the nature of unity . . . This sort of reciprocal relating, this interpenetration of every part by every other part and again by every other part as it has been permeated by all, should be the goal of all attempts at coordination, a goal, of course, never wholly reached.[5]

Scholars after Follett largely ignored her work and took a very different approach. These scholars identified the conditions that favored relational coordination, such as uncertainty and interdependence, but they sought to *minimize* them, favoring a more mechanistic, bureaucratic mode of organization that was assumed to be simpler and more cost-effective. To minimize the need for relational coordination, organizations were advised to build buffer inventories, which permitted each task to proceed independently from other tasks and to be robust in the face of unpredicted changes that might occur in other task areas or in the external environment. Inserting buffers to reduce reciprocal task interdependence minimized the need for direct relationships between workers, and enabled the bureaucratic form of coordination to survive.[6]

However, in the increasingly competitive, high-velocity, unpredictable environment of the 1970s and beyond, buffers came to be recognized as antithetical to quality and efficiency and were removed in the name of just-in-time production.[7] A range of innovations emerged to address the resulting coordination challenges, many of them emphasizing direct coordination among frontline workers. If frontline workers were strategically positioned at the interface between the organization and a high-velocity environment, rather than treated as operatives merely responding to orders from above, then coordination could occur at the frontline level as well as at higher ones. An information-processing approach emerged that shifted the weight of attention to relational forms of coordination and demonstrated their increasing usefulness under these conditions.[8]

Today's performance challenges call for this kind of coordination—coordination with sufficient bandwidth to manage, not only the interdependence of tasks, but also the interdependence of the people who perform them. Traditional management science viewed task interdependence as a complicating factor to be minimized, a view perhaps driven by a desire to keep workers divided and subservient by keeping their tasks independent of each other.[9] Regardless of the motivation, bureaucracy has left a powerful legacy for organizations. Relational forms of coordination have remained the exception rather than the norm. While interdependence has grown, our understanding of relational forms of coordination remains seriously underdeveloped relative to our need for them, thanks to the bureaucratic legacy we have inherited. In other words, we still have a great deal to learn!

QUALITY, SAFETY, EFFICIENCY, AND FINANCIAL OUTCOMES OF RELATIONAL COORDINATION

From the first two studies in airlines and hospitals, we have seen evidence that relational coordination matters for quality and efficiency performance. But these are just two studies. What else have we learned about the effects of relational coordination on performance? Researchers continue to ask this question in many settings, including education, accounting, consulting, pharmaceuticals, criminal justice, and more, and in over twenty countries. As we shall see, relational coordination is associated with a wide range of performance outcomes, primarily positive ones. When relational coordination is strong, interdependencies between tasks are managed with fewer delays, errors, and redundancies, resulting in improved quality and efficiency, greater engagement by customers, and better outcomes for workers. The conditions under which relational coordination is effective are intrinsic to settings in which workers with specialized skills deliver services via ad hoc work teams that need to coordinate with each other—and the client—in both planned and unplanned ways.

Quality and Safety Outcomes of Relational Coordination[10]

- Reduced customer complaints in airlines ($p < 0.001$)
- Increased on-time performance in airlines ($p < 0.001$)
- Reduced baggage mishandling errors in airlines ($p < 0.001$)
- Increased satisfaction of surgical patients ($p < 0.001$)
- Reduced postoperative pain of surgical patients ($p < 0.05$)
- Increased postoperative functioning of surgical patients ($p < 0.10$)
- Increased trust, confidence in care providers by surgical patients ($p < 0.01$)
- Increased intent to recommend by surgical patients ($p < 0.001$)
- Increased psychological well-being for surgical patients ($p < 0.005$)
- Increased quality of life for nursing home residents ($p < 0.01$)
- Reduced wrong-site surgeries ($p < 0.001$)
- Increased recidivism for offenders released from prison ($p < 0.05$)
- Increased patient satisfaction ($p < 0.01$)
- Reduced family complaints for hospital patients ($p < 0.01$)
- Increased satisfaction of hospital patients ($p < 0.01$)
- Reduced medication errors for hospital patients ($p < 0.01$)
- Reduced hospital acquired infections for hospital patients ($p < 0.01$)
- Reduced fall-related injuries for hospital patients ($p < 0.05$)
- Increased well-being of chronic care patients ($p < 0.001$)
- Increased integrated care delivery to elderly hospital patients ($p < 0.05$)

- Increased internal audit effectiveness (qualitative)
- Increased internal audit effectiveness ($p < 0.005$)
- Increased satisfaction of pneumonia patients ($p < 0.001$)
- Increased satisfaction of organ-transplant patients ($p < 0.001$)
- Increased satisfaction of cardiovascular patients ($p < 0.01$)
- No effect on satisfaction of vaginal-birth patients or joint-replacement patients
- Increased quality of chronic care delivery ($p < 0.001$)
- No effect on acute admissions or readmissions for primary care patients
- No effect on ED visits for primary care patients
- Increased satisfaction with care delivered by community health workers ($p < 0.001$)
- Increased staff-perceived quality of care ($p < 0.01$)
- Increased patient well-being, cross-sectionally and over time ($p < 0.001$)
- Increased curricular coherence as perceived by university faculty (qualitative)
- Increase student performance on university exams (qualitative)
- Increased percent of asthma patients with action plans ($p < 0.01$)
- Reduced hospitalization for heart-failure patients ($p < 0.001$)
- Increased ED visits for heart-failure patients ($p < 0.01$)
- Increased product development quality in pharmacy sector ($p < 0.001$)
- Improved on-time performance in pharmacy sector ($p < 0.001$)

Efficiency and Financial Outcomes of Relational Coordination[11]
- Reduced turnaround time of aircraft ($p < 0.001$)
- Increased employee productivity in airlines ($p < 0.001$)
- Reduced length of stay for surgical patients ($p < 0.001$)
- Reduced length of stay for medical patients ($p < 0.001$)
- Reduced total cost of hospital care ($p < 0.005$)

- Increased length of stay for hospital patients ($p < 0.10$)
- Increased overall staff productivity ($p < 0.05$), no impact on physician productivity
- Reduced inpatient and outpatient costs of chronic care ($p < 0.001$)
- Increased workforce productivity in manufacturing sector ($p < 0.01$)
- Increased operating profits in manufacturing sector ($p < 0.01$)
- Increased perceived firm competitiveness in manufacturing sector ($p < 0.01$)
- Increased growth in deposits in banking sector ($p < 0.05$)
- Increased growth in advances in banking sector ($p < 0.01$)
- Increased growth in profitability in banking sector ($p < 0.01$)
- Improved cost performance in pharmacy sector ($p < 0.001$)

We have all been in the position of a client whose personal input makes the difference between a successful outcome and a failed outcome but whose role is often not appreciated, respected, or acknowledged by the professionals we work with. Researchers have found that high levels of relational coordination between co-workers—and with clients—increase the clients' ability to carry out their tasks. We will learn much more about this dynamic in Chapter 3.

Client Engagement Outcomes of Relational Coordination[12]
- Increased family readiness to engage in caregiving ($p < 0.001$)
- Increased family engagement with teachers in early childhood education (qualitative)
- Increased family engagement in evaluation of drug-exposed infant ($p < 0.001$)
- Increased family engagement in enrollment of drug-exposed infant ($p < 0.001$)
- Increased family retention of drug-exposed infant ($p < 0.001$)
- Reduced parenting stress for parents of autistic child ($p < 0.05$)
- Increased parent ability to care for autistic child ($p < 0.01$)
- Increased parent ability to cope with needs of autistic child ($p < 0.01$)

HOW DOES RELATIONAL COORDINATION
IMPACT WORKERS?

But how about outcomes for workers? For years, I simply assumed that relational coordination would be a good thing for workers, based on my observations of the airlines. In that context, relational coordination seemed to be a win-win proposition for multiple stakeholders—managers, investors, customers, suppliers, and workers. In the workplaces where I found the highest scores on relational coordination, workers seemed happier with their work and more proficient in carrying out their tasks. In fact, one reason I was so excited about relational coordination was that it seemed to be a more productive *and* satisfying way to work. But some colleagues argued that this might not be true: workers might have to work harder to achieve relational coordination or might find the new expectations to be burdensome, and as a result, might experience greater stress and burnout.

Why make assumptions about something that is so critically important? Researchers have begun to systematically assess the impact of relational coordination on workers. Across industries, we are seeing evidence that workers who experience higher relational coordination report better outcomes, including greater job satisfaction, less burnout, more proactive behavior, greater engagement, and greater use of competence in their work. These findings have been remarkably consistent across a wide array of workers, and across the spectrum of power and privilege.

Worker Outcomes of Relational Coordination[13]

- Increased job satisfaction ($p < 0.001$, $p < 0.01$)
- Stronger shared mental models ($p < 0.001$)
- Increased proactive work behaviors ($p < 0.001$)
- Increased engagement in work ($p < 0.005$)
- Increased career satisfaction ($p < 0.01$)
- Increased professional efficacy ($p < 0.01$)
- Reduced burnout / emotional exhaustion ($p < 0.01$)
- Increased confidence in collaboration ($p < 0.001$)

- Increased sense of social support ($p < 0.001$)

- Increased involvement in work ($p > 0.01$)

- Increased satisfaction with work ($p < 0.05$)

- Increased sense of competence ($p < 0.05$)

- Increase use of competence ($p < 0.10$)

- Increased motivation, productivity, identification with organizational values ($p < 0.01$)

- Reduced information asymmetry ($p < 0.001$)

- Increased equity ($p < 0.001$)

- Increased resource contribution ($p < 0.05$)

- Increased dual commitment ($p < 0.001$)

RELATIONAL COORDINATION INCREASES ADAPTIVE CAPACITY

Taking all of the previous results together, we can see quite clearly that relational coordination helps to strengthen the day-to-day operational capacity of organizations, as well as outcomes for workers at all levels. But in a dynamic environment, this is not enough. Organizations and their workers need to be constantly learning and innovating—therefore adaptive capacity is also needed.

Interestingly, relational coordination plays a role in fostering adaptive capacity. Much organizational innovation cuts across boundaries, so that when participants are aware of what the other parts of the organization do and of the interdependencies among the parts, they can more easily see the opportunities that exist for innovation. They can more easily develop and implement innovative ideas when they are engaged in timely, problem-solving communication with colleagues throughout the organization. The high-quality relationships found in relational coordination can help to boost psychological safety among participants, reducing identity threat and the loss of face that come with learning new things, thus increasing the potential for learning and innovation.

High levels of relational coordination also predict greater worker satisfaction *with the work of colleagues in lower-status positions*. This finding may not seem like a big deal, but it is. The status hierarchy found in many industries means that people tend to look down on the work done by the colleagues who fall below them. For example, pilots are thought to look down on flight attendants, who look down on customer service agents, who look down on ramp agents, who look down on cabin cleaners, and so on. Similarly, physicians are thought to look down on nurses, who look down on therapists, who look down on social workers, and so on. This status hierarchy often extends across organizations as well: in the healthcare industry, for example, acute care carries the highest status and pay, followed by rehabilitation, then by primary care, then by nursing home care, with home- and community-based care at the very bottom of the pecking order.

This professional pecking order creates a serious dilemma as we come to recognize the need for more community-based care to respond effectively to the growing pressures for increased quality and efficiency. One nursing professor explained the problem, "Our nursing students feel like they have failed us if they don't get placed in acute care—but that's not where they are needed most!" A study of chronic care in the Netherlands found that high levels of relational coordination among nurses, physicians, therapists, and other healthcare professionals predicted higher satisfaction by these professionals with the work carried out by their colleagues, the community health nurses.[14]

Relational coordination has the potential to lower the status boundaries that divide workers, thus removing one major obstacle to the innovations that are needed to move whole industries to higher levels of performance. Perhaps for the same reasons, we are also seeing evidence that workers are more creative and innovative when they are connected to each other through relational coordination. They are more likely to innovate, create new knowledge, learn from each other and from their failures, and to feel sufficient psychological safety to do so, when they have high levels of relational coordination with each other. These developments are very promising indeed, given the need for system change in many industries to meet increasing pressures for performance.

Learning and Innovation Outcomes of Relational Coordination[15]

- Increased psychological safety ($p < 0.001$)
- Increased learning from failures ($p < 0.01$)
- Increased reciprocal learning ($p < 0.01$)

- Increased innovation ($p < 0.001$)

- Increased collaborative knowledge creation ($p < 0.001$)

Taken together, the evidence suggests that relational coordination creates everyday operational capacity in the form of quality, safety, efficiency, and financial outcomes but also a more engaged partnership role for both clients and workers, and greater adaptive capacity in the form of learning and innovation. This is encouraging given the performance challenges we face today.

WHY DOES RELATIONAL COORDINATION WORK?

These findings raise a question: Why does relational coordination contribute in a positive way to this wide range of performance outcomes? Some may not care why—isn't it enough to know the evidence and implement it accordingly? Not at all. If we don't know *why* something works, we will not be well equipped to implement it effectively.

So why does relational coordination work? The most compelling answer, in my view, is one suggested by Follett. Follett argued that relationships are the fundamental building blocks of human identity. "Reality is in the relating," argued Follett, "in the activity between." When we consider "the total situation," we come face to face with the "possible reciprocal influence of the subject and object." Through this reciprocal influence, or what she calls a "circular response," "we are creating each other all the time."[16] Similarly, theologian Martin Buber argued that the self is, by necessity, always constructed as a "self-in-relation," because we are defined through our relationships with other subjects. Buber's argument challenged the foundations of Western ontology, in essence replacing "I think, therefore I am" with "I relate, therefore I am."[17]

As the founder of modern psychology, Sigmund Freud also treated relationships as the fundamental starting point. He treated the broken relationship as the starting point for the human condition, however, arguing that "a primary separation [of infant from mother], arising from disappointment and fueled by rage, creates a self whose relations with others or 'objects' must then be protected by rules, a morality that contains this explosive potential." He points to an urge toward union with others and calls it "altruism," a return, in a more limited way, to the "oceanic feeling" that is left behind on the path to moral development. Connection thus appears to be central to civilized life.[18]

Jean Baker Miller transformed the psychology of human development by questioning the dominant view that healthy human development occurs primarily through individuation and separation. This view is rooted in the male experience, she argued, and either ignores the female experience or interprets it as an anomaly or as failure to fully develop. The prototypical developmental path when considered from the standpoint of the female experience is growth through connection, rather than through separation. The traditional, one-sided view of development ignores the fact that we are socially embedded. In other words, becoming an individual occurs through mutual recognition with other human subjects. Human life itself is possible only through connection with others, starting at birth. We are therefore relational by nature.[19]

How does the relational nature of human identity influence the coordination of work? Just as our identities are created in relationship with each other, so is our work most effectively coordinated in relationship with each other. If human identity is relational, then relational coordination is, quite simply, an expression of our nature as human beings.

Consistent with this view, Jane Dutton and Emily Heaphy defined a high-quality connection as one that is life giving, and a low-quality connection as one that is life depleting. High-quality connections take many forms, but they have in common a keen awareness of and attunement to the needs of the other, and thus are energizing to the individuals involved in them. The energizing nature of high-quality connections comes from the recognition and validation of one's self by others. High-quality connections serve as an endogenous resource for accomplishing work and for creating resilience in the face of stress. These high-quality connections tend to create a positive cycle that is generative of other high-quality connections, just as low-quality connections tend to create a negative cycle that is generative of other low-quality connections.[20]

Although the division of labor is a powerful source of efficiency and productivity, it becomes highly inefficient—and a source of alienation—when we fail to relationally coordinate between areas of expertise.[21] In a landmark study of engineering work, Joyce Fletcher found that relational practices were a key driver of successful performance outcomes, but that these practices tended to be overlooked in favor of individual heroics that were dysfunctional from a systems perspective. Despite the importance of relational practices for achieving high performance, they were "disappeared" from the organizational discourse because they were seen as women's work and as unworthy of recognition or respect.[22]

Relationships can overcome this fragmentation by creating more holistic social identities in place of the fragmented identities that lead people to reject their connections with others. Collective identity at work depends on the recognition by each participant that his or her role is connected to and valued by the other participants. Relational coordination enables us, as workers, to see how our tasks connect to each other's tasks. This systems perspective encourages a greater responsiveness to others, building operating capacity and adaptive capacity for organizations, as well as a more engaging way to work.

SUMMING UP

We have seen that relational coordination is a simple yet powerful process that drives both operational and adaptive capacity. We have also explored the underlying reasons why relational coordination works. The most powerful reason is that relational coordination creates more holistic social identities in place of the fragmented identities that lead us to reject our connections with one another. As a result, it gets directly at the heart of the power and status dynamics that separate us from others and prevent us from coordinating our work. These power and status dynamics also make us rigid in the face of organizational change, given the risk that organizational change will disrupt the power and status dynamics on which our identities rest, helping to explain the well-known threat-rigidity response.[23] Relational coordination promotes collaborative knowledge creation and innovation, helping us to respond more fluidly to everyday performance pressures and unexpected events. Now let's take the process of relational coordination among co-workers and extend it to include clients (Chapter 3) and leaders (Chapter 4).

3 ENGAGING CLIENTS IN RELATIONAL COPRODUCTION

Many people find the concept of relational coordination to be intuitively appealing, and the empirical evidence for its impact on performance to be compelling. But some have asked, What about customers? Shouldn't organizations extend relational coordination beyond co-workers to include their customers? Are customers merely passive recipients of services, or should they be involved in the process in a more integral way? I first heard this question when I presented my research many years ago. Graduate students in the audience were intrigued by the concept of relational coordination but wanted to know why patients were not part of the team. I explained that patients were "outputs" or "recipients" of relational coordination, not participants in it. In retrospect, of course, the students were right.

Organizations have for decades been outsourcing work to their customers as part of a trend toward engaging them as coproducers. The concept emerged in the public sector as a way to avoid passivity on the part of citizens and to enrich their own human potential.[1] Some of the earliest examples of coproduction were consumer cooperatives, along with citizen participation, in public education, in charter schools, and in coproducing local public goods such as safety and community well-being through neighborhood associations and municipalities.[2]

Coproduction by citizens was followed by coproduction in the commercial service sector—via online travel booking, automated teller machines, and online banking.[3] Coproduction is now ubiquitous in the retail sector, where customers search for and purchase items online, often without reflecting on the fact that the work they are doing used to be carried out by retail workers.

In professional service contexts, clients are increasingly engaged as partners in solving problems and creating value. Coproduction now extends beyond service delivery to include collaborative knowledge creation of new products or services, as noted by Venkat Ramaswamy and Kerimcan Ozcan in *The Co-Creation Paradigm*.[4]

One powerful motivation behind this trend is to reduce costs and increase efficiency by enabling unpaid clients to take on more of the work themselves. But another motivation is coproduction's potential to improve quality outcomes to the extent that clients can customize services to meet their own unique needs. Barbara Gutek and her colleagues established through extensive research in the 1990s that clients can add significant value—increased quality and reduced costs—by sharing their knowledge with service providers.[5]

Coproduction is based on the simple recognition that many outcomes cannot be fully achieved without the partnership of the clients themselves. Many important outcomes require high levels of commitment, and even behavior change, on the part of clients. By becoming empowered coproducers rather than passive recipients of services, clients can help to ensure that desired outcomes are achieved. Professor Anne Douglass, for example, found that relational coproduction between parents and early childhood teachers led to greater attentiveness to the child by both parents and teachers in the context of the school, the family, and community life. Together, parents and teachers were able to determine, from a more holistic perspective, what to do and how best to do it. One outcome of parent-teacher coproduction was greater parent engagement and better parenting, benefiting children in ways that no teacher, no matter how excellent, could accomplish on his or her own.[6] As the executive director of a child welfare agency pointed out,

> In the past, agencies like ours minimized the role of family. We could forget to include them or we could even see them as part of the problem. Now we realize that no matter how much we care about the child, we are not his or her family. Rather than try to replace families, we support them as they rebuild themselves. This requires mutual respect and the development of shared goals."[7]

The work begins when professionals invite clients into the process. Douglass explains:

One teacher at Oak Street shared her belief, rooted in her many years of teaching, that parents were not interested in being involved at the childcare program. She reported that, in her experience, parents never participated ... [Then] she invited families to create posters about their family and culture and then to share them with the children. When every family completed and brought in the poster, she described it as "a wakeup call" that parents did in fact want to be involved.

Other teachers shared examples about how readily they had judged parents when children came in hungry or dirty. As one teacher at [one agency] explained, "I think it has had me open my eyes a lot ... It's not that this mom doesn't care" but rather that she needs understanding and support.[8]

Relational coproduction happens when workers and their clients produce desired outcomes together by engaging in high-quality communication supported by relationships of shared goals, shared knowledge, and mutual respect. Rather than workers telling clients what they need, relational coproduction involves reciprocal interrelating between workers and clients regarding what should be done and how best to do it. Although empirical research linking relational coproduction to performance is relatively new, research has found evidence of a positive impact on family well-being and reduced stress for parents of autistic children in the United States, and on greater quality of life for citizens with chronic health conditions throughout the Netherlands.[9]

RELATIONAL COPRODUCTION IS SUPPORTED BY RELATIONAL COORDINATION

No matter how well it is carried out, however, *relational coproduction with clients* does not replace the need for *relational coordination among co-workers*. In fact, co-workers with high levels of relational coordination among themselves are better prepared to build relational coproduction with their clients. Conversely, co-workers lacking in relational coordination are often poorly equipped to engage in coproduction with their clients, as this quote from a frustrated family member illustrates:

I'm in Arizona, she's in Florida, and I'm working long distance to orchestrate home care, oxygen ... the works. There were all sorts of scheduling snafus and miscommunication. The doctor's office sent in the referral for home care, and then closed for the day. It ended up taking thirty-six hours to get home care. Meanwhile my mother—who is very high risk for a frightening and expensive hospitalization—was kept waiting.

The first time we assessed relational coproduction between family members and professional care providers, we found that the strength of their ties—shared goals; shared knowledge; mutual respect; and timely, accurate, problem-solving communication—positively impacted the patient's clinical outcomes and psychological well-being. We found that these positive outcomes were achieved due to family members' greater willingness and ability to engage in caregiving as a result of their stronger ties with the care team at every stage of the care process.[10]

But we found that these family members were also taking on a huge burden—coproducing care in a system with very low levels of relational coordination. Given the lack of relational coordination among the other care providers, family members ended up playing the integrator role in a highly fragmented delivery system. Across hundreds of surgical patients, only the informal caregivers reported strong ties with care providers at every stage of care. Primary care physicians—who were *intended* to be the integrators in the system—reported no strong ties with any role in acute, rehab, or home care.

In effect, family members as informal caregivers were playing the role of system integrators by default rather than by design. Their relational coproduction was not being supported by relational coordination among the other care providers. Given the benefits for patients of the informal caregiver role in coproduction—better clinical outcomes and greater psychological well-being—the solution is not to get rid of this role. Rather, the solution is to better support it by increasing relational coordination among the other participants. In this way, clients can become part of a well-functioning team, instead of trying to make up for the *absence* of a well-functioning team.[11]

If we focus only on partnering with our clients without partnering with others who are involved with our clients, we unintentionally place the burden on clients. Clients must then coordinate a fragmented service delivery process on their own. This default solution results in a heavy burden for clients and also highly inequitable outcomes given the different resources clients are able to bring to the process. Rather, we should build high levels of relational co-ordination among service providers, then invite clients to work with the team to achieve their desired outcomes.

RELATIONAL COPRODUCTION CAN ALSO DRIVE RELATIONAL COORDINATION

Customers can also become the driving force for greater relational coordination when they begin to engage in relational coproduction, making demands that cut across organizational silos, thus forcing co-workers to expand their normal communication patterns with each other to meet customer needs. In the retail banking sector, Loïc Plé found that customers influenced relational coordination among frontline service workers with whom they interacted. As customers began dealing with workers in several different divisions because of the multiple options now available for banking transactions—on-line, in person, by phone, and at the automated teller machine, they created a demand for better relational coordination among banking workers.[12]

The banking workers in this study had not perceived a need to coordinate with each other in the past and did not even see their work as interdependent. But as customer coproduction increased, the frequency, accuracy, and emotional intensity of communication increased among the banking workers. The information provided by the customer sometimes obliged call center advisers to contact branch advisers. Plé explained:

> First, customers do not always accept the new rules that result from the existence of the call center. Many of them refuse to give call center advisors the information needed to handle their demands, forcing call center advisors to send a message to the branch. Impatient customers may demand more frequent communications. . . . Sometimes even though we are meeting with the customer, we receive a second message from the call center. The customer has phoned again and told them, "She did not call me back. Is it normal? Can you please give her the message again?" The emotional state of the customer greatly influenced the intensity of communication between employees. A call center advisor explained, "Sometimes, if they have someone who gets worked up, they call and ask us to deal with the customer because the situation is tense."[13]

Plé found that accuracy of communication was the dimension of relational coordination most strongly affected by customer coproduction, because direct communication between channels was mainly rooted in information provided by the customer. "Sometimes the information [we get from our colleagues in the call center] is too brief compared to what we would need to answer the demand of the customer. But the question is, Did the customer really explain everything clearly enough?"[14]

As customer coproduction increased, banking employees began to develop stronger shared knowledge of each other's work, having started from a very low level. As one said, "When the branch advisers first visited the call center, some wondered if they even work[ed] in the same company. It was a total discovery."[15] They also gained respect for each other's work over time. Shared goals suffered, however, as branch employees found that their commissions were being reduced due to competition with call center employees, who were also selling products to customers.

I have seen relational coproduction have a similar impact in universities, creating the need for relational coordination between professors who have traditionally worked in a highly autonomous manner. When students decide they want to combine different programs of study or simply want to integrate their learning so as to apply it in the real world, their professors are faced with a conundrum. Do they continue to teach in their silos, without concern for how their insights fit with the other frameworks their students are learning? Or do they begin to have conversations with one another, even systematic planning sessions, in order to relationally coordinate what they are teaching? Again, we see that customers' decision to become less passive and more proactive in the production process puts pressure on professionals to engage in relational coordination in ways that were not necessary before.[16]

This same dynamic can play out in crisis situations, when relational coordination is sometimes dangerously lacking. Each party on his or her own may overlook the "cries for help" or danger signals of a troubled teenager who is on a path to committing an act of violence. School leaders, teachers, friends, parents, guidance counselors, and local police each see only part of the picture. Even when they suspect trouble, they may fail to engage in relational coordination with the other parties when there is a lack of role clarity or when they have a sense that they should "mind their own business." It may take one or two active parents who are willing to reach out and contact each party separately, in an act of coproduction, to motivate others to develop shared knowledge and problem-solving communication with one another rather than blaming others and seeking to avoid blame.

LACK OF KNOWLEDGE AND ACCOUNTABILITY AS OBSTACLES TO RELATIONAL COPRODUCTION

Despite the obvious advantages, there are multiple obstacles to creating relational coproduction. Even in the relatively straightforward context of banking and travel, there are challenges as people transition from traditional professional/client roles toward relational coproduction. Customers often have insufficient information about how the delivery system works, with its many silos and disjointed areas of expertise. To make matters worse, customers often require critical services with little advance notice or choice—and at the time of greatest need they are likely to be facing emotional, physical, and other stressors that make it even more difficult for them to engage as active coproducers. Clients and their family members may not welcome coproduction and may prefer to play a passive role, refusing to accept responsibility for the work or for the outcomes.

At the same time, professionals may not recognize the integral role that clients play in coproducing outcomes. They may look down on clients as insufficiently knowledgeable. They may not recognize the complexity of the work the client is asked to perform, and may downplay caregiving as a domestic responsibility, especially when the caregivers are women.[17] In the case of troubled children or elderly clients, professionals may prejudge the families as "problems" or obstacles, rather than partners in the delivery process.[18] In addition, professionals may not know how to engage their clients in the coproduction role or see this as their responsibility. According to Richard Wexler of Healthwise, for example, "I've heard physicians say, 'It's up to me to prescribe the medicine, but I shouldn't be held accountable for whether or not the patient takes the medicine.'"

OBJECTIVITY AND EMOTIONAL DETACHMENT
AS OBSTACLES TO RELATIONAL COPRODUCTION

A second obstacle to relational coproduction is the objectivity and emotional detachment professionals are expected to maintain in their relations with clients. The traditional bureaucratic model that we have inherited has long discouraged the use of caring or knowledge of individual circumstances to guide a worker's decisions and actions. Instead the worker's relationship to customers is supposed to be "personally detached . . . strictly objective," and "not moved by personal sympathies."[19]

Indeed, some emotional detachment is necessary. I have walked through an intensive care unit with care providers who were conducting patient rounds, watched as they discussed a young woman who had overdosed, and heard them say that she did not wish to have any family or friends contacted. As I imagined one of my own daughters lying on that bed alone, I began to feel pain and fought back my tears. Meanwhile, the team of experienced care providers made an assessment regarding the next steps for her and moved on to their next patient. Without some emotional detachment, their work simply could not be done in a timely, effective way. They might also become burned out over time and leave their jobs.

But, taken to an extreme, emotional detachment becomes an obstacle to relational coproduction by preventing the perspective taking that is needed for high-quality communication to occur. Without perspective taking, a worker may simply project his or her own values and preferences onto the client, rather than exploring what the client's values and preferences may be and engaging in dialogue to influence the client's decision-making process. The young woman lying in the intensive care unit would, in effect, become a thing rather than a person, and would thus be deprived of the caring that she needs to recover.

PROFESSIONAL AUTONOMY AS AN OBSTACLE
TO RELATIONAL COPRODUCTION

Workers also fear that engaging in coproduction with clients will undermine the professional autonomy they have been trained to value. Traditional professional/client relationships are shaped by professional autonomy and power based on professional expertise. The possibility that clients may have knowledge that enables them to contribute in a fundamental way to the achievement of desired outcomes may not even be considered.[20] Even once we have entered into a relationship with a client, the "orientation towards doing *for* them rather than *with* them" can create a barrier to developing shared goals, shared knowledge, and mutual respect.[21]

Moreover, traditional patterns of behavior are stubbornly rooted and not easily changed—they are passed down by professional communities and embedded in cultural norms. Relational coproduction disrupts the existing pecking order between professionals and clients—it can threaten one's professional identity and thus be deeply unsettling. Teaching students who have been in medical school for just a few months, I have been amazed by how quickly they internalize and act out the assumptions of the professional hierarchy.

A NEW MODEL OF PROFESSIONALISM

Clearly, a new model of professionalism is needed—and one is slowly emerging. According to Paul Adler and colleagues, collaborative professionals are those who "see other professional communities and non-professionals [including customers] as sources of learning and support, rather than interference."[22] In this new model, professionals are engaged in more equal relationships with colleagues and with clients, offering their own expertise and welcoming the expertise of others.

This new model of professionalism recognizes that emotions are a source of valuable data about the individuals and groups whom professionals are expected to serve.[23] While bureaucracy was invented in part to eliminate unfair differences in treatment, differences can be justified and even necessary from a human perspective.[24] Rather than marginalize emotional ways of knowing and connecting with others, relational coproduction therefore requires emotional intelligence. Let's see how this new model of professionalism plays out in practice.

A PROFESSIONAL'S PERSPECTIVE ON COPRODUCTION

Bill Mundle of Windsor Regional Healthcare Center is an obstetrician who is living through a transition from a system based on a paternalistic, authoritarian doctor-patient relationship to one based on collaboration. Mundle explained how his role has changed:

> Now you're not the sole provider anymore, you're really kind of a consultant for the other care providers . . . We are kind of a coach for the patient too. The patient and family are there and they are wanting whatever is best; the nurse and obstetrician are watching things and feeling uncomfortable with the status of mom or baby, or both. And the neonatologist is not wanting anyone delivered basically early or small or sick or anything like that, and those things are often in juxtaposition.
>
> In the end, everyone agrees they want the mom to be well and the baby to be well, but how to get there has many different routes. Not only in the really extreme cases but even in the everyday cases, there are different paths that could be taken.
>
> What really happens is, it's negotiated. I mean, there are always some educational components and you're always trying to allay concerns, which may be real or imagined. And at the same point, you're always trying to kind of keep your eye on the ball, right? So, I mean, the classic conundrum is you have a mom who everyone finally agrees needs to be delivered pre-term, and she's had deliveries before, so from an obstetrical point of view, everyone thinks she should have a normal delivery. The unit needs to be prepared because the baby's very early.

This evolution toward a more collaborative relationship with clients is occurring hand in hand with the development of a more collaborative relationship among members of the care team. In a sense, relational coproduction with the client is enabled by relational coordination among the care team. Mundle continued:

> I think back in the early 90s, there was still some paternalistic medicine. Even when I was a medical student, things were already turning toward more informed choice, rather than "this is what you need," and that kind of stuff. But it's still a struggle, particularly in *this* area of medicine, it's still a struggle when moms come in with complicated birth plans and things like that, when they've made these decisions based on the advice of someone, often, who has little or no training, and they've made all these decisions based on what's usually needed, and not on what's needed specifically in their case.
>
> If we have the opportunity to review things ahead of time, when we're not in the heat of the battle or having the extra pressures of labor, we can go through and say, "These are the unintended consequences of this thing that you said you

absolutely don't want; this is a potential concern." Oftentimes, this can make people a little reflective. If you refuse to let us assess the baby during labor, this is what could happen. You have to kind of accept that, so if you're taking away that ability, then it means that we only have sound and feel.

So it becomes informed decision making because they are understanding not just that they have choices but what are the probabilities and the risks. The difficulty is, lots of times in those circumstances, if you're not delicate with the approach you can induce animosity and that doesn't help anyone on either side. It can affect the outcome.

Clearly, emotional intelligence is a critical skill for workers when engaging in relational coproduction with their clients. Perspective taking means trying to see things from the perspective of your client rather than imposing your own perspective on that client. Relational coproduction requires workers to share their knowledge with their clients while encouraging clients to share theirs.

SHARED DECISION MAKING AS A FORM
OF RELATIONAL COPRODUCTION

This balance is critical for shared decision making, a form of relational co-production that not only addresses how to achieve the goals of treatment, but allows clients to shape what those goals ought to be. According to Richard Wexler at Healthwise:

> The concept of shared decision making first involves recognizing that there is actually a choice, which many patients wouldn't know unless they were told about it, then discussing what the options are, and what the benefits and harms of those options are. After that, the goal is to have the information about the options, benefits, and harms viewed through the lens of what's important to the patient. All this requires a bidirectional flow of information between the clinician and the patient, where the clinician is the expert on the options, and the benefits and po-tential harms of those options, and the patient is the expert on what's important to them. It's by sharing that information in a shared decision-making conversa-tion that shared decision making can occur.

Wexler acknowledges that these steps, though seemingly straightforward, require a culture change affecting both patients and providers, and also a change in the training of clinicians. While progress has been slow by many measures, Wexler argues the current climate is quite favorable for shared decision making.

> There's been a sort of stuttered history of trying to gain traction for this and we think that now is a good time for shared decision making. There's a growing chorus of voices that are advocating for it and we're cautiously optimistic that it will become more the norm about the way important decisions are made.
>
> So much of our work has really been around how to create change within organizations in order to change the nature of the conversations and, more fundamentally, to change the relationships between patients and their providers and their care teams. As we think about how to create change within systems and in individuals, I am guided by a rather simple yet powerful formulation, rooted in motivational interviewing. The motivation for change basically is driven by a felt sense of the importance of that change and the confidence that individuals and organizations have to make that change.
>
> The importance component of the equation ultimately has to be felt by the individual provider, but it can certainly be shaped by organizational culture, perhaps in response to external drivers like the rising volume of the patient voice in wanting to be involved, and the alignment of new incentives as we move away from volume-based reimbursement. If we can get those levers working to promote the importance of shared decision making, then we also need to raise the level of confidence within the organization and felt by the individuals on the care team and by the patients that they can participate together in a shared decision.

Shifts in payment models have been a key external factor encouraging the movement toward shared decision making by removing the pressure on clinicians to provide more care, whether or not it is clearly needed or desired. This shift has helped to address the "importance" factor in the motivation equation. To address the confidence factor, Wexler and colleagues at Healthwise are working to develop simulation tools to teach clinicians the skills to engage with their patients in shared decision making.[25]

HOW LEADERS CAN SUPPORT RELATIONAL COPRODUCTION

Like relational coordination, relational coproduction enables participants to achieve better outcomes more efficiently, and it therefore becomes even more essential as resources become constrained. Some investments are needed to enable relational coproduction to occur in a regular and reliable way. It is not enough to urge workers to look for windows of opportunity to address the personal concerns of their customers[26] or to urge clients to invest significant personal resources to get their needs met in a fragmented system that does not support their efforts. Dedicated resources and support are needed for workers to partner with customers to achieve the outcomes that neither can fully achieve alone.

There is a need for role and goal clarification—and for interventions to develop shared goals, shared knowledge, and mutual respect between workers and their clients. Given the relational nature of coproduction, leaders do not only need to emphasize what services or kinds of information are delivered but how frequently. Leaders should also encourage and support workers' efforts to attend to the relational aspects of their customer interactions.

The high-quality relationships needed for coproduction do not have to be personal one-on-one relationships, however. Customers with an ongoing need for services need an ongoing relationship with an organization, but not necessarily with any particular worker or set of workers.[27] The role of leaders is to align workers' incentives to engage in relational coproduction with each customer, even though they may never see that particular customer again. Even when services are provided by a network of affiliated organizations, workers can achieve relational coproduction with their customers if the affiliated organizations are connected by high levels of relational coordination, supported by incentives that are properly aligned.

Support for relational coproduction is thus needed at the organizational level, the interorganizational level, and even the industry level. The regulations and reimbursement systems in industry environments often constrain workers' ability to engage in relational coproduction with clients.[28] In healthcare, a reimbursement system based on the number of office visits, for example, motivates workers to schedule multiple short visits that don't allow sufficient time for client education or engagement in shared decision making. The same reimbursement scheme may not allow reimbursement for ongoing coaching and support between office visits to promote client coproduction. These obstacles can be addressed by organizations that unite to create change at the industry level and to negotiate alternative payment schemes with payers.

SUMMING UP

We now understand relational coproduction and its potential for organizational transformation as well as the obstacles to adopting it. We have seen that relational coordination among workers helps to support relational coproduction with customers. Our ability to engage in relational coproduction with our customers will depend in part on building relational coordination with others who are working with the same customers. Otherwise, we will be engaged in a tug of war over our customers instead of providing them with a supportive context for partnership. We have also seen that when customers take the initiative to engage in relational coproduction they can reveal a lack of relational coordination among workers and create a compelling need to develop it.

What kind of leadership is most capable of supporting the dynamic processes of relational coordination and coproduction? If relational coordination and coproduction are strategically important for achieving the outcomes needed to succeed in a demanding environment, we need leaders who recognize their value and are able to support their development. This brings us to the challenge of relational leadership.

4 ENGAGING CO-WORKERS IN RELATIONAL LEADERSHIP

Now that we know how relational coordination and coproduction work, the question arises—What is the role of leadership? We know from decades of research that leadership is instrumental in achieving organizational change, whether through the exercise of power or through the exercise of influence. Using influence rather than power requires articulating a vision that others want to achieve. As Nick Turner, president of the Vera Institute of Justice, pointed out, "If the leader is the only one with the vision, there is no vision."[1] Many organizations are now seeking leadership that goes beyond command and control, and beyond the single heroic or charismatic leader, to achieve a broader, more inclusive process.

In this chapter we explore relational leadership as a process of reciprocal interrelating between leaders and those they lead.[2] Relational leadership creates influence in two ways: by developing shared goals, shared knowledge, and mutual respect *with* others—and by developing shared goals, shared knowledge, and mutual respect *among* others.

Though I was unaware of it at the time, my journey toward understanding relational leadership began when I was observing flight departures and discovering relational coordination. At the time, many scholars and practitioners were arguing that to achieve employee empowerment, organizations had to reduce the number of supervisors to prevent them from getting in the way—taking out unnecessary layers of the organization to allow a more direct connection between frontline workers and top management.[3] Relational coordination looked a lot like employee empowerment to me. So I expected there would be less need for supervisors in airlines with high relational coordination and more need for supervisors in airlines with low relational coordination.

But I found the reverse. In fact, I found that having a large number of su-pervisors relative to frontline workers predicted higher performance—better quality, faster aircraft turnaround times, and higher employee productivity—through higher relational coordination among frontline workers.[4] These un-expected findings opened up my eyes and made me ask the question, What could frontline leaders be doing to *support* relational coordination among their co-workers and what would happen if their numbers were drastically reduced?

ARM'S LENGTH LEADERSHIP DRIVEN
BY PUNITIVE METRICS

American Airlines had reduced frontline leaders over the preceding decade as part of a company-wide effort to create a leaner, flatter organization with greater employee empowerment. Because of their large spans of control—33.8 front-line workers per supervisor on average for airport employees—supervisors had little time to carry out supportive functions. Instead of building shared goals with employees, working side by side with them and providing them with coaching and feedback, supervisors spent their limited time communi-cating performance standards and measuring performance.[5]

One typical comment from workers was that their supervisors "only care about delays. Otherwise, the little report card won't look good that week." The concern with delays, however, was not accompanied by supervisory efforts to analyze and engage in problem solving with frontline workers. Instead, the focus was on identifying the workgroup that appeared to be responsible for causing the delay and "pinning the delay" on that group, in order to comply with reporting requirements from headquarters and to pressure workers to improve performance. This reliance on performance measurement allowed for a largely hands-off relationship between supervisors and workers, consis-tent with the small number of supervisors in this airline.

To the extent that supervisors had time to focus on individual workers, they tended to monitor worker compliance with directives. According to one su-pervisor, "We only have time to focus on the bad apples." Nonmanagement "lead agents" were appointed from the frontline employee groups to assist the supervisors in carrying out supervisory functions. The agents' job was to help the supervisor to direct operations, but they were not responsible for providing discipline, leadership, coaching, or feedback to the frontline employees. Because the lead agents were nonmanagement, and did not see themselves as management, they were not well positioned to align the goals of workers with those of the organization.

The supervisors themselves had little opportunity to bridge the management-nonmanagement divide or to participate in frontline work. They had few opportunities to observe the work process directly or to provide coaching and feedback to workers. They had little contact with individual workers, and therefore little opportunity to build the relationships and know-how that would allow them to play a facilitative role. In sum, at American Airlines supervisors' interactions with workers were quite limited, and tended to be replaced by the use of arm's length performance measures.

RELATIONAL LEADERSHIP THROUGH COACHING AND FEEDBACK

At Southwest Airlines, the supervisory span of control was much narrower it was than at American; each supervisor was responsible for only 8.7 direct reports. In addition, the job of the supervisor went beyond the measuring of performance and disciplining of "bad apples" seen at American. Supervisors had managerial authority but also performed frontline work. "Management will always pitch in at crunch time," said a ramp supervisor. "Whatever it takes to get the plane out." Supervisors were observed to take part in frontline work on a regular basis, even highly physical work like baggage handling, and to wear the clothing appropriate to that work. "A supervisor fills in spots when people are on breaks, or when we are short on a zone," said another supervisor. "We make sure all the gates are manned and that everything is running smoothly, working in a timely manner. When agents see the supervisor working consistently, they give more in a crunch. Also, you get their respect by working with them." Working side by side with one's co-workers appeared to be conducive to building shared goals with them, and to developing the legitimacy and knowledge needed to provide effective coaching and feedback.

Frontline leaders at Southwest Airlines were observed to spend more time coaching and giving workers feedback than their counterparts at American.

Coaching and feedback took the form of problem solving and advising, rather than assessing compliance with performance objectives. "If there's a delay, supervisors find out why it happened," said the station manager. "We get ideas on how to do it better next time. If you've got that kind of relationship, then they're not going to be afraid. Say there was a ten-minute delay because freight was excessive. If we're screaming, we won't know why it was late." A ramp manager confirmed this approach:

> We work real hard to remove that barrier so that agents can come in and talk to a supervisor or manager. There's an open-door policy, so when employees have a problem, they know we can work on it together. It's a totally different environment here. We sit and listen. When that person walks away, he'll have self-esteem. I learned this when I came to work the ramp. Even when you did something wrong, they'll ask what happened. You know you screwed up. They'll tell you what you can do so it doesn't happen again. You walk away so upbeat that you work even harder.

There was some monitoring, but the frontline leadership role was not focused on discipline. "If there is a problem, like one person taking a three-hour lunch," said a supervisor, "they take care of that themselves for the most part. Peer pressure works well." Instead, supervisors told me that the people who reported to them were their "internal customers" and that their job was to help them do their jobs better. As one supervisor described her job:

> We are accountable for what the agents do. It is very difficult sometimes, because it's such a family-oriented company. You might feel like a sister to one of the agents, then you have to bring discipline. You have to step back and put the friendship aside and say, 'I don't agree with what you just did.' But the agents are our customers. We are here to help them do their jobs.

In sum, frontline leadership at Southwest Airlines was hands-on and primarily supportive in nature. It was not arm's length—interactions were intense, and performance measures were not used as a substitute for these interactions.

EFFECTIVE LEADERSHIP IS TIME-CONSUMING AND RELATIONSHIP INTENSIVE

As I tried to make sense of these findings, I learned that an earlier generation of organizational scholars—primarily from the human relations school of thought—believed that effective leadership was both time-consuming and re-lationship intensive. According to organizational scholar Douglas McGregor:

> Roles cannot be clarified, mutual agreement concerning the responsibilities of a subordinate's job cannot be reached in a few minutes, nor can appropriate targets be established without a good deal of discussion. It is far quicker to hand a subordinate a position description and to inform him of his objectives for the coming period.[6]

Even the founder of scientific management, Frederick Winslow Taylor, noted, "More than all other causes, the close, intimate cooperation, the constant personal contact between the two sides, will tend to diminish friction and discontent. It is difficult for two people whose interests are the same, and who work side by side in accomplishing the same object all day long to keep up a quarrel."[7]

RELATIONAL LEADERSHIP NEEDED
FOR INTERDEPENDENT WORK

Just as relational coordination is particularly effective for highly interdependent work, relational leadership may also be particularly effective for highly interdependent work. Supporting this argument, empirical studies have consistently found that smaller spans of control are associated with more interdependent work. The benefits of smaller spans of control do not seem to stem from a greater need for coordination by supervisors. Researchers have found no significant increase in supervisory coordinating activities associated with more interdependent work. Instead, they have found that highly interdependent work benefits from an increase in coordination among frontline workers themselves.[8] So what could account for the benefit of narrower spans?

The evidence suggests that narrow spans lead to a more intimate and informal relationship between supervisors and frontline workers, establishing a context in which shared goals can be developed. Such relationships are particularly useful in highly interdependent work, where shared goals make a difference for performance. Narrow spans of control are also important in highly interdependent work processes because of the difficulty of getting useful feedback from the work itself, compared to independent tasks in which feedback emerges from the work in a relatively straightforward way. Supervisors can play a role in helping workers to interpret the outcomes of their work. Others found that consultative leadership, leader behaviors that promote coordination, and leader initiating structure are particularly valuable in the presence of highly interdependent work. Multiple studies in which frontline workers must work interdependently to achieve a task have reported that groups with greater managerial presence performed better than those with greater autonomy.[9]

ANTI-LEADERSHIP ARGUMENTS PRESUME BUREAUCRATIC HIERARCHY

This idea that frontline leaders would have to be "taken out" in order to achieve employee empowerment was based on the assumption of bureaucracy. In bureaucratic organizations, the worker-manager relationship is defined by norms of hierarchy and power-over.[10] The hierarchy is intended to be a "hierarchy without domination," meaning that within each worker's job description there exists a realm of autonomy for that worker, who is thus protected by formal rules from outright domination. By contrast, the pre-bureaucratic organizational form—the clan—was driven by personal relationships and by personal forms of domination. A clan leader could legitimately command workers to do his or her bidding. In a very real sense, therefore, bureaucracy has been an evolutionary improvement over the clan.

Theories of street-level bureaucracy and job crafting confirm that workers do have a degree of autonomy in bureaucratic organizations, giving them some discretion within the confines of their job descriptions and even enabling them to shape their job descriptions. Workers can use this autonomy to withhold work effort. But they can also use it to take actions on behalf of particular customers, or to increase the meaning of the work, or to create personal connections with employees in other departments to get their work done.[11]

Effective use of autonomy is limited, however, when workers lack understanding due to their subordinate positions in the hierarchy and their disconnected role in the horizontal division of labor. Even in a hierarchy without domination, hierarchical leadership undermines relational coordination by keeping workers oriented toward the vertical lines of authority and unable to systematically build shared knowledge and shared goals with their colleagues across reporting lines.[12] No wonder a generation of organizational scholars believed that to achieve employee empowerment, we would have to reduce the presence of leaders!

RELATIONAL LEADERSHIP AS AN ALTERNATIVE TO HIERARCHY

We are beginning to understand that leaders can play a powerful facilitative role in promoting and supporting relational coordination among frontline workers. How? Supporting relational coordination requires reciprocal relationships between workers and managers, in which managers learn from workers' deeper, more focused knowledge of the work, and workers learn from managers' broader contextual knowledge. Both kinds of knowledge are needed in complex organizations, where no one can possibly know everything in depth, and where each level is designed to have a successively deeper focus on the work—with knowledge and appreciation for what others know as well.

Relational leadership is exercised throughout the organization through reciprocal relating across levels. Mary Parker Follett described this type of leadership as "a coordinating of all functions, that is, a collective self-control." Achieving collective self-control, she argued, requires leadership to be distributed throughout the organization, rather than concentrated in a few positions. Follett observed organizations in which "[w]e find responsibility for management shot all through a business [and] some degree of authority all along the line [such that] leadership can be exercised by many people besides the top executive."[13] At the heart of relational leadership is recognizing the authority in each role, based on the knowledge associated with it. Rather than vesting authority in one person over another based on his or her position in the hierarchy, authority is shared.

After Follett, others argued that "the capacity to exercise a relatively high degree of imagination, ingenuity and creativity in the solution of organizational problems is widely, not narrowly, distributed in the population [but] under the conditions of modern industrial life, the intellectual potentialities of the average human being are only partially utilized." To realize these potentialities, leaders have to rely on integration and self-control by workers rather than on external direction and control, with leaders and workers engaging together to determine the goals of the organization and how best to achieve them.[14]

WHAT IS RELATIONAL LEADERSHIP?

Relational leadership creates influence by developing shared goals, shared knowledge, and mutual respect *with* others and by developing shared goals, shared knowledge, and mutual respect *among* others.[15] But how is this different, if at all, from distributed leadership, shared leadership, connective leadership, fluid expertise, and leading through humble inquiry?

Distributed leadership is a form of leadership that is carried out by both formal and informal leaders throughout the organization to facilitate the achievement of organizational objectives. Deborah Ancona and her colleagues have shown that leadership is a form of influence that can be exercised by participants at any level of an organization, and that leaders are most effective when they can inspire others to engage in the responsibilities of leadership, rather than attempt to carry out all leadership responsibilities on their own.[16] Distributed leadership thus requires facilitative leadership behaviors, more so than directive leadership behaviors, and transformative leadership behaviors more so than transactional or passive leadership behaviors. Lending support to this perspective, others have found that supportive supervisory behaviors predict greater frontline worker engagement in shared leadership.[17]

Relational leadership has much in common with the concept of distributed leadership. However, relational leadership does more than draw on the expertise and unique perspectives of participants throughout the organization; it also fosters the integration of their expertise and perspectives. Participants benefit from a more holistic perspective for understanding their own work and making decisions. This holistic perspective provides a mechanism through which they manage their interdependence. Relational leadership is therefore "connective leadership."

> Connective leadership derives its label from its character of connecting individuals not only to their own tasks and ego drives, but also to those of the group

and community that depend upon the accomplishment of mutual goals. It is leadership that connects individuals to others and to others' goals, using a broad spectrum of behavioral strategies. It is leadership that "proceeds from a premise of connection" and a recognition of networks of relationships that bind society in a web of mutual responsibilities.[18]

Relational leadership is clearly a process of co-creation that requires a particular set of skills, as reflected in Joyce Fletcher's concept of "fluid expertise."

> [P]ower and/or expertise shifts from one party to the other, not only over time but in the course of one interaction. This requires two skills. One is a skill in empowering others; an ability to share—in some instances even customizing—one's own reality, skill, knowledge, etc., in ways that made it accessible to others. The other is skill in being empowered: an ability and willingness to step away from the expert role in order to learn from or be influenced by the other.[19]

Willingness to step away from the expert role in order to learn from others is also known as "leading through humble inquiry."[20] When designated leaders demonstrate this willingness, they help to create a safe space in which all participants can set aside their egos in order to connect for a shared purpose. Recall how Ed Schein created this space for himself, Amy Edmondson, and me to put our heads together to create the Relational Model of Organizational Change, as I described in the preface—putting into action the concept of leading through humble inquiry.

Leading through humble inquiry is foundational to the process of relational leadership. Note, however, that leading through humble inquiry does not require one to be humble in the sense of lacking confidence in one's own contributions. On the contrary, leading through humble inquiry requires having the confidence to recognize that one's contributions, however essential, are not sufficient to achieve the desired outcomes given the distribution of relevant expertise and the need for distinct areas of expertise to contribute to a more holistic understanding of the situation.

Relational leaders develop relationships *with* others in a way that serves to foster relationships *among* others, including relationships among co-workers and with their clients. Together, relational coordination, coproduction, and leadership represent ways of working together that transform professionalism away from protecting one's own expertise toward a collaborative generative process with potential benefits for all stakeholders.[21]

CREATING POSITIVE CHANGE: RELATIONAL LEADERSHIP IN ACTION

Let's consider a case in which relational leadership was used to create a collaborative generative process among professionals and with their clients, replacing a more fragmented hierarchical process.[22] Dr. Michele Saysana, now medical director of quality and safety at Riley Hospital for Children, led the adoption of family-centered rounds in 2008. Riley is part of the eighteen-hospital Indiana University Health system, headquartered in Indianapolis, with a presence throughout the state. Saysana explained:

> We used to do rounds very differently. We would round at the bedside, but it was the old internal medicine model. We talked to each other in front of the patient then told them what we were going to do. Definitely not in ways they would understand. Or we would round in a conference room, then we'd go out and see the patients separately, and try to track down the family.

In the new rounds, residents and medical students were asked to present to the family rather than to the attending physician. Presenting to the family changes the dynamics and the language used, in a way that is beneficial yet highly challenging.

> We are not allowed to talk the way we do in the conference room. It is so hard for medical students. It makes them nervous. They are nervous to be presenting to the family anyway, and nervous to be using regular language—they think using medical jargon is a sign of their knowledge. I say no, it tells me even more if you can translate to the patient. It totally throws the students for a loop. Sometimes they even call the patient "the diagnosis." We have to spend time on that. But we let them know that we're like a big safety net. If they get something wrong, I will correct it right there but in a way that's respectful. Then the family, the nurse, the social worker, and the pharmacist all understand the plan of care and hear the same plan of care. They know how we explained it so they can continue to reinforce it after the rounds.
>
> The other thing is that everybody is there, so everybody hears. That's worth its weight in gold. Especially the families who are having a hard time with social

issues—when everybody on the team hears the same thing, that makes it easier for us to all work together as a team.

And with this way of doing rounds we can do a lot of teaching. We can even teach about conflict resolution. We can discuss conflict resolution in a conference room; but we can really role model it in a room with a family. We can teach medical students and residents how to help a family in need. In the room I can teach about communication skills, about relationships, about having difficult conversations, about giving bad news. You'll have to do these every day.

The new way of rounding also called for new patterns of communication between physicians and other members of the care team. As Saysana summed it up, "You have to engage the nurses, ask them what concerns they have about this patient. You have to be intentional about doing it . . . It's not just having the rounds that makes the relationships good between doctors and nurses—it's *how* we do them."

The new process resulted in more accurate and timely communication, enabling hospitals to discharge patients earlier in the day, and with fewer delays. Soon after the implementation of family-centered rounds at Riley, EEGs and MRIs were being completed in 1.73 hours, compared to the 2.15 hours it had taken prior to the rounds. Moreover, 47 percent of patients were being discharged on the first shift, compared with 40 percent of patients prior to family-centered rounds.

Family-centered rounds represented a new collaborative generative process, requiring new skills and a new kind of leadership. The physicians leading the rounds had to engage in relational leadership to enable them to coordinate with their colleagues, their colleagues to coordinate with each other, and everyone to engage with the family in a respectful way to create shared goals and shared knowledge.

Relational leadership was also needed *outside* the family-centered rounds to bring Saysana's colleagues on board. She described a collective effort that relied on positive contagion rather than formal authority, given that she had no formal leadership role at the time; even if she had such a role, it would not have been sufficient to ensure successful adoption of rounds.

I would say, "Come on! Why can't we do this? Why can't we try this?" The formal leader of our service supported it but really encouraged us to have a discussion about it. He did not tell us we had to do it, but instead he really supported us visiting another hospital and figuring out how we could do it . . . And the other medical services were not really interested in doing it. Then our intensive care unit started it. Those who started it were not the chiefs . . . It was not formal, it just kind of spread on its own.

Relational leadership is a process of reciprocal interrelating that requires respectful consideration of resistance as well as agreement from others. Rather than write off the resistance she faced as "resistance to change" or ascribe it to selfish motives, Saysana saw it as containing potentially valuable information about obstacles that deserved respectful consideration and that needed to be addressed.

> The biggest pushback was from the person who is now my biggest advocate. He wanted to know, How are we going to do this? What if the medical student says in front of the family that the child might have cancer? Well they already do, I said, but you don't hear it. He still didn't want to do the rounds in the room, because he felt it would put the students on the spot. In the beginning some of the residents and students didn't really like it. They said it's going to be awkward, take too long. We really had to sell it to them. We told them, "We're going room to room and we're going to do *all* the work together."
>
> The nurses really wanted to do this. Typically, we as physicians make all the big decisions and they have to do all the work. The pushback we got from some of the nurses was "What about these families that want to take up all your time?" I said, "We can come back." But what we find is, we tell the families up front what's going on and then they don't have so many questions later.

RELATIONAL LEADERSHIP SUPPORTS RELATIONAL COORDINATION AND COPRODUCTION

The successful adoption of family-centered rounding at Riley Hospital for Children involved all three forms of reciprocal interrelating. *Relational coordination* was created in the exchange and collaboration across different professions. *Relational coproduction* emerged as these professionals developed shared knowledge and shared goals with the clients themselves. Finally, these new relational patterns were introduced and sustained by a leadership process—*relational leadership*—that embodied and reinforced the same values. As participants experienced a work environment of greater responsiveness and respect, they were able to turn to their colleagues and clients and treat them in the same way.

RELATIONAL LEADERSHIP IS ABOUT CREATING CONNECTION

Relational leadership is clearly about how leaders connect *with others*—both with their peers and with those who report to them—and it's also about how they connect *others with each other*. According to Carsten Hornstrup, consultant and author of *Developing Strategic Relational Leadership*:

> Strategic relational leadership focuses on how the quality of communication and strong relationships—shared knowledge, shared goals and mutual respect—especially between top and middle managers, impacts the ability to effectively implement desired changes. I have personally found three interconnected elements that play a vital role in creating capacity for change.
>
> The first element is engaging in direct dialogues with key stakeholders. Leaders who do this seem to earn more respect and this respect rubs off on the legitimacy on their decisions. The next element is building strategic competence. It attends to the ways that top and middle managers are able to create clarity around expectations about how people should take part in change activities and how their activities promote or prevent cross professional and cross organizational collaboration. What I find is that in cultures where leaders support and promote attention to supporting the success of others—across professions and organizational columns—they create a vital awareness of the larger whole.
>
> The third element is creating engagement in change activities and ownership of the goals of change. It has to do with how people are invited to take part in change activities from decision making to implementation. What seems to be especially important is how critical voices are included or excluded from these processes.[23]

THE NARRATIVE OF THE SINGLE HEROIC LEADER

Although relational leadership is a powerful process with the potential to support high performance, Deborah Ancona of the MIT Leadership Center argues that it's not easy to get it right. Charles Palus of the Center for Creative Leadership argues that "this type of leadership is just a fact of life now. There's more interdependence and this way of leading fits the new reality . . . But it's hard to move culture. It ultimately happens at the front line, and it's the work of leaders to do it."[24]

One of the challenges is to overcome the narrative of the heroic leader, which has been embedded in many cultures over many hundreds of years. Even collective accomplishments, achieved by hundreds of people through many strategic negotiations, are seen as the accomplishments of a single leader; for example, in reporting the development and promotion of a new national policy by the Obama administration, the media tells it as a story of presidential leadership, whether in praise or blame. In place of the heroic leader, we need to embrace the notion of the "incomplete leader," Ancona argues. Incomplete leaders are strong individuals who understand both their strengths and limitations through self-awareness. Under conditions of interdependence, even the smartest person in the room cannot get anything done by him- or herself and cannot know enough to either set the goals or achieve the goals alone.

Nevertheless, strong individuals are still needed for effective relational leadership. As Palus argued, "Strong individuals make strong collectives, and weak individuals make dysfunctional collectives." Instead of abandoning the notion of the heroic leader, perhaps we need to redefine heroic leaders as those who engage the hearts and minds of others to build collective efforts.

DEVELOPING CAPACITY FOR RELATIONAL LEADERSHIP

How do we develop the capacity for this new kind of leadership? First, we must move beyond the idea that leaders are born, and ask instead how we can develop people's capacity to lead. Becoming a collaborative leader requires taking the time to reflect on our own experiences and to develop our own personal narrative, Palus argues. "To participate in leadership, we have to develop. We have to grow up."

Some youth today are rejecting the word "leader," Ancona has observed, due to the work they perceive is involved and due to the negative connotations of leadership. Youth have grown up observing leaders who fumble and get beaten up in today's transparent world, where confidentiality seems impossible to achieve. They see that it is very easy to go from heroic leader to fallen leader. The paradox is that the youth who reject the word "leadership" often demonstrate leadership on issues they are passionate about, according to Ancona. Millennials may not embrace the idea of becoming "the leader" because of its outmoded connotations. But they are very ready to participate in leadership, creating another reason for organizations to move toward distributed leadership.

> Millennials have had a lot of freedom and do not want to step into an organization where they can't [have] that. If we want to attract and retain them, we will have to change. I would rather have people who want to change the world who don't call themselves leaders than people who call themselves leaders but who aren't passionate about changing the world.

SUMMING UP

In this chapter, we have seen the power of leaders to foster relational coordination among colleagues and to foster relational coproduction with clients by role modeling desired behaviors and by coaching and cajoling others to do the same. But no matter how effective leaders are in supporting the development of relational coordination among workers and relational coproduction with clients, there is only so much they can accomplish through personal influence. Another important role of leaders is to support the development of organizational structures that shape behaviors in the firm. Though they are invisible to the eye, these structures shape and support relational dynamics in powerful ways. For relational leaders, this means that in addition to creating connections through personal coaching and role modeling, they must also support the development of constructive relational dynamics through the design of structures.

Organization design does not mean conceptualizing in a vacuum how the organization should function. It does not mean mandating from above how things will be done. Rather, for relational leaders, organization design means promoting structures to support the connections that are needed to carry out the work effectively, particularly when it spans multiple departments or organizations. Let us turn to this topic next.

5 HOW STRUCTURES SUPPORT— OR UNDERMINE—THE THREE RELATIONAL DYNAMICS

Managers and frontline workers often develop relationships that enable them to get their jobs done. But personal ties are not reliable for achieving the performance outcomes that are at stake for their organizations, especially organizations that must deliver promised outcomes to multiple stakeholders, whether or not a particular individual happens to be present. It is not acceptable to succeed or fail depending on who happens to be present on a particular day or who happens to like whom. While studying airlines and healthcare organizations, I learned that structures such as hiring and training, job design, accountability and rewards, protocols, and information systems can help to promote and sustain relational coordination, coproduction, and leadership—or undermine them—depending on how those structures are designed.

In organizations with traditional bureaucratic structures, relationships tend to be strong *within* functions and weak *between* functions, resulting in fragmentation and poor handoffs between workers in distinct functions whose tasks are highly interdependent. Having observed a number of industries in transition, political economist Michael Piore points out:

> The organizational principles involved in Taylorism and Fordism have pushed us to . . . restrict communication among the people responsible for the way in which the different parts are performed . . . They have led us to divide the internal structure of large organizations into a series of functionally distinct divisions as well . . . But from the cognitive perspective, the problem is that it limits the hermeneutic process, the cycle back and forth between parts and wholes, through which cognitive structures evolve.[1]

Even our ability to engage in systems thinking is weakened by bureaucratic structures, he argues. By contrast, organizations with structures that cut across functional silos promote cohesive and systemic ways of thinking and acting. As Piore observed:

> If one looks at innovations in business practice and the critique of existing organizational structures within the management literature, the thrust is in precisely the opposite direction. The attempt is to break down barriers . . . between divisions and departments, and encourage direct, rich and textured communication . . . forcing people who previously operated at arm's length to confront coordination problems directly and resolve them cooperatively.[2]

It may seem that the simplest option is to get rid of the organizational structures that have become obstacles to coordination and ask workers to rely instead on personal relationships to get their work done. Indeed, post-bureaucratic theories tend to argue that to meet the demands of a fast-moving environment, bureaucratic structures should be replaced with informal relationships. Likewise, network scholars tend to see little room for formal structures.[3]

IF RELATIONSHIPS DRIVE PERFORMANCE, WHY DO STRUCTURES MATTER?

But rather than eradicate formal structures, we need to *redesign* them so they can reinforce and strengthen relationships across the boundaries where they tend to be weak.[4] Why go to such trouble? Why is it not enough to get rid of bureaucratic structures that pose obstacles to relational coordination, co-production, and leadership and just allow people to connect with others as needed? The answer is simple though not obvious. We need structures to overcome our tendency toward "homophily"—our tendency to like best those who are similar to ourselves. When left on their own, people tend to build the strongest relationships with those who are most similar to themselves, and the weakest relationships with those who are least similar to themselves.[5] Yet to achieve desired performance outcomes, strong ties are needed where task interdependencies are strongest, often with those whose work is very different from our own due to specialization and the division of labor.

When we rely primarily on personal relationships, we limit the performance potential of our organizations in several important ways. First, we limit the ability to coordinate across differences, limiting the scalability of our organization beyond a homogeneous group of participants.[6] Second, we limit replicability—the ability to keep doing what we are doing—creating a need to continually reinvent the wheel that wastes both time and resources. Third, we limit sustainability as individual participants come and go over time.

When formal structures are in place to connect participants across their differences, individuals can come and go over time and the positive relational dynamics will persist. Patterns of interrelating are embedded in participants' roles so that the culture becomes stronger than any one individual or set of individuals. Indeed, when we look closely at Ed Schein's classic work on organizational culture, we see that the patterns of relationships that define the culture of an organization are supported and sustained by formal structures.[7] In short, the solution is not to get rid of structures but rather to redesign them to support the reciprocal patterns of interrelating that we need to meet performance pressures.

In this chapter, we explore eight organizational structures that support or undermine the three relational dynamics, depending on their design. We start with structures that are informed by human resource management—selection and training, accountability and rewards, conflict resolution, and leadership roles. We then continue on to structures that are informed by operations and information systems management—boundary spanners, meetings, protocols, and information systems. (See Figure 5.1.)

SELECT AND TRAIN FOR TEAMWORK

In traditional bureaucratic organizations, selection and training are highly role-specific, ensuring that all participants have the requisite knowledge, skills, and abilities to do their jobs. But little attention is given to understanding the roles of others, thus creating silos of expertise. Alternatively, selection and training can be designed to go beyond functional expertise. Participants can be selected and trained for teamwork or "relational competence"—the capacity to develop shared goals, shared knowledge, and mutual respect. Relational

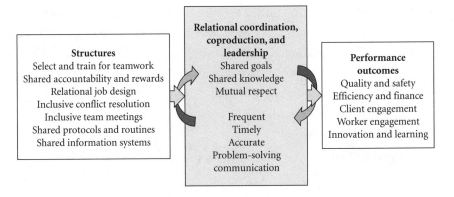

FIGURE 5.1   Relational Model of High Performance

competence involves skills like perspective taking and empathy that are rooted in personal traits but can also be learned.[8] Fluid expertise requires managers and workers to have relational competencies, such as openness to learning from others, enabling them to move back and forth between expert and nonexpert roles.[9]

Selection and training can identify and develop relational competencies.[10] Selection and training can also *elicit* relational competence. Individuals have a range of potential capabilities that can be either elicited or suppressed—for example, we all know people who are not team players at work but who contribute skillfully to their communities outside work. By selecting and training for relational competence, we signal that we expect colleagues to bring their relational capabilities to work, instead of parking them at the door.[11]

Customers can also be selected and trained with an eye to their role as partners in the work process, encouraging them to develop shared goals, shared knowledge, and mutual respect with the workers who serve them as well as with their fellow customers. Southwest Airlines, for example, started this trend in the airline industry by making it clear that customers were expected to play a central role in achieving on-time departures and minimizing turnaround time on the ground by boarding quickly, helping their fellow passengers, and helping to clean the cabin upon arrival—in short, by being attentive to the needs of the overall process. And leaders can be selected for their own relational competence and for their ability to develop it in others. Supervisors, middle managers, and CEOs are often selected for high levels of functional expertise or for their "command personality." But for relational leadership, it is better to find someone who can engage in constructive dialogue with a wide array of internal and external stakeholders and develop the competence of others.

SHARED ACCOUNTABILITY AND REWARDS

Traditional forms of accountability and rewards tend to focus participants on their job-specific goals in order to pinpoint accountability and achieve control. But in doing so, they encourage subgoal optimization—optimizing one's local goal at the expense of the broader goal.[12] By contrast, shared accountability and rewards are designed to connect across all the roles involved in achieving a desired outcome, encouraging participants to focus on problem solving rather than assigning blame. Such an approach reduces finger-pointing and supports the development of shared goals, shared knowledge, and mutual respect across roles.

Shared accountability and rewards also encourage participants to take a broader perspective on their work, paying attention to the quality of the relationships themselves. Organizational experts have suggested ways to align relational work with organizational norms in measurable ways, such as creating measures and rewards for relational work and including relational work in regulatory or reimbursement systems. Performance measures that hold workers, managers, and customers jointly responsible for achieving desired outcomes can encourage the development of shared goals, shared knowledge, and mutual respect. For example, when hospital leaders, support staff, and patients share accountability for the outcomes of care with the clinicians, they are more likely to partner to achieve the desired outcomes.[13] According to one clinical leader:

> We have a couple of different quality improvement processes. One of them we do internally; [it's] nonjudgmental, no names are mentioned. Roles are there but not names. [We ask] is there something that should have been done differently from a management perspective?

But then there's the process that is handled by the patient care team at the hospital. They have less information and expertise, and it seems a little more accusatory. In the end, when things didn't go well, there's an accusation simply based on that fact. Sometimes you need a thick skin, looking at the way this turned out, I wish we had done something differently. There's the notion of shared accountability for the outcome, but the legal system doesn't always support that . . . There's a recognition that everyone has a role to play. But doctors are still seen as the fat cats, so we are the ones that get hit.

Regardless of who is the "fat cat," or the more powerful player on the team, holding one participant accountable for the outcomes of a highly interdependent work process reinforces subgoal optimization, and reinforces a reluctance to share power and coordinate with the rest of the team. To bring about sustainable changes in relational coordination, organizations need to adopt structures of shared accountability, which policy makers can support with changes in the broader legal and policy environment.[14]

This is true for relational coproduction as well. Iora Health is a multifacility primary care model premised on building relational coproduction with patients and supporting it with high levels of relational coordination among members of the healthcare team. To deliver this model of care requires a reimbursement scheme that allows for longer patient visits and ongoing coaching and support for patients between office visits. Iora Health has therefore negotiated alternative payment schemes with individual payers, including private or municipal employers that are financially responsible for the health and wellness of their employees. With these payment schemes, providers are no longer penalized for engaging with patients in relational coproduction but instead are rewarded for patient outcomes.

Traditional structures of accountability also pose a powerful obstacle to relational leadership. Leaders report to their boards, their stockholders, their funders, and their voters. "At the end of the day, the leader is held accountable for the decisions that come from her team," said Melody Barnes, former director of the White House Domestic Policy Council. "This is true in the public sector as well as the private sector." Nick Turner of the Vera Institute for Justice concurred, "At the end of the day I am still accountable as the formal leader. I am the one who bears the risk." There are so many rewards for heroic leadership.

What are the reward structures for collective leadership? "Collective rewards can be designed to reward collective leadership," according to Deborah Ancona of the MIT Leadership Center. "And it's not just financial rewards."

Relational leadership is supported by profit-sharing structures in which accountability for success and failure is shared among participants, as well as by leaders who make a point of consistently communicating the contributions their workers have made to the success of the organization. Leaders at Southwest Airlines appear to do this on a regular basis. A typical news release began with the following statement:

> Southwest Airlines today announced it will contribute approximately $228 million—the largest total dollar amount ever allocated—directly to Employees through its ProfitSharing Plan this year. The payment is an 88 percent increase over last year's contribution of $121 million. Southwest was the first in the industry to offer a ProfitSharing Plan, and this is the Company's 40th consecutive ProfitSharing payment. Through the ProfitSharing Plan, Southwest Employees currently own more than four percent of the Company's outstanding shares.
>
> "The hard work of our People, and the pride and ownership they take in providing outstanding Customer Service, has resulted in four decades of profitability. Our People earned this reward, tirelessly working toward our vision of becoming the World's Most Loved, Most Flown, and Most Profitable Airline," said Gary Kelly, Chairman, President and CEO of Southwest Airlines. "We had a great year in 2013 because of their collective efforts and contributions toward Southwest's success and profitability, and they absolutely deserve this recognition."[15]

This news release provides an example of creating shared rewards—both financial *and* nonfinancial—for shared leadership.

But what happens in the face of failure? It is gratifying to share accountability for positive outcomes, but how can we share accountability for negative outcomes? How can we avoid creating a cycle of finger-pointing and blame and promote learning instead? Several months before Southwest issued this news release, there had been a crisis in its high-performing Chicago hub when many flights had to be grounded, in part because of bad weather and in part because a large number of ramp workers had called in sick. The workers were not publicly blamed, but they were asked to provide notes to document their illnesses. Several union leaders responded by suing Southwest, saying that the workers had built Southwest's success and claiming that now management was ruining it.[16]

Clearly, Southwest workers have shared in the success of their airline. "The average Southwest worker earned nearly $100,000 in 2012, including pension and benefits, compared with about $89,000 at a traditional hub-and-spoke airline, according to MIT. Southwest also shares profits with employees, paying them $228 million last year, or more than 6% of their pay."[17] According to CEO Gary Kelly, Southwest was seeking savings from increased productivity and flexibility in workers' contracts rather than from pay cuts. From the company's inception, the Southwest tradition had been to "share the wealth" with workers by accepting unions and partnering with them. Indeed, when a *Wall Street Journal* reporter asked in 2005 about growing pay levels, Kelly had responded with confidence:

> It's true, our employees are well paid. They've produced the most efficient, well-run airline with the best customer service and they deserve to share the wealth. Our people know what the airline industry environment is like. I am confident they will do what it takes to keep SWA on top. I would consider it a failure if we have to go to our employees and tell them to take a pay cut.[18]

Kelly's words reflected Southwest's long time philosophy of sharing the wealth with employees while keeping executive pay modest relative to that of other executives in the industry. Kelly's words also exuded confidence that Southwest workers and their elected representatives would keep their requests for shared rewards consistent with the sustained success of the organization. This story reminds us that shared rewards must be matched by shared accountability in order to support relational coordination and the desired performance outcomes.

RELATIONAL JOB DESIGN FOR LEADERS AND SUPERVISORS

Leadership is more than a set of behaviors. Leadership is also an organizational role and, as such, it can be designed. In particular, organizations can design leadership roles to enhance the potential for leaders to engage in relational leadership, and thus to support relational coordination among workers and relational coproduction with customers.

A key design feature of leadership roles is the span of control, or the number of direct reports per manager. Although organizations have been striving to become flatter with larger spans of control, small spans of control are more conducive to relational forms of leadership. The evidence suggests that when spans are large, managers find it more difficult to engage in consultation with workers and tend to engage in more autocratic behavior instead. Small spans of control increase the time a leader can work alongside each direct report, creating more opportunities for building shared goals and shared knowledge and for engaging in coaching and feedback.

Consistent with these arguments, researchers have found that managers with small spans of control were more available for coaching and feedback. Managers with large spans had less opportunity to interact with individual direct reports and less time to provide them with support, encouragement, and recognition. Managers with large spans were more likely to handle problems with direct reports in a formalized, impersonal manner, using warnings and punishments instead of coaching and feedback. As spans of control increase, managers tend to make more autocratic decisions. Narrower spans of control allow more contact and create more opportunity for communication between frontline and managerial employees.[19]

We saw examples in Chapter 4 of supervisor-worker interactions at Southwest and American Airlines. The hands-on supervisory role at Southwest was enabled by the selection and training of supervisors, but also by the span of control, which was 1/10 at Southwest (versus to 1/30 at American). In that study, I found that smaller spans of control enabled managers to play a more facilitative coaching role, strengthening relational coordination among workers and increasing performance outcomes.[20]

RELATIONAL JOB DESIGN FOR BOUNDARY SPANNERS

The boundary spanner, whose job is to integrate the work of other people around a project, process, or customer, is another key role to be designed by organizations.[21] Because boundary spanners build understanding between areas of expertise, they add the most value when the existing boundaries are most divisive.

The boundary spanner role only supports positive relational dynamics, however, when there is sufficient staffing to give the spanner the time needed to engage in relational practice.[22] For example, a case management job can be designed with a large caseload and the expectation that it will entail simply managing a checklist of clients. As a case manager who was coordinating the surgical discharge process explained, "I have about thirty patients—with that number I just look at the list for problem patients." Alternatively, the boundary spanner job can be designed with a smaller caseload and expectations of ongoing conversations between the boundary spanner and clients, and the colleagues who serve those clients. A nurse leader described the expectations associated with this job design, "The case manager does the discharge planning, utilization review, and social work all rolled into one. The case manager discusses the patient with physical therapy and nursing and with the physician. He or she keeps everyone on track. The case manager has a key pivotal role—he or she coordinates the whole case." Accordingly, the selection criteria for this job were ambitious. "Case managers have to be very, very, very good communicators and negotiators and very assertive but also have a good sense of timing . . . Willing to be a patient advocate but also be able to balance the financial parameters, think 'out of the box,' and have a system perspective."

In both the airlines and in healthcare, I found that smaller workloads for boundary spanners supported higher levels of relational coordination between the workgroups and higher levels of relational coproduction with customers, resulting in significant payoffs for efficiency and quality performance.[23]

INCLUSIVE CONFLICT RESOLUTION

Bureaucratic organizations are designed with the expectation that all employees will work within their defined work roles with relative autonomy and without undue interference from supervisors, co-workers, or customers. Conflict is reduced by using slack resources to allow different parts of the work process to be decoupled, in effect to be insulated from the need for contact with the other parts.[24] However, these slack resources reduce efficiency and the ability to engage in learning over time. In both airlines and healthcare organizations, I found that the laissez faire approach to conflict resolution between functions was common. Thanks to employee unions, formal mechanisms had been developed to resolve conflicts between workers and managers, but mechanisms for resolving conflicts between workers themselves, or between workers and their customers, have remained less developed.

As Mary Parker Follett pointed out, conflict is not a problem to be suppressed; rather it's an opportunity to bring together opposing perspectives with the potential to generate new insights and innovative solutions. In keeping with Follett, researchers have found that conflicts actually improve performance when they occur in a context that values task-related conflict; however, unresolved conflicts undermine relationships and hinder performance over time. And when participants are divided by power differences or geographical location, conflicts are not likely to be resolved spontaneously. In such a context, the laissez-faire approach to conflict resolution—"we just hope people use common sense and work it out with each other"—only reinforces dysfunctional relationship patterns.[25]

Inclusive conflict resolution structures provide a systematic way to articulate and accommodate multiple points of view, each with the potential to add value to the work process.[26] These structures provide opportunities for building shared goals and a shared understanding of the work process and for identifying and correcting disrespectful interactions. While some have argued that relationship conflict should be avoided in favor of task conflict, relationship conflict appears to be just as valuable. When addressed constructively, both kinds of conflict have the potential to build positive relationships.[27] I once observed a conflict being resolved by a Southwest supervisor at a gate, near the time of a flight departure. A passenger had spoken rudely to a gate agent and was treating fellow passengers in a rude and somewhat threatening manner. After continued efforts at resolution, the supervisor approached the passenger and said, with calm conviction, that this behavior was not acceptable and that the passenger would not be permitted to board the aircraft. The tension among the passengers and employees eased perceptibly.

INCLUSIVE MEETINGS

Although relational coordination, relational coproduction, and relational leadership are often carried out "on the fly," they benefit from scheduled or planned interactions between participants, otherwise known as "meetings." Face-to-face interactions help to ensure effective communication because of their higher bandwidth, immediacy, and ability to build connections among participants through the use of nonverbal clues.[28]

In bureaucratic organizations, meetings are used to bring top managers together to set direction for the organization. Meetings are also held between managers and their subordinates to communicate those directives downward. The alternative design is to use meetings to bring multiple perspectives together at each level of the organization, to assess the current situation and determine next steps, to reflect on performance, provide coaching and feedback, and to learn from successes and failures. Increasingly, these meetings include workers and managers as well as customers. The family-centered rounds established by Michele Saysana at Riley Hospital for Children (see Chapter 4) are an excellent example of meetings that were designed to support relational coordination, coproduction, and leadership.

"Huddles" are brief meetings designed to give workers and managers the opportunity to coordinate their tasks interactively on the spot, often across status boundaries that can make it difficult to speak up. A physician leader in the Boston Medical Center intensive care unit explained, "It's often the person who is closest to the patient who knows where the patient and the family are at. In our huddles, doctors are learning to listen and not feel like they have to know everything. Everybody has a different piece of the puzzle to contribute." The care team used these huddles to share insights and get "on the same page" in preparation for a meeting with family members regarding a sensitive issue, such as transitioning the patient to palliative care when other measures were no longer working.

Researchers have established that meetings contribute to successful outcomes in uncertain or dynamic, time-constrained settings by providing opportunities for distinct perspectives to interpenetrate and influence one another.[29] But meetings can do so only when the relevant perspectives are "at the table." In my nine-hospital study, I found that more inclusive meetings predicted higher levels of relational coordination, which in turn predicted higher efficiency and quality performance outcomes.[30]

SHARED PROTOCOLS

In bureaucratic organizations, job-specific protocols are provided to workers to ensure that they carry out their work in a standardized way, without regard for the unique needs of individual clients. These protocols provide workers with guidance for how to do their own work but not with visibility into how their work connects to the work of others, therefore failing to promote the development of shared knowledge and shared goals with their colleagues in other functions around the needs of customers.

By contrast, shared protocols provide workers with a mental map of how their individual tasks are connected to the overall process, enabling them to more readily adapt to emergent needs over time. Paul Adler and Brian Borys argued that "enabling [protocols] provide users with visibility into the processes they regulate by explicating key components and by codifying best practice routines . . . When tasks are specialized and partitioned, procedures are designed to afford [workers] an understanding of where their tasks fit into the whole."[31] By codifying routines, shared protocols can serve as sources of connections, shared understandings, and shared meanings among participants.[32]

Even in highly dynamic settings, shared protocols can contribute to successful outcomes by providing a common point of reference for workers with distinct areas of expertise.[33] In my nine-hospital study, I also found that more inclusive shared protocols—in the form of clinical pathways—predicted higher levels of relational coordination, driving higher levels of quality and efficiency performance. To my surprise, I found that shared protocols were more important—not less—for achieving relational coordination, as well as quality and efficiency outcomes, when uncertainty was greatest.[34]

How is it that shared protocols can enable the flexible responses that are needed in dynamic settings? Shared protocols help workers visualize how their tasks connect to the tasks of others who are working with the same customer, informing adaptation and improvisation when unanticipated changes occur. For example, organizations can develop "soft and selective standards that do not prescribe how trade-offs must be made but provide direction for making trade-offs."[35] Mass customization offers a model for this approach, integrating the principles of standardization with the principles of customization.[36]

In her study of childcare centers, Anne Douglass found that shared protocols can be designed to support workers' use of flexible and caring responses with clients. Similarly, in mental health clinics, counselors can be trained to follow a prespecified set of rules; or, instead, they can be provided with shared protocols for responding flexibly and sensitively to the differing needs of clients. Shared protocols enable counselors to engage in reciprocal interrelating with the clients, with fellow staff who work with that client, and with managers who can play a supportive, co-creative role.[37]

SHARED INFORMATION SYSTEMS

Information systems are often designed to replicate and reinforce bureaucratic silos rather than connect them. In healthcare, for example, we find that electronic health records are not typically designed to facilitate relational coordination among care providers or to facilitate relational coproduction with patients and families. Rather, they are designed to document activities for billing and quality compliance purposes. In *The Digital Doctor*, Bob Wachter documents in detail the potential harm that information systems can cause due to the mismatch between their design and their use.[38]

Nonetheless, experts have remained optimistic about the potential for information systems to support coordination and coproduction. Rather than simply pass information to the head of one's function to be coordinated with other functions, automated information systems can, in principle, enable frontline workers to more easily coordinate directly with their counterparts in other functions and with customers. Automated information systems can also enable customers to participate directly, for example, through customer portals. Some researchers have argued that indeed the primary purpose of information systems is to provide a common information infrastructure to support coordination. Consistent with this view, some studies have shown information technology to have a positive effect on performance outcomes.[39]

But automated information systems have the potential to demotivate, deskill, and disempower workers by obscuring the relationships underlying the production process.[40] Information systems are also limited in their ability to exchange feelings and emotions. To the extent that feelings and emotions, in addition to other information, are valuable inputs to work processes, there is a limit to the effectiveness of automated information systems. Researchers have found that electronic networks are more conducive to building extensive weak ties than to building intensive strong ties.[41] Perhaps for these reasons, most studies of information technology and productivity fail to show a significant relationship between them.[42]

Consistent with these findings, I found very different uses of information systems at American and Southwest Airlines, as well as differences in how the boundary spanners used each system to coordinate flight departures.[43] American relied heavily on automated information interfaces to bring together the information required to dispatch a flight. Operations agents playing the boundary spanner role were expected to coordinate up to fifteen flight departures at a time. They relied on a computer interface into which each workgroup was responsible for entering the relevant information. Though they played a central role in coordination, the operations agents lacked familiarity with the particular features of the flights they coordinated and lacked the time to dedicate to each flight. "Our biggest problem is communication," said an operations agent. "Getting [the other workgroups] to talk to us, tell us what's on the airplane." From the point of view of other workgroups, the problem was more basic: "We don't understand their process, and they don't understand ours." The information technology interface obscured shared knowledge and undermined accurate communication instead of supporting them.

At Southwest Airlines, there was comparatively low reliance on automated information systems. Although automated systems were used to track flight information, they did not serve as the primary means of communication among workgroups. Instead, communication was carried out largely through personal interactions with the operations agents—the boundary spanners—

who were staffed sufficiently to allow each to coordinate *one* flight departure at a time. The goal was for the operations agent to engage in face-to-face interaction with each function before, during and/or after the turnaround of that flight, then focus attention on the next incoming flight. Notably, this role included face-to-face interactions with passengers as they boarded the aircraft. The more intensive use of personal communication to *complement* digital communication was associated with higher levels of relational coordination across workgroups and with customers, driving higher quality and efficiency performance. In sum, even well-designed information systems need to be counterbalanced by personal communication.

SUMMING UP

In this chapter we have explored organizational structures that influence the development of relational coordination, coproduction, and leadership, for better or worse, depending upon their design. When these structures are designed to support the three relational dynamics, they form a relational work system in which participants can build shared goals and shared knowledge across diverse boundaries in a mutually respectful way, enabling high performance in the face of uncertainty.[44]

Yet these relational work systems are not yet widely implemented in most industries. The bureaucratic model of organizing persists, reinforcing silos that separate participants, undermining the potential for high performance. Economists theorize that organizations make rational decisions and adopt the structures that optimize performance, yet there is much evidence that this does not occur.[45] Why? What are the challenges of getting from here to there?

In Part II we will explore these challenges and see how change agents overcome them to create positive organizational change. In the Relational Model of Organizational Change, we will see that even though organizational structures can shape the three relational dynamics in a positive direction, they are difficult to implement unless those relational dynamics are already in place. Organizational change therefore becomes kind of bootstrapping process where new structures and relationships are each needed to support the development of the other. We will learn how this works in practice by following four organizations along their journeys of change.

PART TWO

GETTING FROM HERE TO THERE

Now we get to the heart of the transformation challenge. We will see that organizational change is a bootstrapping process in which new structures and new relationships are each needed to support the development of the other, as reflected in the Relational Model of Organizational Change. We then use this model to analyze the real-time journeys of four organizations, witnessing the challenges, setbacks, and triumphs they experience as they transform their relationships for high performance. Given the challenges currently faced by the health sector, I have chosen to focus on four highly innovative health systems:

- Group Health in Seattle, Washington, illustrates efforts to build relational coordination among co-workers (Chapter 7).

- Varde Municipality in Denmark illustrates efforts to build relational coproduction between workers and the citizens they serve and among citizens themselves (Chapter 8).

- Dartmouth-Hitchcock Medical Center in Hanover, New Hampshire, illustrates efforts to build relational leadership from the top management team to middle managers to the frontline (Chapter 9).

- Billings Clinic, headquartered in Montana, illustrates efforts to "bring it all together" with the most comprehensive—and inspiring—approach I have seen thus far to building relational coordination, coproduction, and leadership throughout their organization and with partners in the communities they serve (Chapter 10).

These four cases were selected from twenty-five cases documented in a study called "Interventional Uses of Relational Coordination: Early Evidence from Four Countries."[1] In all twenty-five cases, relational coordination was used as a principle to guide organizational change. I selected these four cases to explore in detail the use of relational coordination, coproduction, and leadership to guide organizational change, and to show the kinds of interventions that are used in this change process. I captured the data for each case by interviewing change leaders, frontline workers, frontline leaders, middle managers, and top managers. I reviewed baseline relational coordination survey data, interviewed participants about their plans for sharing the data, learned how they actually shared the data, how the data were received, and what happened as a result. In each case I describe the broader organizational context, then describe the change process in detail.

These four cases illustrate the emergent nature of how the change process unfolds and how relational, work process, and structural interventions are used to achieve relational coordination and relational coproduction, supported by relational leadership. In each case, I model the principles of relational coordination by drawing on many voices to tell the story. In each, we will see both incremental and disruptive changes. We will see that changes are sometimes resisted by participants initially due to perceived threats to their power or professional identities or due to outdated structures that continue to reinforce the existing dynamics and ways of thinking. At times, participants are simply overwhelmed by the pace of change, given the workloads they bear. Let's see how a dedicated group of change agents emerges in each organization, and how they move forward in response to these challenges.

6 A RELATIONAL MODEL OF
ORGANIZATIONAL CHANGE

Change agents looking for ways to improve organizational performance are often relieved to learn that the problems they currently observe in their organizations are not simply caused by "bad people." They are relieved to learn that outdated organizational structures contribute to the siloed behaviors they observe, and that these structures can be redesigned to better support relational coordination, coproduction, and leadership.

These same change agents can be overwhelmed, however, by the sheer number of structures that influence relational coordination, from hiring and training to performance measurement and rewards to information systems and protocols to job design and conflict resolution practices. Sometimes they glaze over and disengage, or they seek to achieve relational coordination in their own way based on their hunches about how to build it. Oftentimes they ask, "How do we get from here to there?"

TRANSFORMING STRUCTURES

At first, I thought the answer to that question was obvious, based on the research we learned about in the previous chapter. With a fair amount of confidence, I would respond, "If you adopt these organizational structures, the three relational dynamics will be transformed, and your performance will improve." Often, the change agents responded, "Sure, that makes sense but where do we *start*?" I would explain further that changing one structure at a time was not sufficient—that because of the interactions between the structures, the whole set of structures must be changed at once to reinforce the new relationship patterns in a consistent way. It makes no sense to invest in new structures to hire and train for relational competence, for example, if accountability and rewards continue to be based solely on functional expertise.

At this point, they would look at me warily and ask, "How can we possibly change all of these structures at once? We would need a lot of buy-in and a lot of resources—and these ideas are still new for our organization." My response was, "Of course, you will need support from top management to move forward."

Given the looks I got, I began to feel that my responses were not helpful and therefore not "true" in some important sense.[1] I started to wonder. The responses I was giving were consistent with a large body of research. As we saw in the previous chapters, researchers, including myself, have found that organizational structures shape relational coordination—for better or worse, depending on their design—and that these dynamics are associated with high performance on a wide range of outcomes. This research accurately captures a snapshot of organizations at a given point in time, based on cross-sectional research methods. However, we had not captured the dynamics of change over time, and we had not yet learned much about *how that change occurs*. People who study organizational structures, like myself, tend to be experts in human resource, operations, or information systems management with a good understanding of structures and performance but with less understanding of organizational change.

Many change efforts do indeed begin with structural interventions—the adoption of a new information system or a new accountability or reward system, or a new training program. Often, these structural changes are initiated by top management in response to competitive pressures, management trends, shifts in the regulatory environment, changes in technology, or changes in customer demand. There are good reasons for the new structures to work, based on the evidence. Yet workers often reject these structural innovations like shoes that don't fit, or they simply go through the motions of compliance. Worse, these innovations cause resentment and resistance when people feel forced into new behaviors that do not fit their well-established patterns of interaction or their professional identities—or when the changes take up valuable time when they are already feeling overstressed and overworked.

TRANSFORMING RELATIONSHIPS

My colleagues with expertise in organizational learning, culture, and change had a different perspective to share. Together, they helped to focus more on the relational dynamics of organizational change. They did not seem to believe one should start with structural change, even if you *could* change all of the necessary structures at once and even if you *could* get all key participants to support those changes.

These colleagues reminded me that relationship patterns are embedded in our professional and personal identities and in our organizational cultures. In fact, this relational perspective was already part of how I saw the world. My undergraduate thesis many years earlier was titled "The Socially Embedded Human Subject: A Moral Standpoint for Achieving Social Justice."[2] As a political philosophy student, I had argued that even our identities as individuals are created through mutual recognition with others, and that these relational identities create obligations to one another.

Ten years later, my dissertation on the flight departure process and then my follow-up study of the patient care process identified the dynamic of relational coordination, along with new ways to "see" relational networks and to assess how they shape performance outcomes. My reading of Mary Parker Follett, as well as of Jean Baker Miller and her colleagues at the Stone Center, deepened the relational perspective I had developed in my younger years. But while I took relationships quite seriously, I saw them as shaped by structures and therefore as changeable primarily through structural change.

I came to realize, by talking with my organizational development colleagues, that changing structures would not be sufficient. To the extent that our existing relationship patterns are siloed and hierarchical, it is difficult for us to fully embrace or even to know how to make use of the new cross-cutting structures that support relational coordination, coproduction, and leadership. Because these new cross-cutting structures don't fit our existing relationship patterns, we are likely to adopt them only superficially and temporarily, like a new flavor of the month. The new structures are like transplants that are poorly matched to the organization and its participants. It is therefore no surprise when they are ultimately rejected, leaving people cynical when they don't work.

Whether workers have high status or low status in the organization, and whether they have much power or little, they cannot be forced to do things that do not fit with their existing relationship patterns and identities. Workers typically have sufficient power to resist, whether actively and verbally or passively and silently. Even when they do choose to use their power to embrace change rather than resist it, they may lack the relational networks needed to effectively implement the new cross-cutting structures.

An alternative approach is to start our change efforts, not by transforming organizational structures but by transforming ourselves and our relationships with each other. The established methods range from T-groups to appreciative inquiry. At the heart of these methods is establishing psychological safety—creating cultural islands, relational spaces, safe containers, or holding environments in which participants can develop new ways of connecting with one another, aided by skilled coaching, role modeling, and facilitated dialogue.[3]

These insights struck me as powerful. Inspired, I agreed to partner with colleagues who had the relevant knowledge to turn relational coordination from a research tool into a tool for organizational change. With them, I founded the Relational Coordination Research Collaborative. I wondered whether they would see as I did the need for systemic structural changes in addition to relational interventions. I also wondered whether a focus on relational interventions could become too disconnected from the work—producing good interpersonal connections among participants but failing to transform the way people work together on an ongoing daily basis.

PAYING ATTENTION TO THE WORK ITSELF

As we know, relational coordination, coproduction, and leadership are not about relationships in a generic sense—rather they are about communicating and relating for the purpose of integrating our work.[4] Recall that relational coordination was first discovered in the context of flight departures, a process in which twelve distinct functional workgroups interact to achieve the goals of on-time performance, baggage handling performance, and customer satisfaction while, at the same time, seeking to achieve high levels of employee productivity and efficient aircraft turnaround times at the gate. The relational interventions needed are transformations in the ways people work together. This means we need to "do" relational interventions in the context of transforming the way we work.

My colleagues in operations management had their own distinctive and compelling perspective on organizational change. Process improvement focuses on transforming the work itself through structured problem solving, using the tools of total quality management, Plan-Do-Study-Act, process reengineering, lean, six sigma, and so on. As a professor who had taught operations management for over a decade, first at Harvard Business School, then at Brandeis University, I had a great deal of respect for the field. I had also been influenced by process improvement thinking as a student at MIT.[5] Reading Deming and other authors had helped me to "see" the flight departure process when I first visited American Airlines at Logan Airport and to notice the task interdependence between the twelve functions and the coordination challenges it posed. Listening to frontline workers and their managers, I could see that American was organized into silos that were at odds with the performance outcomes they were seeking to achieve.

When we look at the history of process improvement, it is evident that its founders placed a great deal of emphasis on the relational dynamics underlying effective process improvement. "Measure the process, not the person," Deming advised decades ago, attentive to the hazards of blame and blame avoidance, wanting to avoid the narrow functional goals and siloed thinking that performance improvement can foster and wanting instead to foster process-level goals and systems thinking.[6] In that simple phrase—"measure the process, not the person"—Deming showed an appreciation for the importance of improving work processes in ways that foster problem-solving rather than blaming communication, shared goals rather than subgoal optimization, and shared knowledge rather than fragmented knowledge. The Toyota Production System incorporates many of these elements and goes a step further by including "respect for people" as one of its core principles. Even Steven Covey points out, "A cardinal principle of Total Quality escapes too many managers: you cannot continuously improve interdependent systems and processes until you progressively perfect interdependent, interpersonal relationships."[7]

Practitioners sometimes lose that appreciation for the relational underpinnings of process improvement, applying the lean and six-sigma tools in a vacuum. Some have learned from experience, however, that process improvement tools do not work particularly well by themselves. My colleague Robert Hendler, as chief medical officer at Tenet Health Systems in Texas, noted, "We've been doing process improvement for several years, and we think we're on the right track. But we've tried a number of tools for process improvement, and they just don't address the relationship issues that are holding us back."[8]

Don Goldmann and Gareth Parry from the Institute for Healthcare Improvement pointed out that, in their experience, the organizations that struggle most with process improvement are those with low levels of relational coordination, in which participants lack a clear sense of shared goals, shared knowledge of each other's work, and respect for each other's work. Their communication is neither frequent nor timely, nor focused on problem solving. The organizations that adopt process improvement with greater ease and more successful outcomes, they believed, were those that started with higher levels of relational coordination.

Consistent with this insight, Earl Murman and his colleagues from the MIT Lean Advancement Initiative developed an approach to lean that includes relational coordination explicitly, labeling it the "Soft Side of Lean." Walter Lowell and Kelly Grenier of the Maine Department of Health and Human Services Office of Lean incorporated relational coordination into their lean training, inspired by Murman's work, their reading of *The Southwest Airlines Way*, and their own experiences. The fundamental premise of process improvement is its focus on horizontal cross-cutting processes, following the value stream through while value is created. This method thus has the potential to counteract and provide insight into overcoming the vertical silos of traditional bureaucracy, to create a new organization design. However, it does not always work that way, according to critics. As systems thinker Russell Ackoff notes, "Most applications of improvement science are directed at improving the parts, but not at improving the whole . . . [As a result] the parts don't form a system because they don't fit together."[9]

Perhaps this is true because we often use process improvement methodologies to achieve a narrow definition of efficiency without having a sufficiently broad view of what the problem really is or what our purpose or goal really is. This analysis suggests one other potential limitation of process improvement as it has been conceived and implemented—the focus on identifying and eliminating defects. According to Ackoff, in order to improve the whole rather than simply the parts, "improvement programs have to be directed at what you want—not at what you don't want." This means a fundamental starting point for an improvement process is to achieve clarity on the shared purpose.

It is essential to engage in this systems thinking without losing sight of the fundamental contribution of process improvement—seeing and strengthening the horizontal connections through which value is created. I am not suggesting that we reject process improvement but rather that we expand its scope. I am suggesting we need to cast our nets wide enough to see the potential upstream drivers of the processes we are trying to "fix"—to avoid fixing a piece that is too narrow to address the real goal or purpose that we might ideally want to pursue for the sake of efficiency and quality more broadly understood. In some cases, a large group intervention may be needed to visualize the overall work process and to identify the most promising levers for change.

FIX THE PEOPLE, OR THE WORK PROCESS, OR THE STRUCTURES?

In organizational change efforts, these three perspectives—people, work process, and structures—often clash. When organizations face performance challenges, leaders sometimes debate whether they are due to incompetent people or poorly designed work processes or poorly designed structures. Some leaders will blame their people, while others will examine the siloed work processes and structures that make it difficult for even "good people" to be effective without constantly inventing and implementing workarounds. Often, these people and process issues are difficult to disentangle. Much of the science of process improvement has been designed to focus our efforts on improving the processes instead of blaming the individuals who are caught in those processes, consistent with the teachings of Deming.[10]

I observed this debate in one of my early interviews in the airline industry, talking with the Boston station manager for American Airlines, Lynn Heitman. A few years earlier, Heitman had been a promising mid-level financial analyst in the human resource department at American Airlines headquarters, when she found herself in a heated argument with CEO Robert Crandall. He had just spent a day in the field at Dallas/Fort Worth International Airport, presumably to show support for the frontline and to gain insight into the nature of their work. Upset by his experiences, Crandall convened his management team that weekend and argued with conviction that American had too many incompetent employees.

Heitman had been observing another airline headquartered in Dallas—Southwest Airlines, which was building a reputation for cross-functional teamwork, superb operational performance, and highly satisfied employees and customers. Based on what she was learning from colleagues there, Heitman suspected the problems Crandall had observed went much deeper than incompetent employees. She questioned his conclusion and asked whether American might need to change its systems of accountability to better support teamwork. She argued that American should not be organized in such a way that heroic efforts were required to achieve performance outcomes, and that instead its systems should be designed to support teamwork. Surprised by her ideas—and also by her willingness to articulate them—Crandall challenged her to prove her argument and to submit a report to him within a week. The vice president who was Heitman's immediate supervisor was very upset with her; Heitman told me later that she suspected she was facing imminent demotion. She was right.[11]

A similar argument occurred more recently at the Lehigh Valley Health Network in Pennsylvania. The primary care clinics there had recently begun a journey of organizational change toward the so-called patient-centered medical home, intended to coordinate care around patients' needs to promote health and wellness in a more holistic way. This new patient care model is part of a larger trend in the United States and beyond, but it is challenging to achieve.[12] Toward the beginning of the project, one frustrated physician leader argued that "we have the wrong people—we need to start over."

Krista Hirschmann, who directed a center at Lehigh Valley Health Network that supported the development of patient-centered medical homes, responded that the problems the physician leader had observed were sufficiently widespread that they might indicate problems with the clinic's systems—not just its individual employees. She pointed out, "There were no standards for how people were doing their work. It was very inefficient. The relational coordination data also showed a huge gap between the front office and the back office. We needed to develop our work processes, not just get rid of people."

According to Hirschmann, her lean colleagues shared her view of the importance of relationships:

> Relationships are absolutely essential for lean. We can set up these beautiful processes, but if people aren't communicating well, the processes we develop will not be sustainable. You need the shared accountability, the clarity that it's about the patient, the ability to have the conversations about what we need to do to achieve our shared goals, for lean to work.

Both arguments made sense. Sustainable success on the people side is likely to depend on having supportive structures and high-functioning work processes in place. But to develop high-functioning work processes—and to develop supportive structures—requires positive working relationships.

In the same clinic, it turned out that there were numerous areas for improvement, with one role in particular that was in need of repair. Hirschmann explained:

> One of the staff members was playing a kind of negative boundary spanning role. She was talking with the back office [clinicians], undermining the front office [administrative staff]. She was talking with the front office, undermining their confidence and undermining the back office to them. We needed to help her see how what she was doing was breaking down coordination between front office and back office. Ultimately, she needed to move elsewhere in the organization to get a fresh start.

Hirschmann and her team of practice coaches realized there was more to change than this particular role or the particular individual in the role. In this clinic, as in several of the others, it turned out goal alignment was a problem in part because of the existing structures of accountability and rewards:

The goals are not in alignment. The goals for physicians are based on patient satisfaction. The goals for the front office are based on workflow. They are not mutually supportive of one another's goals. Physicians are graded on their patient satisfaction, but the rest of the patients and the practice can fall apart. Who is getting rewarded for what is not consistent with good relational coordination—or achieving the desired performance outcomes. Physicians are fully engaged with their patients but not with their colleagues. So we got physicians and nurses and front office to identify their shared goals.

Pressures from healthcare reform more generally were pushing physicians and other clinical disciplines from their highly valued autonomy toward interdependence, just as pressures from deregulation and global competition had pushed pilots and their colleagues in other functions from autonomy to interdependence. Managing that interdependence required attention to the whole system. One of the primary care physicians at Lehigh Valley Health Network explained, "It's not just about what happens between you and the patient in your exam room anymore—it's about the you, the patient, and the whole team." However, there was an invisible power dynamic that was preventing communication between physicians and other members of the patient care team. Hirschmann reflected, "It was such an 'ah hah' for the physicians to see the disparities in perceptions and experience. They didn't even see it before. They asked, 'How could anyone be afraid to give me feedback? I'm one of the most approachable people I know!'"

This blindness is often associated with invisible privilege, which occurs when people with power do not see that they have it or how it affects their interactions with others. In Hirschmann's view:

> By having conversations about new processes for standard work, like how to take a phone note, participants got a glimpse into each other's worlds and saw what details made a difference to the other and how the lack of consistent training and process among the staff made them look incompetent to the physicians. Once the process was consistent, communication improved, trust built, and feedback was easier to offer both ways because the data was now about the process and the not the person. I think that's the heart of how lean and relationship work mutually reinforce each other.

Through this combined relational and work process intervention, Hirschmann and her team were able to help the physicians to see—and address—the impact of their power and privilege on communication patterns.

ANTICIPATING THREATS TO HIERARCHY AND PRIVILEGE

Clearly, there are advantages to paying attention to both the social system and the technical system. But there is a potential stumbling block. Will changes to the social system have any chance of succeeding given the hierarchies that characterize many of our organizations? Recall the obstacles to relational coordination introduced in Chapter 1. All of these obstacles, at their core, were about the disruption of identities shaped by hierarchy and privilege. Alasdair Honeyman of the King's Fund in the United Kingdom reported finding that relational coordination was perceived as threatening in hierarchical organizations that he worked with.

I observed this firsthand a few years ago when I was invited to introduce relational coordination to a multidisciplinary group of about sixty participants from the Japanese healthcare industry, led by several powerful physician leaders. As participants engaged in a relational mapping exercise, identifying areas of strong and weak relational coordination, the nurses, pharmacists, therapists, and case managers in the group played a particularly enthusiastic role, especially the younger ones. But when they reported back, sharing their insights openly with the larger group, I began to sense tension in the room. Several of the physician leaders requested to meet with me at lunch, when I was told, "We don't need relational coordination in Japan. Doctors here communicate very well with each other." It seemed that they felt threatened by the conversations that had opened up.

Perhaps this is not surprising. When we introduce the three relational dynamics, we invite participants to reflect on their current patterns of interrelating and to recognize that co-workers create value through these patterns of interrelating with each other, their customers, and their leaders. Why is this a threat? Once workers see how value is created, they may ask to be recognized for their central role in creating that value and to receive a greater share of that value. This sharing of power, recognition, and rewards can be threatening to people throughout the hierarchy. Those who embrace the new developments may risk being marginalized or even penalized by their peers, their boards of directors, government regulators, the financial analysts who recommend that their company's shares be bought or sold, and by other stakeholders they rely on for resources.

A former corporate executive described his experience as the leader of a unit in a large multinational corporation. Under his leadership, the unit had achieved unusually high levels of customer satisfaction. By sheltering people from the corporate hierarchy and giving them the freedom to innovate, he observed high levels of relational coordination emerge within the team and high levels of relational coproduction with their customers, driving performance to previously unattained levels. Then, the arrival of a new CEO posed a threat to this experiment.

> The new CEO was a very strong central control guy—he had no interest in people whatsoever. And so my ideas made no sense to him. My direct boss was a board member who had much bigger fish to fry. So, as long as we were keeping our customers happy, he didn't care how we did it. And so I basically had unusual latitude to do whatever I thought made sense.

It was a bubble in which he had been able to innovate without being subjected to external critiques. "A couple of my customers' managers were really intrigued by what we did, and they liked it, so when the new CEO tried to shut it down, they got up in arms and tried to keep it going, but they didn't have any influence." As his unit was being shut down, he became acutely aware of the limitations of innovating at the frontline without active support from top management. The lesson, from his perspective, was that top managers who do not believe in this new way of leading and creating value will make it difficult to sustain and nearly impossible to roll out beyond a single unit.

> What you are doing in a case like this is you are taking a blood type A organ and trying to put it in a blood type B system, and that system—that hierarchical control system—is going to reject it. It's not exactly clear how it will reject it, but it is a very powerful system that's going to reject anything that threatens its core assumption, which is that management control of employees is essential to create order and prevent chaos.

For this approach to succeed, he argued, "the CEO has to truly believe that there is no need for hierarchical control and that there is tremendous potential here if I can help my employees self-control and self-coordinate their activities."

In short, relational coordination, coproduction, and leadership can be threatening to top management because they challenge the deep-seated belief that hierarchical control is needed. This belief is at the core of bureaucratic organizational cultures. Moreover, paying attention to the three relational dynamics shifts the focus to workers' and even customers' role in value creation, challenging the view that leaders are the primary force in value creation.

If relational coordination threatens the identities and interests of some participants—especially those at the top of the hierarchy—how is this obstacle to be overcome? The answer is not rocket science, but neither is it easy. As Ed Schein and others have suggested, *not* changing has to be seen as more threatening than changing for progress to be made.[13] One example arose in a Brandeis University workshop for the American College of Surgeons. One senior surgeon leader looked quite frustrated and impatient during a seminar I was leading on relational coordination. At one point, he burst out, "Sure this all sounds great, and sure I'd love to share power with the rest of the team. But I can't. No matter what happens, it's just me who is responsible for the outcome." Several of his fellow surgeons raised their hands and argued, "Yes but you can't do it yourself—it's too complex. The only way you can get the outcomes you need is to share your power." His colleagues were right—there is often a need to shift to relational leadership in order to achieve the desired performance outcomes. But existing structures of accountability also need to be changed to better support the three relational dynamics. To address these complex challenges, a multi-interventional approach to organizational change is needed.

A RELATIONAL MODEL OF ORGANIZATIONAL CHANGE

The Relational Model of Organizational Change, first developed by Amy Edmondson, Ed Schein, and myself, proposes that three types of interventions—relational, work process, and structural—are needed to transform role relationships in a positive and sustainable way.[14] *Relational interventions* enable participants to transform the way they see themselves and their role within their organization. Relational interventions include building a safe space in which to experiment with new ways of interrelating. By identifying shared goals and expanding shared knowledge, it is possible for participants to become more respectful of one another's roles, supporting more frequent, timely, accurate, and problem-solving communication among themselves.

Relational interventions are not expected to be sufficient, however. To achieve positive sustainable changes in role relationships, the model suggests that *work process interventions* are needed to apply the new dynamics to the work itself. Participants can use work process interventions to assess the current state, identify the desired state, and experiment to close the gap between the two states. Work process interventions enable participants to visualize the work they are engaged in and identify opportunities to redesign that work to achieve the desired state.

Even this is not expected to be sufficient. Combining relational and work process interventions can be powerful for changing dysfunctional ways of working together. But what happens when we get "back to work" and the structures we encounter for accountability, rewards, conflict resolution, meetings, protocols, and information systems put us right back into our little boxes? Each of us has likely heard of changes that cannot be sustained in the face of the traditional structures that pull people back into their previous ways of being, leaving them disillusioned, disappointed, and cynical. Organizational structures have an importance that we overlook only at our peril. These structures must often be redesigned to support and sustain the new culture and new ways of working together that are beginning to emerge. *Structural interventions* are needed to embed the new relational dynamics into participant roles.

Figure 6.1 illustrates how the three types of interventions are expected to work together synergistically to support changes in role relationships. In the Relational Model of High Performance shown in Figure 5.1, there was a one-way arrow between structures and relational dynamics. In Figure 6.1, the arrows in the Relational Model of Organizational Change go in both directions, suggesting that structural interventions do not create new relational dynamics, but rather are co-created with them, in a kind of bootstrapping process. Moreover, the Relational Model of Organizational Change suggests that new relational dynamics are themselves jumpstarted by relational and work process

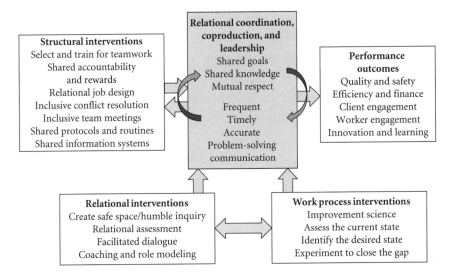

FIGURE 6.1   Relational Model of Organizational Change

interventions. While structural interventions are critical for embedding the new relational dynamics into roles of workers, clients, and leaders, these structures are not sufficient to create the new relational dynamics. Figure 6.1 thus builds from Figure 5.1 but reflects a more complete and nuanced understanding of the change process.

SUMMING UP

The bottom line is that each of these three interventions—relational, work process, and structural—is unlikely to be successful on its own. As we will see in our cases, *relational interventions* include creating a safe space to reduce the risks associated with trying out new role relationships, then diagnosing current relational patterns to open up a dialogue, learning among participants, supported by coaching and the role modeling of positive relational behaviors by leaders and change agents throughout the organization. *Work process interventions* include the use of process mapping, role and goal clarification, and structured problem solving to support changes in the work itself. *Structural interventions* include the implementation of cross-cutting organizational structures to hardwire the new teamwork dynamics into roles, to achieve sustainability. The Relational Model of Organizational Change illustrates how these three types of interventions together can transform the dynamics of relational coordination, relational coproduction, and relational leadership, thus increasing the capacity of organizations to meet the performance pressures they are facing. Now let's follow the real-time journeys of four organizations as they put this model into action.

7 RELATIONAL COORDINATION AT GROUP HEALTH

The story of Group Health gives us a chance to explore, up close, efforts to enhance relational coordination for the purpose of achieving quality performance more efficiently. Founded in 1947 in the Seattle, Washington, area, Group Health is a consumer-governed, nonprofit healthcare system and health-plan provider. By 2014, Group Health was serving more than a half million patients in twenty-six outpatient clinics. The founding of Group Health "is a great story about a small group of people in the late 1940s who wanted to serve people who did not have access to healthcare by offering a consumer model of governance with prepaid coverage. These were very radical ideas at the time," explains Diane Rawlins, longtime consultant and executive coach for Group Health. "This basic idea has continued to be the bedrock of the organization and the reason that many people went to work there."

NEW PRESSURES ON THE HORIZON

In 2012, Group Health was experiencing new performance pressures, as were health systems across the United States and around the world. Like other industries in previous decades—autos, apparel, airlines, telecommunications, banking—the healthcare industry now faced a need to improve quality outcomes in an increasingly cost-sensitive environment. By 2013, Group Health leaders had already taken $250 million out of the system and were planning to reduce costs by another $100 million in 2014. Morale had traditionally been strong but was at risk as substantial layoffs—nearly 1,000 full-time equivalents—were carried out to bring costs in line with revenues.

As an integrated delivery system with its own physicians on staff, a network of community providers, and its own insurance products, Group Health had some leverage to align goals across diverse stakeholders. Owning each of the key pieces is not sufficient for achieving alignment, however. Group Health leaders were therefore working hard, seeking new ways to achieve true alignment in an increasingly competitive and dynamic environment.

Ten years earlier, Group Health had reorganized into service lines, with primary and specialty care providers reporting to different vice presidents. The upside of this service-line approach was an ability to more fully align primary care with a patient-centered medical home model, to assure reliable processes via standard work, and to reduce variation in practices and processes across the primary care clinics. The downside was a perceived disconnect between primary care and specialty care providers working in the same clinic. According to one primary care leader, "With the need for more integrated care, especially for our complex patients, we needed to change. Now we are reorganizing so people working with the same patients will be reporting to the same person ultimately." It was not clear whether the new reporting structures alone would result in aligned and integrated care, however. Indeed, research thus far suggests that regardless of how reporting structures are defined, relational coordination is strengthened by creating shared accountability *across* reporting structures.[1]

In the meantime, reorganization was causing anxiety at Group Health. According to one mid-level leader, "We keep going forward with the work we know we have to do, knowing that all is changing soon. It's a very strange place to be." Another employee confided, "It's a very anxious time. There are many people who have worked here for thirty or forty years and who've never experienced so many things changing at once."[2]

SUCCESSFUL PRIMARY CARE EXPERIENCE WITH LEAN

There were many bright spots as well. Innovation at the frontline of care had been quite successful. Using lean methods to standardize roles and work, a patient-centered medical home was piloted in one clinic in 2008, with multiple positive outcomes. On the efficiency side, the clinic achieved a 10 percent to

15 percent reduction in the utilization of emergency and urgent care, a small decrease in the hospitalization rate, and a large increase in the use of virtual medicine. On the quality side, the pilot clinic achieved greater improvement in quality and service than other clinics, improved both patient and staff satisfaction, and increased its utilization of specialty care, perhaps due to improved handoffs between primary and specialty care.[3]

Following its successful implementation in the pilot clinic, the new model was rolled out across all twenty-six primary care sites as Group Health's Patient-Centered Medical Home 1.0. But, as is often the case with change efforts, the early successes were not easily replicated across the system. According to one observer, "People got better at performing their own tasks, but when they had to go beyond and connect with each other in response to an unexpected event or patient need, it didn't work as well." Why? Lean consultants at Group Health had come to see lean as more than a set of tools. When used effectively, lean represents a shift toward a systems perspective. This does not happen automatically, they discovered. Group Health's internal consultants took several lessons from their implementation of lean:

> We did some things that were top down. We didn't engage all the frontline staff.
> We did a lot of design and spread, and even though frontline teams initially
> designed the work processes, if you weren't on that frontline team or weren't
> a pilot, what you received was a toolkit with 150 pages of detailed process
> descriptions. We've had undeniable successes with the use of lean to develop and
> improve processes, but we are still reflecting, learning, and improving our practice
> and approach.
>
> I think we got a little dogmatic in our approach around standards and standard
> work. Some staff had a negative experience because of that, and because of
> the inflexibility. We were saying lean is all about frontline-driven continuous
> improvement toward customer responsiveness, but we did some things counter
> to that, in some cases putting in place rigid structures that didn't make it easy for
> frontline staff to take that baseline and make it better and better. So we lost sight
> of that true north and became overly focused on adherence instead of the ultimate
> outcome we were trying to achieve.

As with any improvement methodology, people can lose sight of the outcomes they are trying to improve. A lean consultant shared:

Our leader has been out talking to all sorts of different leaders around Group Health and interviewing them to ask, "What was your experience with lean?" We learned some key lessons. First, it's not about the tools. An overly dogmatic approach will not serve you well. Perhaps most important, we embarked on improvements without a responsive and timely method for frontline-driven continuous improvement. Leaders spent inordinate amounts of time monitoring compliance rather than developing the skills of a lean leader—coaching, humility, and developing people.

Putting improvement work in the hands of the frontline workers would require a new level of attention to relational dynamics. An operations manager in one of the primary care clinics explained:

> We started a frontline improvement effort in 2008 to get more participation in lean. So we've had a little bit more time to feel that out, figure that out. It really didn't have a lot of oomph, though, and I think everybody was looking for that next piece. We were great at going through a process and saying, "Okay, let's try this; let's try that," but it didn't have a relational dynamic in it.

Together, these insights reflected an opportunity for Group Health to add another dimension to Medical Home 1.0. Medical Home 2.0 was rolled out in 2013, with several goals—to build the capacity to serve a growing number of patients, to manage the growing use of virtual medicine, and to continue reducing the costs of care. To achieve these goals, high-performing teams would play a critical role.[4]

GROUP HEALTH DISCOVERS RELATIONAL COORDINATION

Several key players at Group Health had learned about the relational coordination theory and methodology and were intrigued by its potential to foster high-performing teams. Claire Trescott, the medical director of primary care at the time, and Barbara Trehearne, vice president of primary care, had learned about relational coordination from Diane Rawlins. They were looking for a way to measure and improve what they were calling "teamness." Rawlins explained:

> What they liked best about RC is that the model is fairly intuitive; it's measurable, and it's evidence based. These are the qualities that organizations are looking

for. What makes RC unique as an intervention methodology is that, when used thoughtfully, it doesn't get imposed upon people as a ten-step toolkit. The only way it's truly useful is when we give teams their own results in a way that invites them to own and act upon what matters to them. This is as opposed to the expert model in which results are given, and people are told what to do. It's a deeply respectful way to engage the people who know the work best, and then give them the time and support to create local solutions.

Michael Parchman had been recruited to play a leadership role at Group Health Research Institute, after having for years led innovative research on primary care at the University of Texas Health Science Center in San Antonio. Following that, he had also worked at the US Department of Health and Human Service, in its Agency for Healthcare Research and Quality, as a senior adviser on primary care transformation, implementing policies that would support primary care transformation. Parchman's research in nearly forty Texas primary care practices was used in the development of a practice improvement model centered around implementing a team-based model of chronic care delivery, supported by coaching, reciprocal learning, and relational coordination. One finding from this study was that the level of relational coordination in primary care practices significantly predicted their ability to adopt team-based care by increasing participants' ability to learn from each other across roles.[5] Parchman hoped to bring insights from that improvement effort to his work with Group Health.

BUILDING SUPPORT FOR RELATIONAL COORDINATION
AT THE LEADERSHIP LEVEL

Other teamwork methods were already under development at Group Health when Parchman arrived, however, and it was not completely clear what relational coordination would add to the mix. Trescott and Trehearne decided that the members of the primary care leadership team should take the RC survey so that they could understand what was involved. In addition to learning about relational coordination in order to support its implementation in the clinics, there was a potential side benefit—improving the functioning of the leadership team itself. "It was a leadership driven decision," Rawlins reflected,

Trescott and Trehearne said basically, "We're going to try this with our frontline teams, so doing it ourselves first is a way to look in the mirror. It will help us to improve as a team, and to inform us as we engage with our frontline team." Some of these folks have worked together for twenty or twenty-five years. A lot of patterns were already ingrained. But they were highly motivated to make Medical Home 2.0 work, so there was a strong desire to improve.

After introducing the concepts and measuring relational coordination in the leadership team, Rawlins and Parchman led a four-hour retreat in which they provided feedback on the results and allowed participants to begin designing solutions as a team. According to Parchman, "Diane and I spent a lot of time with the leadership team that day, going over their results with them and explaining the concepts and the interrelationships between the concepts, and giving examples of what this means and what that means and why is this area scoring higher than other areas."

Respect was one issue the team wanted to address. They already had the ground rules, but these were not followed in a consistent way. Rawlins said, "We didn't have a big group discussion on this topic. Rather we asked people to reflect individually about, what are the kinds of things you need from others to show up and do your work, to feel respected? People wrote their answers on sticky notes—quite poignant—and from these, we came up with behavioral standards." One leader reported that behaviors changed following the retreat:

> The primary care leadership team is following the behavioral norms that we established in the retreat. These standards are now listed on the back of every meeting agenda. We do a check during the meetings to see if the standards are being followed. We've also implemented communication systems with each other to address shared knowledge, making sure our communication is aligned and consistent.[6]

BUILDING INTERNAL COACHING CAPACITY
FOR RELATIONAL COORDINATION

Some members of the primary care leadership team also attended the Roundtable at the University of California, Berkeley, hosted by the Relational

Coordination Research Collaborative. They began to share ideas about relational coordination with colleagues from other health systems and from industries beyond healthcare. The following month, ten primary care leaders from Group Health, along with organizational development and clinical leaders from the nearby Kaiser Permanente Northwest health system, participated in a workshop, co-led by Tony Suchman of Relationship-Centered Health Care and Diane Rawlins, called "Improving Work Processes with Relational Coordination." The purpose of this workshop was to prepare participants to use relational coordination principles to create positive, sustainable organizational change, using the following frameworks:[7]

- *Relational coordination.* Explicitly linking communication and relationships for the purpose of task integration
- *Adaptive leadership.* Providing a map and a way for teams to measure success when work is unprecedented, complex, and requires experimentation
- *Process consulting.* Creating a safe setting in which group members can reflect, share feedback, re-engage, and hold each other accountable
- *Appreciative inquiry.* Focusing on stories of already existing strengths and successes as a means of building on those elements

CHANGE IN THE PRIMARY CARE CLINICS

As Group Health's primary care clinics prepared for the changes, some participants were concerned about how the changes would play out. Each clinic was organized around primary care teams of thirteen to fifteen people, consisting of a mix of physician assistants and nurse practitioners; pediatric or family practice physicians; physicians trained in internal medicine; and registered nurses (RNs), licensed practical nurses, and medical assistants. Each clinic also had a nurse leader and a physician leader. Some of the clinics were about to pilot a new kind of care team for their most complex patients—Level 3, or complex care, teams—that would incorporate several additional team members, including an internal medicine physician. One of the clinic chiefs described what he was observing in his clinic:

Our staff are a little bit nervous about seeing these complex patients, but I've told them, "You know, we've been doing this for a decade. What are you uncomfortable with? If you have a problem you need an internist for, go ahead and refer the patient to them. The patient can go downstairs to their clinic and see them and get the consult, then come back to us."

The RNs are concerned, too, because we've been low-staffed on RNs for years now. And so they are actually very overstretched and overburdened. But none of us really know what all the other work is that they do, and they don't know enough yet about what the other people on the team can do. That's been a silo for a long time.

That's where this relational coordination, I thought, would be very useful to help everyone understand what everyone else is doing. And have the team and the leadership of the clinic go and look at these RNs and their jobs, and say, "These last five things on the list that you've been told to do or you think you have to do, we don't need you to do that anymore. We can give that to somebody else who can do it, so you can do this other work."

The contribution he hoped for was quite basic:

I think it is really going to be powerful to have people learn how other people do their jobs. And I'm trying to figure out, which of these interventions would we use to build the shared goals, the shared knowledge, and the respect. Those are things that the group needs to get some traction on. Especially shared knowledge—What are we all doing and what are our strengths [and] what are our weaknesses? It's been hard because we have to see patients, and we haven't had a whole lot of time for team development.

Insufficient time for team development was a common constraint in primary care and throughout the healthcare industry, and Group Health's primary care leadership team was committed to addressing it.

LAUNCHING RELATIONAL COORDINATION IN THE PRIMARY CARE CLINICS

By January 2014, the primary care leadership team was ready to take the next step. Three clinics were selected to participate in this change process. Lean coach Lindsay Pappas explained the kickoff:

The coaches have gone and met the teams in the three clinics where we will be doing the initial work. We spent about an hour with each of the teams, introducing them to relational coordination as a topic: how the pilot [i]s going to work and how the survey process works. We could see that they [we]re already interested in RC and how it [wa]s going to work. And the feedback from the teams, that was really helpful to know. They had questions and they started thinking, just from that kickoff.

"At one of the clinics," one leader recalled, "we had a little bit of pushback from people saying, it's the organization's fault that we're not a good team, and things like that. So we had anticipated some people being stuck there. But none of the teams were."

As the primary care teams began to measure their baseline relational coordination, Rawlins and Pappas began to plan the intervention process. Despite the agreement in principle about potential synergies between relational coordination and lean, it was not clear how these relational and work process interventions would be combined in practice. From Rawlins' perspective as an organizational development practitioner:

We are thinking that the first intervention will be more focused on the relational aspects, probably emphasizing respect, trust, and safety, and also shared knowledge, which could begin to touch on process improvement. The team members will also get a good chunk of time to make sense of their data and—hopefully—to own their improvement ideas and questions. It is in the second intervention session that I believe we will focus more on process improvement, based on their ideas from the first session.

As a lean practitioner Pappas also had ideas about how to integrate the approaches:

We've been talking about it borrowing a process from lean, called A3 problem solving, which is a four-step approach to understand root causes and to then propose countermeasures. We would first look at the actual RC survey results, and after some sense-making time, we would look at target versus actual: Where do we want to be? What does that look like? When we have great relational coordination and things are working really well, what does that look like? A positive deviance sort of perspective. And, in terms of metrics, maybe that's a score of 4.5 or above on relational coordination. Then the team would discuss, Where are we right now? What was our score? What's my current experience with this? Where do we want to be versus where are we now?

Then the second stage is delving into the why. Why is it that we're here right now? We're thinking about using the Relational Model of Organizational Change to guide this discussion. If they have really low respect, we're probably not going to be diving into work processes. We're going to need to talk about relational issues. So this could set us up to be able to focus where the group's energy goes. If it's a relational intervention they need help with, we might pull in our HR experts. If it's more of a work process intervention needed, I would take that on from a lean perspective.

FEEDBACK, INTERVENTION, AND CHANGE

As the coaches reviewed the baseline relational coordination data, they found that the response rate was nearly 100 percent in all the clinics. These high response rates were seen as an indication that leaders and frontline workers in the clinics were engaged and interested. Rawlins coached the coaches, by walking through each team's report one by one. From her perspective, "It was a rich and nuanced discussion, filled with inklings, hypotheses, and clues about how to proceed with feeding back the data to the teams."

Janice Wharton had been supportive in her role as a nursing leader on the primary care leadership team, but she was somewhat wary of how this would work in practice. She attended session 1 with the coaches and was quite surprised to see how the teams responded to their data.

> We had a four-hour session in each of the clinics where we reviewed the high-level results with them and then had the staff identify what they wanted to work on over the next few months. We got good reactions and we saw that the survey really helps people focus on the work and on getting outcomes in the work.
>
> They went right to their working relationships with each other, having really good conversations about their jobs and helping each other understand their jobs, how to work together, and how this work could help them achieve results in the workplace. So that's very interesting, very different than what we've done in the past, where the team building has been more touchy-feely. RC has seemed to help us focus on getting results as a work team versus just liking each other in the workplace. We were a little surprised but delighted that they focused on work issues around coordination, not just their interpersonal relationships with each other.

A key physician leader agreed:

I've been participating with the coaches in planning the sessions and doing the debriefs afterward. I've been very pleasantly surprised how focused the conversations have been among the teams. Staff are jumping right in to what seem to be the right topics. They're getting energized. They're coming up with actionable work plans and they're following through on the work plans.

The primary care project director recounted:

One of the things they all did was to make this visual that Lindsay and Diane helped build—it's a tree with the roots having the different elements of RC. So the roots of the tree are shared knowledge, shared goals, mutual respect, et cetera. And each of the teams has leaves where they can write down when they've observed RC behaviors and they can recognize the team member who demonstrated the behavior and put it on the tree. So each team receives fifty leaves, and it'll be interesting when leaders round in the clinic to see the trees and how they're being built.

All three teams decided to work on reducing inventory at the end of each day. "Inventory," a lean concept, means different things to different teams, but basically a team is asking whether their inboxes are empty at the end of each day or whether they have leftover tasks and, if so, how to communicate that to each other. They were also thinking about timeliness for the patient, how to make sure that the flow each day is going well, and how to communicate that to each other to help achieve their shared goal of reducing inventory, so patients can flow through on time.

Looking at their relational coordination results, one team had identified the need for better problem-solving communication in place of blaming. They developed a process that would help them identify specific issues in need of problem-solving communication. They decided to do additional problem-solving communication in their daily huddles, even though they don't have a lot of time in the mornings. They also decided that if something required more time to resolve than they had in their daily huddle, they would bring the issue to their weekly huddle using a yellow-slip system at the whiteboard. They decided to get a portable phone so that they could talk to specialists when the patient was still in the exam room, to do a virtual consult and improve the timeliness of communication.

Two teams also invented new approaches for dealing with stress and conflict. In one team, Wharton explained:

> Their theme was "game day" so that when they already know that the day's going to be hard because of access issues or staffing issues, they will implement a set of strategies ahead of time so that they will have mutual respect and good communication on those days, so that they'll be ready. Instead of saying, "Today's going to be a really bad day, what do we do about it?" it was more like, "Put on your game day. You know, we all have to work a little harder and faster and how important it is to be positive to each other when we have to do that."
>
> Then the other team came up with a hot-tub theme. And it was because someone on that team had said, "When I'm busy at home with my husband, or whatever, and we can't talk about something but we know we need to, we say, "Well, we'll talk about this at the hot tub." And so that clinic decided, instead of a gripe session, it would be the "hot-tub talk."

This reframing was potentially powerful from a psychological perspective, given the finding that people tend to shut down and become rigid under negative stress, while they open up and become more creative under positive stress.[8] This reframing was also consistent with the focus of relational coordination on problem-solving versus blaming communication. In effect, the teams were designing interventions that would enable them to solve problems, as needed, rather than blame others for what was going wrong.

Conversations of interdependence were seen as one of the most useful tools for creating new conversations and building shared knowledge. A clinic operations manager explained:

> We did about twenty or thirty minutes of these conversations among all the different roles, and it was great. Just three simple questions we had to ask. The conversations were lovely. I mean they were fabulous. People said very honest things, "Hey, I don't know why you do this." And people were open and listening. Even our brand new staff felt comfortable to engage in those conversations. We got to say, "You know, honestly, I don't know why you do this. I'd love to understand, because it really makes it hard when I have something to do." And one of the RNs was doing something with a medical assistant, but the medical

assistant was saying to her, "I don't know why you do that. It makes it really hard when I try to do this." And the nurse was like, "Oh, I didn't realize that." It's just honest. I'm trying to figure out how we can do this on a regular basis, because it really does matter.

Everybody went away with a homework assignment to have two conversations of interdependence with people in other functions on their team. Based on session 1, the coaching team developed an agenda for session 2, to be held one month later.

EARLY EXPERIENCES WITH RELATIONAL COORDINATION INTERVENTIONS

Two months after session 2, when the interventions were still very new, one clinic operations manager was seeing positive changes in her clinic. In particular, she noted employees' willingness and ability to participate proactively in organizational changes intended to improve quality and efficiency outcomes for patients. Her clinic was exploring how medical assistants could become health coaches for patients with obesity issues, and how to improve productivity by reallocating tasks across roles in the clinic.

> We are diving into how to get to that high-functioning team and looking at some of our work processes, and how do we get the waste out essentially. And we had a little kickoff event at the same time that our baseline relational coordination feedback was complete. During their first session, they decided to see what the medical assistant does, so they had the physician provider actually play the role of everyone else. So, he was the medical assistant; he was the LPN [licensed nurse practitioner]; he was the RN; he was the physician, and we had one of the participants be the patient. And as they're going through that, the providers were like, "Oh, you do this? Oh, you do that? Well, that's not very efficient; I should do that." And there were great learnings from the providers' perspective.
>
> The providers took ownership of things that had been in the medical assistant's pool, but that were maybe not the right work to have in that pool, because it was medication review. We realized the providers were repeating the process again, without taking into account what was already being done. There was also a lot of that mutual respect part of relational coordination of "Oh, this has really got to be hard for the medical assistant to do this without having the training." You know,

even the providers were saying, "Hey, there are some meds on here that even I have no idea what they are." Right? Because they're specialty meds, and it's like, "Oh, okay, maybe there's a better way to do this."

Staff also decided to reallocate some of the work that was involved in virtual medicine. Some providers were overloaded with entering notes and doing the follow-up with patients and providers afterward. According to the clinic operations manager:

> I have one provider who routinely does two-hundred-plus emails in a week time, and then we'll do ten to twenty phone calls of prescheduled phone calls, and then he has the other calls that he does. So, there's this flood of virtual work that we weren't using our other staff to triage and we weren't finding a different path for the patient to use appropriately."[9]
>
> When we started using the electronic health record, we somehow lost the conversation they used to have with the medical assistant—"Call Mr. Smith and have him do this, have him do this, have him do this, and call me back if it's not getting better, or make an appointment with me." A very detailed message, and they used to do that verbally, and then do a scratch note, and the telephone call happened. Then it went away. With Epic [the electronic health record used by Group Health], it's the provider having to write that note, and then sending it on to the medical assistant to make that phone call. For some reason, that was lost, and we didn't have a lot of medical assistants doing phone calls out to patients.

As a clinic operations manager, she perceived a growing level of comfort between the different roles to have these conversations and to create something new.

> There was comfort in the team's ability to communicate, and they felt the trust. They felt like everybody was listening to their ideas. So, whether it was the provider, the medical assistant, or the nurse—LPN or RN—they felt like they were able to speak and that communication was effective . . . It all comes down to that mutual respect, shared knowledge, shared goals. It's having all of those pieces in place to make sure it's happening. And doing that across an entire organization is difficult.

From her perspective, participants reached a relatively quick consensus on how to reallocate tasks across their roles—providers would do more of the reconciliation of medications, while medical assistants would do more of the after-visit summaries at the time of discharge from the clinic and the follow-up calls to the patients. Just one week later, 90 percent of the after-visit summaries were being completed by the medical assistants.

These primary care teams seemed to be building *adaptive capacity*, a capacity that was becoming more important as the rate of change was accelerating. "We need to get more comfortable with change," a nursing leader explained.

> One shortcoming in our use of lean before was that we focused on the standardization part but not on the experimentation and learning part—that was too messy. We were under the understanding that, "We all need to do standard work." But now we see, "No, that's just the starting point. Let's figure out how we get to the next step, which is we've all got to start experimenting."

According to a physician leader on the primary care leadership team, "We're starting to see that RC interventions help teams implement what they're trying to implement. The RC survey is actually a catalyst rather than a new initiative. The survey tells us how we can do things better. It doesn't add to change fatigue, it actually helps."

BUILDING LEADERSHIP CAPACITY THROUGH TRAINING

Because relational coordination is a dynamic that plays out among colleagues in different workgroups, the intervention methodology taught by Suchman and Rawlins encouraged frontline staff to take responsibility for the current state of their own teamwork and do something about it. Group Health's primary care teams appeared to be doing just that. Even the team that had started by blaming the organization for the fact that their teamwork was not strong had moved quickly to take ownership of the relational patterns they observed in their data.

Relational coordination is not just about frontline staff taking responsibility, however. It is also about a new way of leading. Before the RC launch, the primary care working group had developed a new team-training program for the clinic chiefs and clinic operations managers. The curriculum was deeply informed by the Lencioni team effectiveness model, providing insight into individual communication preferences and conflict styles to enable clinic leaders to build teamwork among staff members by better understanding and adapting to their personal differences. A Group Health human resources business partner explained:

> I was part of the subgroup that worked on team development using the Lencioni model. We focused on things like conflict resolution, communication. Having those difficult conversations. We've done Myers-Briggs assessments and strength finders, all as ways of having people appreciate the differences on the team and recognize that if you have an idea or if you need accomplish something, you need to tailor your message to your audience, because not everybody receives information the same way. By sharing our differences, by making those more transparent and having people be more self-aware of their own preferences and styles as well as those of others, it breaks down some of those things that can get in the way of coming together as colleagues and team members.[10]

Relational coordination added an important new dimension to Group Health's team training, in her view, by offering clinic leaders an opportunity to go beyond individual differences to address *roles.*

> With relational coordination we are going beyond individual differences to look at roles. Recognizing that if you look at service to the patient, everyone has a role to play, and we should think about how I can play my role in a way that makes the job of the next person easier, so it appears seamless to the patient. And everybody can go home feeling like we all did our best work. Not to go home exhausted, and even if they are exhausted, to feel like it was worth it because they accomplished something.

Relational coordination also provided an opportunity to link team-building activities directly to Group Health's lean improvement work. The relational coordination interventions underway in the clinics were helping leaders to reinforce the skills that the teamwork training was designed to build. A physician leader on the primary care leadership team was particularly hopeful about this potential, "I think it would really help us to think about connecting the dots between leadership development and linking it directly to improving the patient experience and quality process outcomes. How do we do that? How do we make that link? Because right now, people still think of these as separate silos."

We know from existing research that training programs are more impactful when training is connected directly to something participants are doing in the present. This connection helps to overcome a traditional training challenge—transferring what participants have learned into their daily work. More and more training programs are designed to engage learners in some kind of project in their own workplaces, where they can put into practice almost immediately what they are learning. The coaching and intervention work was beginning to make this link. According to a physician leader on the primary care leadership team:

> The clinic leaders are definitely involved in the RC interventions. They're getting the concepts. They're working on the homework like everybody else. They're working on specific improvements in their work area. So in a sense these leaders are already learning by doing. I think it would really help us in terms of spread and sustainability to think about a better way to integrate RC within our quality improvement framework here at Group Health so we can use this as an opportunity to learn new ways of leading in our clinics.

DESIGNING STRUCTURES TO SUPPORT RELATIONAL COORDINATION

One way leaders influence relational coordination is through their role in designing, shaping, and implementing the organizational structures that support relational coordination (see Chapter 5). Through the teamwork training described earlier, leaders gained new tools for supporting teamwork among staff and implemented weekly huddles to coordinate and improve their work on a regular basis. But there are other key structures that either support or undermine relational coordination depending on their design. These structures historically had not been designed with a view toward supporting relational coordination, and their design would ultimately impact the sustainability of the relational coordination interventions.

Consider employee selection. How do we select people in our organizations? Do we pay attention to teamwork when we hire new employees or promote existing employees into positions of greater responsibility? Do we have policies and practices that enable us to deselect people who turn out to be relationally or otherwise ill-suited for their roles? What is the nature of our training policies and practices? Do we design our ongoing training programs in a way that adequately supports teamwork? What are our conflict-resolution processes? And are people held accountable for broader outcomes, not just for their own immediate tasks?

What about other organizational practices? What are our meeting structures, and do they include the key roles in the continuum of care? Do we design protocols for care delivery that encompass the continuum of care beyond the immediate tasks of a particular role? Do we design our information systems so that information is shared easily and visibly with other key roles in the continuum of care? These organizational practices are all influential in shaping relational coordination, for better or worse. Some can be shaped by leaders of individual clinics, and some must be changed in partnership with leaders elsewhere in the organization.

Selection and Deselection for Teamwork

"Most important, probably, is hiring the right people in the first place," according to one clinic operations manager. "I think if we've had any kind of management role, we've all hired and then realized, 'Oh, okay, that was a mistake.' It's usually very painful learning." The human resource management department also plays a role in selection through a centralized recruiting process for all staff. According to an HR business partner:

> We've done some work in recent years to get more clear about, not only the clinical and experience requirements, but interviewing—we do behavioral interviewing. And trying to pull those soft skills out. The things that people either have or they don't, in some respects. And we're getting more clear, as are managers, that that's important. There are a lot of skills you can train, but there are certain attitudes that, if people don't come with them, they're hard to transplant into a person.

At the clinic level, managers were looking for similar attributes:

> For the medical assistant staff I've hired, I do a preliminary screening on the phone and look for fit. I look for service, service, service, service, service. And how they address conflict. I look for willingness to speak up to other roles, and not be

overly subservient. Even if you are a new grad, we teach you many of the clinical skills you need to know. It's these other things that I can't necessarily teach . . . To find out, we do a behavioral interview.

Though it is less obvious, part of selecting for teamwork is deselection, as we know from other high-performing organizations like Southwest Airlines.[11] "If the mission, vision, and values in this organization don't work for you, you might be a better fit for a different organization," said one leader. "We might have a conversation about, 'Is this really working for you?'"

Shared Accountability and Supervision

Shared accountability is another critical human resource practice for supporting relational coordination. When work is highly interdependent, it is crucial to hold people jointly accountable for outcomes that can only be achieved by the team as a whole. Doing so is a time-intensive relational process for frontline leaders, as we saw in Chapters 4 and 5 and as extensive research has shown.[12] According to a clinic operations manager:

> The first thing I tell somebody when I hire them, I say, "If you hear from me at a monthly one-on-one that you're not doing your job, then I'm not doing mine." So you should have heard before that. One of the things that the organization has done really well is set up our workplace rounding. My boss is in my clinic once a week. I am on my floor daily, and if there is a conversation that needs to be had, we have it in the moment, because if you're waiting for the annual review that's just too late.
>
> It's a lot of work. It can be really hard, and it can be draining. But I also find it really rewarding. I do actually get back from it. And it helps that I have eighteen direct reports—I don't have forty-five.

This kind of hands-on interactive leadership—characteristic of relational leadership—depends on a relatively small span of control. As we saw in the airline industry, frontline leaders with large spans of control gravitate toward a focus on "the bad apples." Frontline leaders with smaller spans of control gravitate toward a more proactive focus on the medium to high performers. One leader explained, "I found that by focusing on the ones who are here and are happy and are doing everything that they need to be doing and want more,

the high performers have become more high performing, and the low performers are now striving to get into that." This leadership approach is consistent with the principles of relational coordination articulated in *The Southwest
Airlines Way* and the principles of positive deviance that we will see in action
at the Billings Clinic in Chapter 10.

Performance review at Group Health was focused on achieving both business outcomes and relational outcomes. An HR leader explained, "We have
an evaluation tool . . . with a section on what your personal career goals are,
what the business outcomes are that we expect you to contribute to, and to
create a line of sight between your job, whatever your role is, and the business
outcomes."

> But it's not sufficient to achieve the business outcomes. There are ways you need
> to behave while you are accomplishing those business outcomes, and one without
> the other is not okay. So if you meet your budget every year, or if you hit all your
> clinical outcomes, but you are not a respectful colleague, then that is a separate
> section with its own separate rating . . . These behaviors . . . contribute to the kind
> of culture that we want to work in and that we want patients to experience.

THE ROLE OF INFORMATION SYSTEMS

As with human resource practices, information systems can either support
relational coordination or undermine it, depending on how they are designed
and implemented. A leader in Group Health's information systems department pointed out the potential for information systems to better support coordination.[13] The problem list, for example, was intended to give providers an
overview of a patient, facilitating the coordination of their care, "The problem
list is meant to be a patient-level summary of their key, important medical
problems. It's a place where anyone working with a patient should be able to
come and get an overview of what is happening with that patient."

Instead, the problem list can be quite cumbersome, difficult to sort through,
with too much detail in some cases, and critical missing information in others,
due in part to a lack of a shared responsibility to maintain it.

> Historically, for better or for worse, the maintenance of the problem list has usually
> been the job of the primary care doctor. Since our sickest patients deal so frequently

with our specialty physicians, it's not realistic that the primary care doctor be the only one responsible for maintaining that problem list. You want the specialist to be looking at that so they can see their patient in a context, and you want the specialist updating that problem list and maintaining it. So that when the patient does come back to primary care, the problem list would be an accurate portrayal of all of their specialty care. But that has not happened—specialists, historically, have just ignored that and just continue to put all their stuff in free text notes.

There was this feeling at one point that better use of the problem list in a patient's chart is fundamental to shared understanding of the complexity of a patient's medical condition. So, maybe there are some technical things that we could do to improve the problem list or sort the problem list or something like that. But, until there is a leadership goal set to say, "We think coordinating care between primary care and specialty is important for these reasons. We're going to be measuring it in this way and you're are going to be held accountable in this way"—in the absence of that, simply doing technical things to the problem list and hoping that people use it in the right ways does not make sense. We've done that and it just doesn't end up having the effect that you want.

THE NEXT FRONTIER: RELATIONAL COPRODUCTION WITH PATIENTS

Along with efforts to build relational coordination, another fundamental change occurring at Group Health was a move toward greater relational coproduction between care providers and patients. Group Health had been an early pioneer in shared decision making in the specialty care arena.[14] Now relational coproduction was expanding to include everyday health decisions, as medical assistants expanded their roles to become health coaches for patients. According to a nursing leader:

> In shared decision making, you're feeding the evidence-based information to the patient, and then the two of you are making that choice based on individual situations. Whereas with health coaching and motivational interviewing, it's really about finding out where this patient lives with their chronic disease and setting goals that they can accomplish themselves, because they really drive the care. They're the ones you can tell to not eat cake a hundred times, but unless they make that choice, it won't work. You have to really engage what they're interested in and what they're ready for.

NEW RELATIONSHIP WITH KAISER PERMANENTE

As these change efforts played out, Group Health was being acquired by its powerful sister organization to the south—Kaiser Permanente. The new relationship seemed likely to succeed given shared values and a shared history. Recall that Group Health started its relational coordination journey together with its colleagues from Kaiser Permanente, with both organizations focused on improving complex chronic care for their members. Eighteen months after its launch in the Northwest Region, the Kaiser Permanente relational coordination journey had achieved improvements ranging from patient satisfaction to employee engagement, thanks to leadership support from management, frontline workers, and the Labor Management Partnership. A regional vice president summarized the learning thus far:

> Capitalizing on the opportunity requires leadership that accepts the opportunity to be boundaryless and to focus on improving the care continuum versus departmental performance. And when you provide the leaders who are passionate about moving in that direction with a great tool like relational coordination, you have the ability to truly transform our culture and delivery for even greater value for our members.[15]

SUMMING UP

Moving into its new relationship with Kaiser Permanente, Group Health was making progress on the complex challenge of coordinating primary care.[16] Reflecting on their efforts, an HR leader noted:

> This has been a long journey. Group Health has for a long time recognized the value of developing teams, but at the beginning we weren't very good at it. The first part is recognizing the potential. We have done a lot of working in silos. We have teams within silos. We've had success stories of people working across silos on particular pieces of work. But the most evolved state of integration that we could achieve, we're not there yet.

Looking forward, the primary care leadership team anticipated additional areas where relational coordination could potentially add value, based on the emerging research. First, if the pilot was successful, relational coordination initiatives might expand beyond the initial three clinics. Second, relational coordination could be used to help new complex care teams form successfully. To do so would require a paradigm shift, toward teams that go beyond face-to-face interactions to include colleagues working in other locations with the same patients. These teams would increasingly include patients and their families to engage them more fully in promoting their own health and wellness. This paradigm shift was well under way at Group Health. Let's see how this same paradigm shift was playing out half way around the world in a Danish municipality called Varde.

8 RELATIONAL COPRODUCTION IN VARDE MUNICIPALITY

Relational coproduction is the production of outcomes by workers in partnership with their clients, through relationships of shared goals, shared knowledge, and mutual respect. Although relational coproduction is a simple concept, it can be challenging to achieve because it departs from traditional professional/client relationships in which clients comply with goals established by professionals, passively receiving their expert knowledge.[1]

Promoting health and wellness is both more holistic and smarter from the standpoint of shifting investment from downstream consequences to upstream causes. But investing upstream creates a need for relational coordination and coproduction across a greater number of sectors. While many organizations were working to make relational coordination stronger internally, as we saw at Group Health, municipalities in Denmark were working to build relational coordination across sectors in the community. According to Danish municipal leader Max Kruse, "We see the challenge, and we don't have a lot of answers for that challenge right now. But we're working on it." The movement was profound, according to organizational consultant Carsten Hornstrup:

> In Denmark we've had public organizations taking care of a lot of issues, such as healthcare, education, social service, et cetera, but we can't afford that to the same degree anymore. As citizens, we have to take over vital parts of these services ourselves—for our kids and our elderlies—so that the professionals are taking care of the more difficult citizens, for example, severe mental illness, elderlies with dementia, et cetera. And even here, a much more collaborative approach to taking care of these citizens is needed, collaborating with the relatives of the citizen. Some cities are handling these challenges by setting up a coordinating body within the municipality to coordinate across groups of professionals, or they

bring together relevant professional groups in a direct form of dialogue to address the needs of a particular population—troubled kids, or the elderly with dementia, or families with severe social issues. This new approach will require everyone working together in a new way.

Rather than simply cutting services, on the one hand, or simply making everything the responsibility of the public sector, on the other hand, the Danish model was about supporting health and wellness in the community by promoting care for oneself and for one another.

RESPONDING TO NEW EXPECTATIONS AND PRESSURES

Responding to new expectations and pressures, leaders in Varde Municipality began this journey in 2013 to make municipal services more proactive and more of a partnership with the citizens. Varde Municipality is in the Region of Southern Denmark, on the west coast of the Jutland peninsula. The main town and the site of its municipal council is the town of Varde. In the healthcare revolution of 2007, Varde Municipality merged with several other municipalities to achieve the scale needed to meet its new responsibilities for health and wellness in the community. Kruse explained the impact of the healthcare revolution:

> With the healthcare revolution in 2007, we set up a clear separation of duties between regions and municipalities. We formed five regions that are responsible for health and psychiatric care, and ninety-eight municipalities that are responsible for taking care of people before they get sick [e.g., preventive care] and after they are out of hospital.

These new responsibilities were supported by a new approach to payment.

> We have been increasing the part that municipalities pay when citizens are in hospital or visiting a doctor. We started out in 2007 being responsible for 9 percent, on average, of the total cost of the hospitals and the general practitioners. Now we have something close to 20 percent of the cost. Because of the 20 percent and because of our citizens, we have incentives to take care of our duties.

Varde had a historic commitment to health and wellness, which gave its leaders a platform to build upon. Kruse explained, "Local health issues are a priority for Varde Municipality. It started with an earlier leader—he set a high priority and [had] a high ambition for local health. It's our history—and we've provided the resources to make it possible." At the national level there were debates about the move toward community-based care. Some of the public unions were engaged in the national debate. However, the Danish municipalities tended to be highly pragmatic and consensus based. As Kruse noted, "In Varde, we have a lot of consensus in what we do because we work together for the best of our people. We make a written plan for the coming year once a budget has been decided upon by our mayor and city council. We are close to the users and we are very practical."

Varde's efforts were supported by the new mayor, Erik Buehl Nielsen. Nielsen had taken a deep interest in relational coordination as a way to shift municipal services toward a focus on health and wellness in the community, starting with root causes like workforce participation.

EXPANDING WORKFORCE PARTICIPATION

In Denmark, which has one of the highest rates of workforce participation in the world, workforce participation is considered a key ingredient for health and wellness. Helping people to get the right skills and find a good match was considered to be a responsibility of the municipalities. Now, with an aging workforce, every worker was needed more than ever. Some of the younger citizens were hard to place in jobs, but it was also a challenge to place older workers after an extended illness or a job loss. According to Erling Pedersen, director of Social Health and Employment:

> If you lose your job and lose your relationship to your workplace, within six months we find you are very, very tough to get back into the workplace again. You can lose your health, too. So we need to be very actively involved in helping people hold on to their workplace, and getting them healthy again. So we do rehabilitation for those who are out of work. This takes collaboration between a lot of different people.

HEALTHY AGING

Another change in Varde was the increased expectations for healthy aging. Since the healthcare revolution, the municipality's goal has been to enable people to age at home, providing them with more support to stay healthy and active but less support for having their houses cleaned. Housecleaning services were to come instead from the citizen and his or her family and neighbors. Kruse explained:

> Mastering your own situation—I think that's been a change in concept in Denmark in very short time. In a few years there has been a movement from feeling like you have the right to have your house cleaned. You have been working hard and now you are seventy-five years old. And so the municipality has to come and clean your house. That was, at least in some areas, the feeling some years back, but not any longer. I think that has changed quite dramatically over the last three years, probably. People are now proud of managing their own situation. And our staff are now telling elders that's how they can stay fresh and young and healthy.

This shift represented a significant cultural change that took place in a very short time, according to Varde's leaders. The trigger for this cultural change was not just the budgetary cuts, according to Kruse, but also a realization that there was a better way to live:

> I think that for each individual, you have to have something more than money to make these changes. There are good stories, and it seems, at least here in Varde, that everybody has the same agenda. The government has the same agenda, we have the same agenda, and nearly e[very] family has the same agenda—to keep healthy as long as possible. It's very easy for us to find somebody that will sit with a newspaper and give an interview and say, "Yeah, this has been fantastic. I've thrown away my helping support, and now I'm on my own again. And it's a much better life."

To make it possible for aging citizens to live healthier lives at home, Varde established a health center, where existing services were co-located and new services were developed, including yearly wellness visits to all citizens aged seventy-eight and older. These wellness visits were part of an effort to keep people healthy and in their homes as long as possible throughout their aging years, with the needed supports. Varde also built a transitional unit in one of the local elder centers to reduce hospitalizations and readmissions by providing physical therapy to strengthen elders who were too weak to return home safely. It was difficult to get people out of the hospital when they were still too sick to go home. The transitional care unit at the nursing home was an attempt to meet this challenge. According to Pedersen, "That's an example of working with the patients and with the wallet, too. Because we save money and we believe that we give good care too."

HEALTHY BEHAVIORS AND MANAGING CHRONIC DISEASE

In addition to supporting healthy aging, the new payment system also encouraged municipalities to take a new approach to promoting healthy behaviors and managing chronic disease generally. Under the leadership of Margit Vest Thomsen, the head of Health Promotion, Varde Municipality began offering courses to help citizens learn to live with chronic diseases, depression and anxiety, chronic pain, and so on. Thomsen's department also offered supervision to citizens who had lifestyle problems, whether with diet, alcohol, or drugs. Supervision involved skilled coaching from nurses and other professionals, using an approach that ran counter to the traditional professional/client relationship. According to Thomsen, "It doesn't work to say, 'Do it because I am the nurse and I said so.' It has to connect to something the citizen cares about."

Nurses and therapists in the Health Promotion Department were learning to act as coaches by engaging in motivational interviewing, talking with citizens about healthy behavior and managing their chronic conditions. Motivational interviewing is a technique that helps patients or citizens to identify life goals that can motivate them to engage in healthier behaviors, such as "I want to be around to see my grandchildren graduate from school." In effect, motivational interviewing was intended to establish shared goals between workers and their clients. Relational coproduction—the production of outcomes by workers and their clients through high-quality communication, supported by shared goals, shared knowledge, and mutual respect—was thus becoming part of the new care delivery system in Varde, with the goal of supporting health and wellness in the community while minimizing costly visits to doctors and hospitals.

This new approach to behavioral health and chronic-disease management was part of a deeper cultural change. In the past, there had been a belief that healthcare and medications could solve everything. Now it's different. According to director of health Kirsten Myrup, "Say you had a stroke—we know it's better to have exercise than pills. That is part of this change—that you take responsibility for your own health. You cannot just go to the doctor and say, 'Cure me.' Instead, it's 'take responsibility for your own life.'"

The downside was that this culture change was differentiated by income level, at least initially. Myrup explained, "It's strange because exercise is better for everyone. But exercise is much more income differentiated. The wealthy are running and the poor are getting fat." Her colleagues agreed:

> The poor sometimes have mental illness, and typically they don't have a healthy life. So that's an area where we have to offer extraordinary help by helping these people with mental illness to get healthy. Stop smoking, stop maybe drinking, get out running, et cetera . . . To do the exercise, it's not about getting everyone out to run. But rather, How can you do the moving in your daily life? It's got to be natural. That's one of the ways we can get to social equality in health. It's the way of thinking. It's not just exercise; it's the way of thinking—the way of living that's natural.

One thing they were learning was that these behavior changes could not be externally imposed. Myrup explained, "We are from a part of Denmark, where if you say to people 'do it,' they don't do it. We have to have to take the message to the private part of our citizens to take it inside and do it." One solution, they agreed, would be more concerted efforts on the part of citizens to notice when something is going wrong with family members, neighbors, or colleagues and to offer help. Pedersen argued that this would require a first-responder mentality:

> The first person who spots someone taking the wrong path should react. I think that comes from inside you. So that's how I see it. Instead of saying I'm not a manager, I should notice that one of my colleagues is not doing what he should. It's often a colleague. It's a member of the family. So, how can we do it? Because if we're starting to go a little bit in the wrong direction—if we get a small push in the very early days it might be easier. I think that's some of the philosophy that's underlying this. How could we make it so that the first person who sees something could take just a little bit more responsibility before it gets out of hand?

This call for citizens to act as their "brother's or sister's keeper" was reminiscent of the bystander training that US colleges had begun to promote in an

effort to prevent sexual assault. By establishing the skills and the expectations
to intervene to protect another's well-being, communities may be able to tap
into an effective and cost-effective way of addressing unhealthy or threatening
behaviors.

Leadership was also responsible for creating this culture change. Mayor
Nielsen, who had been a political representative in the municipality before
becoming mayor, was known for organizing an annual bike tour and other activities to promote healthy living. Kirsten Myrup was also credited for leading
this culture change. According to Kruse:

> Our life would have been much easier if Kirsten had not been a busybody, but
> we know it's good for ourselves that she comes around and tells us, "Have you
> thought about [this]? Have you thought about [that]? You could also do . . ." And
> then the political backup is important because we could just say, "Well, Kirsten,
> this sounds very interesting. You might be right."

RELATIONAL COORDINATION ACROSS BOUNDARIES

Despite a high level of agreement regarding the municipality's role in promoting health in partnership with their citizens, and despite significant financial
incentives, Varde's leaders admitted that implementing the new approaches to
health promotion remained a challenge for them. Doing so would require far
greater coordination than they had achieved thus far, across boundaries that
previously did not need to be spanned. The number of silos in municipal government was significant, as Figure 8.1 illustrates. Kruse reflected:

> Now we have the challenge of working across sectors, and we don't know how to
> do it yet. These people have to get along and work together. Sometimes it works—
> especially at the start of the week [*laughter around the table*]. They need to have a
> good relationship between each other and a good dialogue—they need to know
> what is going on in the other silos. Otherwise nothing works.

There was a challenge with creating relational coordination across municipal government more broadly. Kruse explained:

> I think if you look at relational coordination, if there's not mutual respect inside
> the organization, the chance is that our citizens experience that when they meet
> the frontline staff . . . And that's where we are now in our management team. We

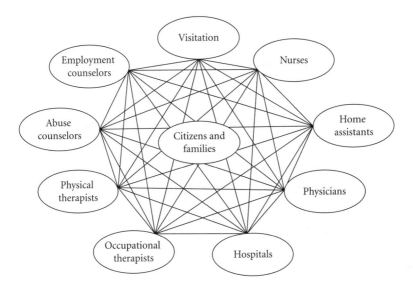

FIGURE 8.1   Health and wellness in the community: a coordination challenge

spend more hours together than we used to do because we have just been brought together. So, we are trying to build it from the top. There is no script for this.

Just as Myrup had played a leadership role in getting Varde to focus on promoting community health and wellness, she was also playing a leadership role in the efforts to improve relational coordination. As the director of health, Myrup was responsible for health and rehabilitation; the work of the nurses and therapists; health policies and strategies; coordination across sectors in the municipality; and coordination with community-based physicians, hospitals, psychiatric hospitals, and the Region. Myrup brought a broad set of skills to her leadership role. According to Hornstrup:

> Kirsten was in our training program for relational leadership. I was assessing one of her papers, and she was pointing to some of the challenges there in Varde, and she had already read about relational coordination. So I met with her and said, "I have a bit of a provocative proposition for you. I think you could do this in a more effective way using relational coordination." And she told her boss about it, and they invited me to come and talk. They were really quite interested in finding out how they could do more relational coordination in their work.

Building from this initial interest, Myrup and her colleagues worked with Hornstrup to strategize how they would build connections across their silos. Given the perceived need for cross-sectoral coordination in almost every area of the municipality, where would they start?

IMPROVING COORDINATION OF CARE FOR ELDERS WITH DEMENTIA

Myrup argued that care for the elderly with dementia was the place to start due to its complexity and due to the need to involve the citizen and his or her family in the care process. So many players were involved in the care of elders with dementia. If they could find a way to build relational coordination in this complex area, Varde would have a strong start on its journey. Myrup explained her thinking:

> Relative to the whole overall budget, dementia is not a huge area for Varde. But it's a very complicated area. And so it's a good area, I think, to start out on. I think we will do a lot of good observations and find out [about] a lot of obstacles that we will be able to transfer into the larger organization. That's my expectation.

To achieve the initiative's overall performance goal—enabling elders with dementia to remain in their homes with their families and with neighbors nearby as long as possible—involved many players.

> We will be developing relational coordination among those who are working with elderly citizens with dementia. These include nurses, nurse assistants, physiotherapists, dementia consultants, general practitioners, hospital staff, relevant administrative staff, and most importantly for us, the relatives of the elderly citizen. For citizens with some other conditions, relatives are optional—for dementia, their involvement is essential.

Given the aging of the population, and given Varde's goal to reduce hospitalization and keep citizens at home as long as possible, it seemed sensible to target dementia as an area to target for improvement. But given the complexity of the cross-cutting relationships and the multiple sectors involved, solutions would not be easy. One key element would be building relational coordination among the professionals, and then going further to build relational coproduction with the citizens and their families. It would also be critical, in Myrup's view, to involve leaders at every level of the municipality in the journey.

Myrup and her colleagues also sought support from municipal union leaders. Danish public sector unions in some parts of the country had opposed the new approach to health and wellness, concerned that "fewer warm hands" were needed when citizens became more active in the care of themselves and their family members. In addition, there was a change in the nature of work itself. The job of nurse assistants and helpers in particular had changed from helping the citizen by doing everything for him or her to helping the citizen to do the work for him- or herself. According to one nurse assistant:

> It's just that, before when I came to the house, it was like Christmas. If I come with a wheelchair and push them around, they like that. What I'm doing now is, I give them a pair of running shoes. So, I have to accept being unpopular in the short term to reach the goal in the long term.

Hornstrup reflected:

> The leaders are saying, "I have to push people into new frontiers that they would not just do themselves." They say we've got the right culture. And we've got the incentives. But I think this is about pushing that culture, because they need to meet their clients in a new way. When working with everyday rehab, the moment of truth is, "Do I give them the wheelchair as they want, or do I give them the running shoes in that moment?" Because the pressure from each individual and their families is to give them the wheelchair.

The lowest-skilled workers would experience the greatest changes in their jobs, education, and mindsets. As nurse assistants prepared to work at a higher skill level, they would have to be listened to in a way that was not currently the norm. As Hornstrup explained:

> A lot of time the nursing assistants—the largest group of employees and the ones with most client time—are not listened to. They are the ones with the shortest education, and I find that they seldom have a chance to speak. At a meeting with a mixed group of nurses, physical therapist, leaders, social workers and nurse assistants, one of them came up to me and said, "I am a sixty-year-old nurse assistant, and I weigh 100 kilo. I'm one of the guys you never listen to." There are

some things built into the culture, and the way we organize. We have a visible leadership hierarchy, but we have a real—maybe even stronger—professional hierarchy that almost disables the ones with the lowest education.

These professional status hierarchies would have to be considered in designing interventions to build relational coordination and coproduction across the existing silos.

DESIGNING AND IMPLEMENTING THE RELATIONAL COORDINATION INTERVENTION

When planning the relational coordination intervention for Varde, Hornstrup reflected on previous experiences, "It is usually the people with a more positive outlook who willingly participate, but it is important to pay as much attention to the critical voices. Much resistance to change can be generated by managers not taking the critical voices seriously."

In the dementia care improvement initiative, Hornstrup trained frontline municipal leaders to serve as coaches in the change process. He and Myrup designed a three-day workshop to develop frontline leaders' knowledge and capacity to lead relational change; each workshop was followed by time in the field when they could act upon what they had learned. Hornstrup reflected on the process:

> We've run one three-day workshop so far. We've worked with internal coaches and frontline managers and introduced them to relational coordination. We've worked with the survey results and introduced different dialogic intervention tools. We taught them to do team-performance dialogues, a very structured dialogue that helps bring out every voice on an equal basis. We gave people the seven questions of relational coordination and produced a map of the different groups involved in dementia care—it's a relational mapping exercise. We asked everyone to look through the questions while looking at each group—where do they think they are currently strong, medium, and low on RC. We did it in a dialogic form. I interviewed people one at a time in the group; and we create the map together. Each individual can say what they think. We use that to prioritize the most obvious area for improvement and to prioritize next steps. Then these cross functional teams can use this map with a white board for status meetings as a way to monitor how they are doing on a regular ongoing basis.

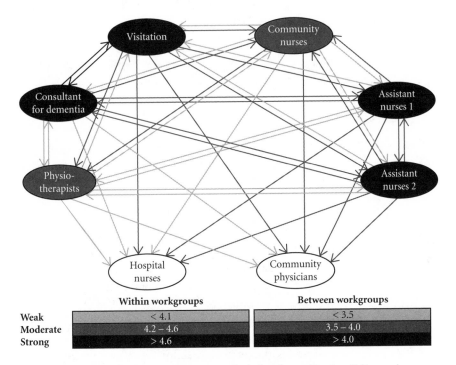

FIGURE 8.2   Frontline leader assessments of relational coordination: RC mapping
SOURCE: Joint Action, Inc., adapted from Relational Coordination Analytics.

The mapping process, in effect, allowed frontline leaders to anticipate and imagine how relational coordination was working across the various teams they were responsible for leading, specifically around the task of dementia care. See Figure 8.2 for the results. A key part of the method was for the coach to notice the workgroups that might have respect issues or feel that their voices were less likely to be heard within the broader cross-functional team, and to get the input of these workgroups separately.

The next step was to incorporate the voices of the workers themselves by conducting a survey assessment of relational coordination. According to Hornstrup, "The dialogue is the mechanism through which the goal is ultimately accomplished, but the survey gives the dialogue an edge because it provides hard data for people to use in the dialogue." Because the survey was carried out across multiple municipal sectors and organizational boundaries, it was challenging to achieve a high response rate. The response rate for the baseline survey was 65 percent, respectable but lower than the response rates of 70 percent to 100 percent the unit-based surveys at Dartmouth-Hitchcock and Group Health had achieved. Still, given the size of the workforce involved in dementia care for Varde—nearly 400 workers—there were around 260 survey responses.

When measuring relational coordination for interventional purposes, a key factor to consider is feedback of the data—when, to whom, and in what format. Previous experience had suggested the importance of timely feedback. Hornstrup explained:

> We did the survey four weeks ago, then did a final check of the data Sunday night to make sure the numbers were right. And Monday morning I was there feeding back the data to the frontline leaders, the same ones who had done the relational mapping. We wanted to do a quick feedback due to research that says how and when you feed data back to the system is part of the actual learning and determines how quickly you are able to move them along.

The survey results summarized in Figure 8.3 revealed some patterns. First, frontline leaders discovered that they were directionally correct in their assessments of the strength of relational coordination across their workgroups, but that their assessments were more positive on the whole than the assessments made by their frontline workers. Second, they could see that the lower status workgroups—for example, the nursing assistants—experienced lower levels of relational coordination than colleagues who were higher in the professional status hierarchy.

The frontline leaders were prepared to move along quickly, in part because they had anticipated the results through their own relational mapping exercise and now felt they owned the data.

> I just put the data out there and said, "Here's the pattern that I see—What do you see?" I find that one of the important things about feeding survey data back to the leaders is that they are the ones who have to do something about it. So I'm not coming with the data as the expert. I did that the first time I worked with this survey, in another organization, and it's really obvious that the leaders became much more passive because I was considered the expert and the "owner" of the numbers. They basically said, "It's your data. You know the numbers." In this case,

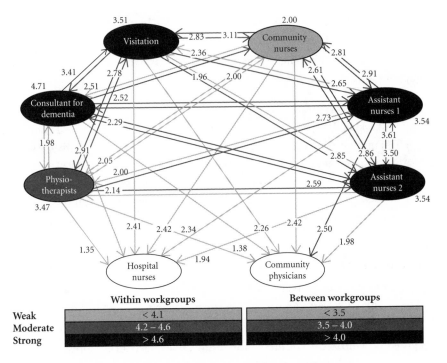

FIGURE 8.3   Worker assessments of relational coordination: RC survey
SOURCE: Joint Action, Inc., adapted from Relational Coordination Analytics.

I asked the leaders to compare the numbers with the map they produced. They could see it was actually pretty close.

The survey data revealed that there were many weak ties in the care of citizens with dementia—particularly with community-based nurses, hospital-based nurses, and general practitioners (community-based physicians). The data also revealed that the relational dimensions—shared goals, shared knowledge, and mutual respect—were stronger overall than the communication dimensions—frequent, timely, accurate, problem solving. Hornstrup felt this result suggested that work could move forward relatively quickly, "Even if the numbers are relatively low, which they are in this case, if respect is not one of the lowest dimensions, then it's easier to move forward with solutions.

Hornstrup's approach to sharing data with participants had evolved over time. "I guess my approach has actually become more blunt and upfront, saying, 'These are your problems,' being more confrontive simply because if you don't, it tends to take longer."

> Maybe I'm not a sensitive guy, but this survey is not asking, "Do you love me?"—it's just asking, "Do people respect each other's contribution to how we do our job?" I mean it's the voices of people, so I would probably turn it the other way around. I think not to use the data rather openly would not be sensitive to the people who answered this survey. And of course, I've had separate discussions with those groups that have really low numbers. But they are not surprised. Because they know. The ones who are going to get the lowest score, they knew before they got them. That's often why they're a bit defensive.

Hornstrup had been careful about sharing the data with frontline leaders first, before sharing with top leadership or the frontline employees themselves. "That's where I'm very careful," he explained, "who to share the data with first. Don't go senior. Don't go to the employees. Instead, go to the people who are pointed at, who are accountable for results, who have all the pressures—the frontline leaders. We need to talk to them first."

FRONTLINE LEADERS REFLECTING ON THE RESULTS

Based on the mapping they had done together before conducting the relational coordination survey, frontline leaders found the results were similar to what they had expected but a little worse. They began to debate the nature of the challenges and potential solutions. Hornstrup described the feedback session:

> We discussed the map and simply brainstormed possible initiatives that could handle this thing, and so we're now talking about two different things—role clarification, and building spaces for cross professional collaboration. Those are the two main things they identified to work on.

Specifically, frontline leaders acknowledged the lack of shared knowledge:

> The hardest thing right now is to find out who's doing what. So everybody thinks the other one is doing it. It's also hard to find out *how* they are doing it. And for the people doing the work, it is a problem that the relatives do not always live

close by, or they're coming in the weekend or in the evening, when we don't have so many people working at that time. So sometimes we are just leaving little notes. And that's not the best way to do it.

We don't have a stable team. We work in ad hoc teams, established for a particular citizen based on wherever the citizen lives, and what the needs are. We've got different districts in the Varde municipality. And the nurses and the occupational therapists are assigned to different districts, but those districts don't line up. Sometimes I have to work with you. And sometimes I have to work with you. And it's quite difficult to find out.

Part of the problem, they realized, was lack of visibility around the need to coordinate—and a lack of knowledge about what the others were doing.

It's our tradition . . . not coordinating with each other [or] taking responsibility for doing it. We're very good at coordinating internally. I am fine coordinating with the ones who I work directly with. But the ones who I don't see, that's the problem. And we don't know enough about the others, what they can help with, how they can support me. We don't take so much time to sit down and talk about what we are doing.

Frontline leaders also acknowledged the lack of shared goals. Goals for the care of a citizen often evolved based on the professional perspective of each caregiver, and perhaps in conversation with the family, but there was no mechanism for developing shared goals *across* caregivers. "When you meet the citizen you are going to work with, maybe you see something else than what I saw. And then you say, hey, that gets me thinking I should do this and this and this. Because you're not involved in the goal setting from the start. The goals keep changing because every person sees something different based on their training."

Frontline leaders noticed particular areas of weakness in the results. In particular, they noticed that the ties between nursing assistants and nurses were weaker than they had thought. They also recognized the importance of this tie, given the increasing complexity of the citizens.

Often, the citizens are very weak and their dementia is very progressed. So our staff are taking care of very sick elderly people in their own homes. A nurse assistant recently told me that it's not rehabilitation, it's people who are still in intensive care when they come back home. And she explained that even her nurse colleagues don't feel that they are up to it because the patients we get from the hospitals are so complex and not really ready for going home.

And often it's the ones out there who have the lowest education [who have] to care for the elderly with dementia. Because for dementia care, we don't send nurses. We send nursing assistants. But the job is very complex. In addition to the physical care, sometimes it's almost like being a family therapist.

Despite the challenges they face, the nursing assistants are often reluctant to call other members of the team for help. According to a manager of the nursing assistants:

Nursing assistants don't feel they should call the nurses. If they do call, the nurses are not very happy, because there is a cultural thing that says nurses should not be called upon to take care of dementia. Nursing assistants tell me, "I don't call nurses because the nurses are just as busy as I am. They have a lot to do. So if I call them for help I interrupt something that's also important. And the second thing is, I don't really know them. They're so far away. I don't see them very much, so that it's hard to just call and ask for help."

Her colleague in nursing agreed, "And maybe you just don't think about doing it because we are not used to it. To call each other and say, 'Hey, I need your help. Just come and help me.'"

COMPLEX CASE MEETINGS TO SUPPORT
RELATIONAL COORDINATION

One method was working well to generate creative solutions for individual citizens, though on a fairly limited basis—the simple process of meeting around a table with the relatives and caregivers of citizens with dementia. Varde dementia consultant Karin Viuff explained:

We meet around the table with the spouse or the kids, and everybody who's taking care of the citizen, and we talk for a few hours. We get ideas for how we can actually work with this particular case. Often we succeed. As a dementia consultant, it's a big part of my job, and I take it very seriously because I've had experience with it, very good experiences with it actually.

I think it's because everybody is heard. And even the nursing assistants can actually tell us about things they know about the person, things they don't know about the person, things that are difficult for them when they meet these people in their home. Sometimes there are conflicts, and there are families that really don't think we do our jobs very well. Then it's hard. But if we do it on time and early enough, it's actually good. And I find when we meet in that way, we can also coordinate with what each other says. Typically, all of us are documenting why it is hard for the citizen to stay at home, but we don't see the bigger picture. We don't have a clue that this or that is a problem. And all of a sudden we can see that, "Oh, if this is the case, we can do something here. We'll help you out." It's easier to talk the same language when we sit together.

But often these conversations don't happen, her colleagues agreed. As a result, caregivers don't know what others need to know, so it is difficult to create shared knowledge. Everybody is operating in a vacuum. Still, if they were to use complex case meetings more extensively, they would need some kind of agreement about when to convene a meeting, given that meetings could not happen on every question that arose for every citizen. As one nursing leader offered:

Maybe the fact that the complexity is growing is asking us to make sure that we are getting together in the beginning, all together, and make the plan together. And saying I'm doing this and you're doing that, and we're going this way. I think the complexity is calling for something other than waiting for someone else to decide—instead we need to talk to each other. But if we meet about all the complexities, we will meet with each other half to death [*laughter*]."

The same nursing leader had another concern:

It's a problem when we have very old, very sick people with complex nursing needs. It's not the nurses who see the problem or challenges. It's the helpers. The helpers spend the time with the citizens, so they have the information, but they don't know how to use the information. Or, to see when things get wrong with the elderly. They are very, very good at taking care of them, but not at diagnosing their needs.

To bring together the knowledge of assistants and family members, along with their own knowledge, nurses might need to play a facilitator role, a role they were not currently trained to perform. According to the same leader, "I agree that we have to bring nurses and helpers and assistants together. But my point is that the nurses are responsible for facilitating these meetings . . . And I think that, unless we have special training in that, it's just not something we do."

To better support coordination, this facilitator role could become part of nurses' training. In effect, they would become boundary spanners, bringing parties together to solve problems and coordinate care (Chapter 5).

INFORMATION SYSTEMS AS AN OBSTACLE TO RELATIONAL COORDINATION

Information systems have great potential to support relational coordination, but in Varde as elsewhere, these systems often fell short.

> Our information system does not help us very much at this point. One of the big challenges is, we've got a new IT system in Varde. We're trying to make it a basis for coordination, but it's not working yet. It was the vision of this system to be good for coordinating care. But we had a lot of challenges in forming it. We haven't given up. We are working on it now. You have to have ways of working that are captured in the system and well known by everybody.
>
> Most of our workgroups are using the IT system to input their data. But it's coming from many perspectives. If you had to read it, it's very long story. So you don't have one way you can get a view and say, 'Okay, this is the problem, or this is what we need to do together. And what's my colleague supposed to do about this?' Often, we work [on] the same things and the same citizens, but we don't know what each other is doing about it. So it's hard to coordinate our own work with the other. But it's also how we do our work. We do it in different ways in different organizations. You do it one way, and you find it good. I do it another way, and I find it good. But we are not doing it together. Yet.

These challenges with automated information systems were common, as we saw in Chapter 5. Information systems are often poorly designed to support relational coordination, but at the same time, the lack of relational coordination also makes it difficult for participants to use the systems well. Participants often don't know enough about the roles of others to know which information would be most helpful to share.

REWARDS, ACCOUNTABILITY, AND JOB DESIGN
AS OBSTACLES

There were additional obstacles to relational coordination. Rewards, account-ability, and job designs had all served to discourage relational coordination by discouraging time spent working in the *spaces between* areas of specialization. According to one nursing leader:

> The problem is that coordination is not seen as part of our work. So that we only have to do this one thing. But in fact, we also have to collaborate with the others. And that takes a little bit of time. People are being measured only for doing that one thing, so that's all they are doing, as opposed to seeing the big picture.

Some of the obstacles were quite specific.

> The way we get the money is that my people have to be face-to-face with the citizen for a certain percent of their working time. And the rest of the time, they drive from one home to another. So I think we have a tradition not to do the personal coordination very much. And we forget sometimes that it's better to be involved at the start—you can save time afterward. So we are starting to change that tradition.

The accountability structure also worked against relational coordination.

> There's a conflict because Karin has to document that she is delivering 70 percent face-to-face time. And at the same time, she has to coordinate a lot, and that's not face-to face-time. And yet, that time might save you other time. It might be worth it. But I still have to be somewhere else because that's what I get the money from. If we were measured by how we coordinate, we would do something else, I think. If we had a bonus for doing coordination, maybe we'd think differently.

TOP LEADERSHIP LEARNS FROM RELATIONAL
COORDINATION SURVEY RESULTS

After sharing the survey results with frontline leaders, Hornstrup took the re-sults to Varde's top leadership team. Gathered around a table were Pedersen, Myrup, Thomsen, Mayor Nielsen, and several others. As they viewed the base-line relational coordination survey results shown in Figure 8.3, I listened to their reflections. They were intrigued by the measurement tool and its ability to make visible in a more concrete way the networks through which services were delivered. Pedersen was intrigued:

> We haven't had a tool before for measuring this. One thing is talking about networks; now we can see it. Now we can simply ask the physical therapists, "How well do you work with the nurses?" Now we have tool we can follow up [with]— and we can go out there and measure, Did it work or didn't [it]? So now we don't have to just talk, we can do something.

Myrup noticed that the network map "creates a different image of what the organization is. It looks very different than the chart where everyone is reporting to someone else. A lot of those empty spaces on the organization chart, [this] is where we need the communication. And the organization chart never really shows that."

They were concerned when they saw the experiences of those who work most directly with the citizens. The data showed that the participants who are lowest in the hierarchy had the worst experience of coordination, while the ones at the top of the hierarchy had the best experience. Hornstrup reflected:

> That's a problem. Because those at the top set the agenda. But in numbers and in contact with the citizens, the assistants and the helpers are really outnumbering the other workgroups. And they have it the hardest. It's harder for an assistant nurse to say, we have a big problem, than it is for a nurse or leader. Often the assistants see the problems first, because they are out there the most.

Their big takeaway was that the map and the weaknesses it showed were a result of the mixed messages that they as a leadership team had been sending. According to Pedersen:

> This map and the red ties we see here just reflect the way we told our employees to work. We tell them, you have to go and work and do your job. We think we have told it and we think it's the way we work, but if those closest to the citizens still are saying, "Well, does that mean we can call for somebody else if we need it," then we haven't told it enough. It's a big deal just to give permission for people to talk.

This experience brought to mind a recent conversation I had with a vice president of a US healthcare system who was asked by a frontline worker, "Why should I be communicating with so and so? She reports to a completely different person!" On reflection, the vice president's reaction was, "We are responsible for giving this message. We are sending mixed signals. We want our employees to coordinate with others, but we also want them to focus on their jobs and stay within their reporting lines. We have to decide what we really want."

INCLUDING THE CITIZENS: DESIGNING AND IMPLEMENTING RELATIONAL COPRODUCTION

An additional concern when top leaders and frontline leaders reviewed the relational map in Figure 8.3 was that citizens and their families were absent from the map. Given that one of the goals of the Danish municipalities was to get citizens to do more for each other, this was an important missing piece. Citizens and their families had not been included in the baseline survey because that would have required obtaining additional permissions from the municipal authorities. (Those permissions were under way and the data would be available before long.) However, Hornstrup anticipated that building stronger ties among the professionals would strengthen—not weaken—involvement by citizens and their families:

> We see when there's better coordination among the team, it's easier for the family to know what to do. It makes it easier for them to be a player on the team because it's not so confusing. Because right now, with all the weak ties, they have no idea. They have no information. They don't know what to do. If we're having good teamwork with each other as professionals, then the family can do a lot more because it's clear what they can do.

In the meantime, frontline leaders had begun to generate ideas for strengthening coproduction with citizens and their families simply by taking the citizen's perspective. Thomsen shared:

> I'm a relative, too. My own father is nearly 100 and has a little bit of dementia. Sometimes, what I see as a relative is that I get absolutely no information. I've been to a case meeting—one and a half years ago—and I haven't heard a thing since. That is the main problem. Couldn't you just leave some piece of paper and write something to me sometimes? I visit him mostly on the weekends because it's 100 kilometers to drive.

Then, in the evening, they know absolutely nothing; if you call one of them and ask, they say, "No, you have to ask those who are here in the day." And I don't see the ones who are here in the day. So why can't we give some information just on a piece of paper? It doesn't have to be that complicated. It doesn't have to cost money or involve meetings. Just give me some information. I need that.

As a professional, Thomsen's experiences had already shown her, "When we do get the family to be a part of the team we get so much information from them that we can use and we can make things much better for the citizen."

One potential solution was to expand the information system to include an interface for family members. There were some legal restrictions to be considered, and perhaps legal changes would be needed to support the more open sharing of information. But even within the legal constraints, there was much more information that could be shared beyond what was already shared.

Another possibility was to meet with families, not only to solve a crisis, but also to build their capacity early on to form a helping network around their family member, even drawing in neighbors and other community members to make the existing social networks more helpful. Viuff explained:

Right now, it is mostly conversations with the relatives about what are their own strengths, what would they like from the municipality, what kind of life have they had, what resources do they have, how could they bring in their own help? So these are conversations with relatives about their own wishes for the future, with this disease coming in. Because what they're coming into now is pretty rough. And I try to help them be able to stand in the storm . . . To do more I would need to know more about what others are doing, and what they can do. I don't want to promise something I can't deliver.

There was the potential for complex-case meetings to build a broader helping network, but the meetings would have to include additional stakeholders, and Viuff and other leaders would have to learn more about how to convene them.

TOP MANAGEMENT TAKES RESPONSIBILITY

An important turning point had occurred when Pedersen said to his leadership team and to the mayor, "I think we have to admit that we, as leaders around this table, we have a responsibility for what we see on this map and for its development." As the top leadership team for the municipality, it was tempting for them to propose solutions. However, they agreed it was best for the frontline leaders and their workers to create solutions based on their own insights from the relational map, and for top leadership to support those solutions with their authority. Myrup explained:

> Because this relational map is a diagnostic tool, it can give people ideas and make the solutions more obvious. We might see that we need structures that cut across, and not just structures for the silos. So it doesn't give the solution but it gives a framing. A way to identify solutions.
>
> That's what happened yesterday in my group. They were saying, well, we don't get paid to go to meetings with the nurses. But we decided we will do it whether or not we get money for it because we think it's a good idea.

Another leader agreed that bottom-up initiative was important but argued that top-down role modeling and support was also required. "As top management, we have to point the direction. Say this is the way we want to go. And support it. Walk the talk. And in order to do that we can't demand something from our co-workers that we don't do ourselves." From her perspective, new structures would be needed to sustain the new culture of collaboration.

> It's more than the cultural dimension. It's also a question about tools. Do we have some procedures for how we deal with these kind of questions we face when we realize that one of our citizens is becoming weaker in some dimension? Who do we bring to a meeting about it? What's happening next? And so forth. This might include a screening device so we know *when* to call in other people. And then a routine for who do we call.

Others agreed enthusiastically. Other supportive structures could include changed budgeting, so people would get paid for doing the right thing, and revised job definitions. "What is my job? Maybe for a nurse the job is not just to deliver care but also to deliver support to the other functions. Is that written down? I mean, you can't *just* write it down, but it would be helpful to write it down as part of the job definition."

SUMMING UP

The Varde Municipality initiative was off to a very robust start. Underpinning the initiative was a newfound awareness of how to assess and build relational coordination across the silos of service delivery. It was not rocket science, but it was certainly a new way of thinking and learning. Reflecting back on the relational map in Figure 8.3, it was clear that there was more work to be done in Varde. Hornstrup expressed his hopes:

> Hopefully, it will be all blue lines [moderate ties] when we're finished—and some of them green [strong ties]. And then the ability for these people to work together will be better. Then when the new problem comes up, the next problem we don't know yet, they will be much quicker in finding solutions, because they will be used to that. I think that's an underlying culture that we can build, both as leaders and frontline people.

The good news was that top leaders, frontline leaders, and frontline workers were all taking responsibility for change, and were creating structural solutions to support the relational changes that were beginning to emerge. After building relational coordination across the municipal sectors, the next frontier for Varde and the other Danish municipalities would be to extend it to include the hospitals, who reported to the regions, and the general practitioners, who were loosely governed at the national level. These new frontiers would require them to address some of the same concerns that they were already beginning to address within the municipality, building the culture of relational coordination as well as the structures—information systems, rewards, accountability, and job designs—needed to support and sustain it.

Having started with a focus on transforming the role of the citizen toward greater relational coproduction, Varde Municipality had turned to building relational coordination among workers to better support the citizens. Now Varde was addressing the need for transformed leadership roles. According to Hornstrup:

> Discussions in Varde are now very much focused on the leadership dimension—how leaders can develop collaboration among themselves as an important step in creating sustainable relational coordination across professionals. This includes all levels of leaders from the director of the municipality to leaders at the frontline.

The task of frontline leaders would be to share the results with the workgroups they led, and to generate solutions with them. Hornstrup told them:

> Go back. Talk to your employees, assess, map out what's on your plate in terms of the role you as a group have in relation to these other groups and to the citizens with dementia and their relatives, in order to be able to build stronger cross-professional collaboration. What are the kinds of spaces that you think you should exploit more or build to be able to do this?

Given the other demands on frontline leaders' time, he knew this was a lot to ask.

> Frontline leaders are under an extreme amount of pressure all the time. A lot of people want their time and their attention, and they really feel reactive to everyone else's needs. And they each supervise maybe forty or more employees. Plus, a lot of the citizens come directly to them if something doesn't work. You really need some strong leaders out there, but they're under a lot of pressure. It's the place in the organization that, when you think about it in relational coordination terms, the largest number of relationships goes through.

Let's see what our colleagues at Dartmouth-Hitchcock Medical Center in northern New Hampshire were doing to build relational coordination at the frontline, and how they were building relational leadership to support it.

9 RELATIONAL LEADERSHIP AT DARTMOUTH-HITCHCOCK

Relational leadership, the third dynamic in the Relational Model of Organizational Change, is a radical departure from the traditional leader-follower relationship. Instead of top-down control, relational leadership is a process of reciprocal interrelating between leaders and the people they lead.[1] As we saw in Chapter 4, relational leaders create influence by developing shared goals, shared knowledge, and mutual respect *with* others—and by fostering shared goals, shared knowledge, and mutual respect *among* others. Relational leaders draw on the expertise of their colleagues throughout the organization—and help them to integrate their expertise *with each other*—to produce better outcomes more efficiently, with greater engagement, and with greater capacity to adapt and innovate. Let's visit Dartmouth-Hitchcock and observe efforts by our colleagues there to meet the demands of a dynamic and highly competitive environment.

EXCELLENCE AND INNOVATION IN CENTRAL NEW HAMPSHIRE

The Dartmouth-Hitchcock health system in central New Hampshire has long enjoyed a sterling reputation for healthcare delivery and innovation. As an academic health system treating populations in New Hampshire and neighboring Vermont, Dartmouth-Hitchcock provides patients with access to nearly a thousand primary care doctors and specialists in many areas of medicine, including more than eleven surgical specialties, and conducts world-renowned research through the Geisel School of Medicine at Dartmouth. In addition, Dartmouth-Hitchcock has a children's hospital and a specialized cancer center.

The system is anchored by Dartmouth-Hitchcock Medical Center, with major clinics in both states.[2]

Across the street from the Medical Center is the Dartmouth Institute for Health Policy and Clinical Practice, noted birthplace of many health delivery system innovations.[3] The Dartmouth Institute was founded in 1992 by Jack Wennberg, whose pioneering work documented substantial regional differences in clinical practice, resulting in the Dartmouth Atlas. These regional differences suggested that it was not primarily the patient's voice that was producing differences in clinical practice; rather, it was differences in physician training and organizational norms, which resulted in cost differences that were unrelated to differences in quality. Building on this awareness of unjustified disparity, the shared decision-making movement was born, fostering awareness of the patient's and family's roles in the coproduction of care outcomes.[4]

Dartmouth-Hitchcock was also on the forefront of the accountable care movement in the United States, as one of the first systems selected to be a Pioneer Accountable Care Organization. CEO James Weinstein served as leader of the High Value Healthcare Collaborative, a coalition of healthcare organizations seeking to achieve higher quality at lower cost in an effort to meet the challenges of accountable care.[5] Shared decision making with patients and families was one element of this work. As Weinstein pointed out:

> We know from our experience at Dartmouth-Hitchcock that involving patients and families in their treatment decisions, with evidence-based, objective information, results in higher patient satisfaction, superior clinical outcomes, and often, lower costs. When patients are well-informed about the risks and benefits of a test, procedure, or treatment, they have more confidence in their decisions and are more satisfied with their outcomes. Our studies have shown that the process also greatly reduces the decisional regret that can occur when patients make treatment choices without good information.

CHALLENGES AHEAD

Despite Dartmouth's impressive resources and accomplishments, there were challenges as well. The work done at the Dartmouth Institute had not been consistently adopted by the Medical Center. Participants on both sides agreed that there was an opportunity for greater translation of the Institute's work into clinical practice. A new wing was under construction at the Medical Center to house the Institute, with the hope of minimizing geographic obstacles to collaboration.

Another challenge was that many communities in southern New Hampshire and in the border regions of Vermont looked to Boston and its network of Harvard-affiliated teaching hospitals, rather than to Dartmouth-Hitchcock, for their out-of-the-ordinary healthcare needs, drawn by proximity and the powerful Harvard brand. Weinstein was seeking to change that perception and behavior and, through affiliations and collaborations, to extend the Dartmouth-Hitchcock network across the region more broadly and create "a sustainable health system that will improve the lives of the people and communities we serve, for generations to come."

THE DEPARTMENT OF SURGERY

In September 2013, the Department of Surgery embarked on a transformation of surgical care, led by Richard Freeman, from the traditional model of academic medicine driven by silos of expertise to a team-based model of care. This effort was launched against the backdrop of national payment reform, which was pressuring healthcare organizations to optimize both quality and efficiency. The broader impetus for change included "a few wrong-site surgeries and near misses [which] happened despite compliance with the checklist and timeout. The issue was a rote completion of the checklist, and there wasn't any communication and feedback," according to associate quality officer Giri Venkatraman. There was a perceived need for enhanced teamwork, both within each of the eleven surgical sections—cardiothoracic surgery, dermatology, general surgery, neurosurgery, otolaryngology, ophthalmology, pediatric surgery, plastic surgery, transplantation, urology, and vascular surgery—and in the flow from patient intake to patient discharge.

Freeman had arrived in 2010 as the new chair of the Department of Surgery. He explained, "Healthcare reform is driving the imperative for change— at Dartmouth-Hitchcock we are responding to these reforms proactively by moving away from the predominant piece-rate payment model toward negotiating contracts in which we will be paid for the overall cost and quality outcomes of the populations we serve." At Dartmouth-Hitchcock, as in many surgical departments across the United States, there was misalignment between the surgery department's traditional role as a money-maker for the institution and the new competitive environment of accountable care, in which surgery was changing from a revenue center to a cost center.

It was not an easy change. Dale Collins Vidal, section chief for plastic surgery and former director of the Center for Informed Choice at the Dartmouth Institute, reflected, "I think morale across the organization is troubled. And I think, within surgery, some of the sections are particularly troubled because for the first time ever they're having trouble making budgets. Normally surgeons are the ones who bring in the bulk of the money for institutions—sort of prized and highly valued, and right now they're just expensive."

Freeman's challenging mandate from Weinstein was to bring the surgery department into alignment with the new strategic environment. Weinstein was reported to be a hard-driving leader with a vision. According to Vidal, "Jim's pretty clear about where he wants to take things. And then he expects people to get it done . . . He really is a pace setter." In addition to the demands for productivity that Freeman faced as a new leader, he also set out to accomplish a broader set of mandates. According to one of Freeman's section chiefs, "It's not just increased productivity at this point because I think he basically topped the volumes that are accessible to us. It's really more trying to expand into the region so that we can broaden our population base and have a more coordinated impact on population health and cost."

To reach these goals would require coordination on many levels. It would also require a new kind of systems thinking in place of the local optimization that the Department of Surgery had learned so well. How should the Department of Surgery respond? "I think it's by doing the right surgeries," Vidal explained.

> There's enormous variation in practice because surgeons don't necessarily
> know the right answer for every problem, and a lot of times we treat problems
> excessively. Maybe we do too many surgeries in some areas and maybe not enough
> in another. If we could actually get that balance right and operate on the people

who really need those procedures and not operate on the ones who don't, and don't impose complications that are costly and provide value for the work that's done, then we are right-sizing our efforts.

To do surgeries well, with less waste and fewer errors, would require better teamwork, not just within each surgical section but with colleagues upstream and downstream, and with patients and their families.

Freeman's first step was to increase the surgical leaders' awareness of the challenges they faced and to develop a unified approach that was better aligned with the goals of Dartmouth-Hitchcock. Yet this teamwork was not yet solidly established, even within the surgical units themselves. The results of a recent employee engagement survey had suggested that there were fairly deep problems in the Department of Surgery. Freeman noted that the results were "pretty lousy, actually."

As was true elsewhere, many physicians at Dartmouth-Hitchcock followed the traditional professional model: they were relatively autonomous players who could exercise veto power simply by not acting. Increasing the challenge, the Department of Surgery, as well as the Medical Center more broadly, was perceived as inhospitable to the advancement of women, a perception that was supported by national comparative data.[6]

LEADERSHIP IN THE SURGICAL DEPARTMENT

Freeman had arrived at Dartmouth with strong academic, clinical, and leadership credentials. Most recently, he had directed the transplant fellowship program at Tufts New England Medical Center and had also taught and served as vice chair of surgery at the Tufts University School of Medicine. Freeman articulated his goals as an incoming leader when he was first hired in late 2009: "I reviewed all of the department members' CVs, and I was very impressed by the fact that there are many extremely accomplished people here—a lot of them, across the board. One of my tasks is to stimulate them to grow their careers and become more widely recognized experts." Based on his experience with transplants, Freeman also recognized that surgery required more than individual experts. "It's a team sport, for sure," Freeman said of transplant surgery. "So many fields are involved—surgery, medicine, molecular biology, ethics, international politics, states' rights versus federalism . . . As a [medical] student, I didn't appreciate all of the intricacies."

Three years into his tenure, Freeman began looking in earnest for a way to shift the culture of the surgery department to achieve greater alignment with the changing needs of the organization. Freeman and Jack Cronenwett, a trusted colleague and former vascular-surgery section chief, considered leadership feedback as a potential avenue for achieving this goal. They invited Eddie Erlandson, coauthor with Kate Ludeman of *Alpha Male Syndrome*, to meet with the leadership team. A former surgeon turned executive coach, Erlandson conducted 360-degree feedback and coaching for corporate leaders with the intent to help them "become vulnerable and hear from others how they could do better." For Freeman, the goal of the leadership coaching would be to create a culture and practice of teamwork beyond what already existed. He decided to be the first to receive 360-degree feedback to show his surgical chiefs that there was nothing to fear and to demonstrate his personal commitment. Moreover, he wanted the change process to be measurable, consistent with the high value that Dartmouth as an academic teaching hospital placed on research.

Freeman had learned about relational coordination in fall 2012 from Vidal. In addition to leading the plastic surgery section, Vidal had previously led the Breast Center and the Center for Shared Decision Making. She had recently served a term as the faculty representative on Dartmouth's Board of Trustees and was well-respected at the senior level of the organization. Vidal had learned about relational coordination during her time with the National Cancer Institute's Working Group on Management Science and Engineering. She was attracted by its evidence base and its practical relevance to her as a leader, "Relational coordination makes so much sense to me as a leader. Ever since learning about the concept I have used it to run meetings in my section. I ask everyone to consider how we are doing on shared goals, shared knowledge and mutual respect, and I put it on the board to keep these questions in focus."

As Freeman's plans for creating change began to unfold in spring 2013, he saw relational coordination as a way to measure the teamwork that he sought to foster. He liked the fact that relational coordination could be carried from the surgical microsystems he was starting with to the mesosystems that included perioperative and anesthesiology departments, all the way up to the larger macrosystem that would soon need his attention. "I want to first use relational coordination to measure the baseline of our teams' impressions about their level of coordination," he explained. "I was also interested in seeing how these measurements would change after we offered 360-degree leadership feedback to our section chiefs. The idea would be that this is like a clinical trial where we measure teamwork and outcomes, then intervene, then measure teamwork and outcomes, as far down the hierarchy as we can get." Freeman reflected:

> There are many outcome measures that we would like to move—and we measure everything—clinical performance, errors, economic performance, patient satisfaction . . . We would essentially be testing the hypothesis that improving self-awareness of leaders will improve relational coordination across their departments. In other words, we wanted to see if self-awareness coaching affects the state of team functioning.

However it was not yet clear *how* leaders' self-awareness would affect their team's functioning. Should leaders not also become more aware of their team? The team might also need enhanced understanding of its own functioning, to foster self-reflection and inspire initiatives for change.

RELATIONAL COORDINATION AS A METHODOLOGY FOR CHANGE

Rather than simply measuring relational coordination before and after the executive leadership coaching, Freeman embraced the idea of using relational coordination measures and principles as part of an intervention that would more directly influence team functioning. Using the seven relational coordination measures—shared goals, shared knowledge, mutual respect, and frequent, timely, accurate, problem-solving communication—feedback to leaders could include "How am I doing from my team's perspective?" and also "How is my team doing with each other?" Using these metrics, frontline workers in each section would be able to receive direct feedback about how well they were meeting each other's coordination needs, within and across their roles.

There were different ways to provide this coaching and feedback. After considerable study and discussion, Freeman and Cronenwett chose an approach that focused on building internal capacity in Dartmouth-Hitchcock. Their decision was predicated on the goal of creating a self-sustaining program within the department that was not dependent on outside paid consultants and that would instead utilize existing internal resources. The primary consideration was to create a sustainable model for improving relational coordination over time.

A key decision was to engage Marjorie Godfrey and Tina Foster, co-directors of the Microsystem Academy at the Dartmouth Institute, to serve with them on the change team. Godfrey had been a nursing leader within Dartmouth-Hitchcock prior to becoming a pioneer and internationally recognized leader on microsystems and coaching. Foster, an obstetrician within Dartmouth-Hitchcock and a leader of the Preventive Medicine Program, brought her insights on leadership and improvement to microsystems when she joined Godfrey.[7] Godfrey explained, "Microsystems are all about starting at the smallest unit where care is delivered and being attentive to the role of frontline workers—then building out from there. Relational coordination has the same philosophy. It helps participants to see the connections through which work gets done—and strengthen them."[8]

Godfrey and Foster agreed to deliver a coach-the-coach program that would support ongoing organizational change—not just for a single project. Jack Cronenwett, whose years leading a national vascular quality initiative had given him valuable experience overseeing a data-driven change process, would serve as co-leader of the relational coordination initiative and the 360-degree leadership feedback initiative.

As Freeman prepared to launch these change initiatives in fall 2013, however, some perceived a disconnect between what he claimed to want and what he was asking for. Although he was talking about the need for leadership among his section chiefs, to some it sounded as though he was asking for compliance instead. One colleague noted, "We never get those kind of messages about how things are changing and what is our vision for getting there. It's always about, 'This is what I've been told to do and this is what I need you to do' . . . It's not clear what the ultimate goal w[ill] be." What kind of leadership would Freeman offer to achieve the engagement he needed from his section chiefs and their staffs in this challenging environment?

LAUNCHING THE CHANGE PROCESS

One Friday in early September 2013, the operating rooms were closed for several hours for an event that introduced about two hundred members of the Department of Surgery to the need for a new kind of leadership and relational coordination in the accountable care environment. The operating rooms were almost never closed down, and Freeman was gratified by the response.

> We had 180 seats and it wasn't enough. I wish we['d] had a bigger room. We drew a crowd, so that was fantastic, that was great. The residents were all there and everything. Those are the malleable minds we need to work on. We can't do this all the time, but I like to really wake people up with a change. I like disrupting and bringing world-class experts on something that has nothing to do with how you cut and sew . . . There are a lot of collaborators here now.

About the same time, Freeman received his 360-degree leadership feedback from his direct reports—the surgical chiefs—in a process facilitated by Erlandson. The process included a detailed written synopsis of the feedback provided by others, which Erlandson had helped to interpret. After reading it, Freeman confessed, he was shaking. His first reaction was, "What? I understand that's bugging you, and it may be something I did, but this is the first I ever heard about it. Why does it take some high-powered consultant to get that feedback?" On further reflection, he noted:

> It's been interesting. You learn so much about yourself when you get this feedback from people. So Erlandson had an executive summary for me, because the whole thing was forty pages long. I told him, "You sugarcoated the executive summary." When you get into the individual comments, there's some tough ones in there, for sure. So we had this meeting with all the section chiefs . . . and they were reading the negative comments, some of which they wrote themselves, and it really coalesced the group. In fact, they all started saying, "You shouldn't feel so bad. Those comments could be written about any one of us."

So we got into it. "What can we do to be a team, and how can we be a team more." It was actually very gratifying to me . . . It became a very positive team-building thing. One of the section chiefs said to me, "That was the most constructive section chiefs' meeting we've ever had." We didn't talk about any budget or operations or anything. It was just my 360 review.

Out of that leadership feedback session came a plan to move forward. There would be a retreat, and the section chiefs would together create a vision statement answering the question: "What are our principles?"

Leaders from all eleven sections convened in December 2013 to take the next step. Facilitated by Freeman and Cronenwett, Erlandson introduced the leadership coaching process, then Godfrey and Foster presented the frontline coaching process. Afterward, Godfrey reflected on what happened:

I was impressed that Rich and Jack had communicated in advance of the meeting with two of the section chiefs—Dan [Morrison] and Dale [Collins Vidal]—to alert them to the agenda. At the meeting they publicly stated their support. Dan had worked with a coach to develop his surgical microsystem so he could speak to the usefulness of that approach. Dale was already using relational coordination as a leader so she could speak to the usefulness of that approach.

As Foster saw it, "There was also a good job setting up the idea that there will be a survey that will provide us with some data and provide a way to measure the current state, then launch us into some work and an opportunity to address the issues that we find." Cronenwett agreed that the launch meeting had been "very positive." While there was some skepticism about the effectiveness of this kind of work given that surgeons tend to be objective and results-oriented, there was a willingness to try.

BUILDING LEADERSHIP AT THE FRONTLINE

The next step was to identify leaders within each of the eleven sections to take on the coaching role. Selecting the right people to play the coaching role was an important success factor for the change process ahead, from Godfrey's perspective. She explained:

I spent a bit of time with Jack talking about which past experiences make a good coach and that, particularly in this team coaching model, it's about raising

up an interprofessional improvement group within a section that then has a
responsibility to be a bridge to their roles. Like, if I was the nurse, I would be
bringing information back and forth to the other nurses, and that the goal
would be for the lead improvement group to understand the basic improvement
methodology in relational coordination. But the responsibility for the coach is to
create a bi-directional flow of information and to recognize that everything we do
as a lead group is a draft. And I pointed out the number of hours that it takes to
become an effective coach because it's based on action learning.

The real surprise for everyone was the number of section chiefs who vol-
unteered to become coaches. "Despite all those stipulations, we had all these
surgeons sign up to be coaches!" Godfrey related. "And so then I went back to
Jack, and I said, 'Jack, I'm really worried about this list. Surgeons already have
so many constraints and problems and a limited amount of time.'"

And so Jack talked to each one of the surgeons individually, and they still insisted
on doing it. It's everything I would say don't do, but they were insistent. And then
some of them have co-coaches. I like the co-coaching model where they've got the
surgeon with the practice manager working with them. Ideally, to me, the practice
manager or somebody else on staff should be the coach. But in all but one of the
eleven sections, the section chiefs became coaches, because they wanted to. So
now we are looking for experiences to guide them about how to move from being
the formal leader to being the coach.

Through their training as coaches, these surgical leaders would have the chance
to learn new behaviors that could change how they led their sections.

The 360-degree leadership feedback overseen by Erlandson continued, so
that by late February, every section chief had received feedback from Freeman, his or her colleagues, and other members of his or her section. Erlandson also led two off-site meetings for all the section chiefs to improve their
sense of being a team and to create a strategic plan for growth of the Department of Surgery. Reports from several of the section chiefs suggested that a
sense of teamwork among the leaders was beginning to emerge. The process
of receiving feedback from others, as well as observing their own leader sub-
mitting himself to their feedback, helped the section chiefs achieve a sense
of vulnerability—or psychological safety—that opened them up to learning

from each other. Receiving feedback in this novel way may have put them in a humbler frame of mind that was conducive to developing relational leadership.

MEASURING BASELINE RELATIONAL COORDINATION

The next step was to conduct a baseline assessment of relational coordination in each of the eleven sections. Setting up the survey involved asking a number of important questions, including (1) What is the work process in need of coordination? (2) Which workgroups are involved in that work process? and (3) Who will be invited to complete the survey? These choices, while seemingly minor, were impactful because they would begin to set the parameters of the change process itself. In that spirit, Cronenwett advocated framing the focal work process as broadly as possible, "It's really hard for us to define at this point exactly which process that group may want to ultimately focus on improving—and we don't want to define it for them." In the first three sections Cronenwett visited, for example, each articulated a different priority for what they wanted to improve.

> In the first section, the practice manager said, "Well, the most important thing in our section is that people don't like to work here. They're not getting along well. And I really want to improve just job satisfaction. That's my number one goal. And we have ways of measuring that here. So let's do that." The other group said, "Well, you know our problem is that our clinic is really inefficient. We can't coordinate anything, and our numbers are really low. We have to increase the number of patients we see." The third group said, "You know we work together pretty well. But at the end of the day, we've just got to increase our revenue. And so everybody's got to work together to increase our revenue."
>
> So we could encourage them to have their specific focus, but be open to changes in other measures too. Some measures may change faster than others—certainly depending also on the intervention that's chosen and how well it's implemented. But you should be open to seeing changes in a range of measures above and beyond the one that you are most interested in.
>
> At the same time, we probably need to have some discussion with the central leadership [at Dartmouth-Hitchcock] about the outcomes we are seeking here.

Because they obviously have some perspective. And at the end of the day, of course, in most of these cases, there's going to be some outcome that involves money. Because that's just where medicine sits right now.

Ultimately, the decision was to measure the work process broadly as *the work we do together*, to include every workgroup in each section, and to survey every person in those groups. In effect, the baseline survey was designed to be a highly inclusive assessment of relational coordination.

To identify the workgroups correctly, Cronenwett met with each section chief for an hour. The section chiefs then selected representatives from each workgroup, usually by asking each workgroup—nurses, physicians, secretaries, technicians, and so on—for volunteers. When the survey was launched, there were concerns in more than one section that the workgroups had not been correctly identified. These concerns were acknowledged, addressed, and ultimately allayed as frontline workers throughout the eleven sections engaged in completing the baseline survey; but Godfrey saw it as an important lesson about the need to involve the workgroups in setting up the survey.

Survey response rates were some of the highest that had been experienced to date. Relational coordination surveys typically have response rates of 60 to 70 percent, quite high for an online survey considering the growing survey fatigue in the healthcare industry. But across the eleven surgical sections at Dartmouth-Hitchcock, the response rates—75, 85, 86, 90, 92, 92, 93, 94, 97, 100, and 100 percent—were exceptionally high. Posters, e-mail, and verbal reminders were used. It helped that the change team had already provided a timeline for sharing the data back with the sections, thereby overcoming the usual cynicism among frontline employees that this would be just another survey. It also helped that the section chiefs endorsed the initiative, and that the staff themselves wanted to improve relational coordination and saw this initiative as a way to do so.

COACHING THE COACHES

Cronenwett, Godfrey, and Foster spent many hours becoming familiar with the data and thinking hard about how best to share it with the coaches. Not surprisingly, the baseline data showed variation across the eleven sections. Of the seven dimensions, the most consistent area of strength was frequency of communication, and the most consistent area for improvement was shared knowledge. They wanted to engage the coaches in a dialogue about the seven dimensions of the survey specific to their daily work before presenting the data. Godfrey explained:

> Two sessions were held to prepare the coaches to share the scores with their sections, including rehearsals of what they would say and do. Because most were surgeons, with a mindset that leaned toward diagnosis and prescription, it was particularly important for them to practice coaching the group. It was not yet clear how the coaches themselves would respond to the data. Whereas physicians were accustomed to being measured, these numbers were very different from what they were used to—they measured relationships and included the whole team, not just themselves.

As it turned out, however, the coaches reacted positively to the data. "We were surprised," Godfrey admitted.

> These coaches are almost all surgeons. We expected them to be a bit gruff about the data. But they were very engaged and very curious and asked great questions. Jack had sliced and diced the data every way and could answer every question that came up. And the fact that Rich was there both days making it clear that he was there to support the work in any way necessary, was powerful.
>
> It's a huge statement when your leader is there [at] every meeting. When we were talking about the next steps, and that the coaches would be convening their colleagues in their sections, that they would have to select who's going to be on the improvement team and decide how they will communicate to the rest of the section and when they will meet, there was a realization that "wow, we've got a lot to do," and "how will we meet every week?" Rich stood up and said, "You guys decide. You're the leaders. Make it happen." They responded, "Well, this might affect productivity." And Rich said, "Tell me what's going on, and tell me what you need."

According to Vidal, "People are starting to feel comfortable talking about these things. I give some of the credit to Eddie Erlandson and the leadership retreats he did with the section chiefs. The eleven chiefs are starting to feel like a team and that was never true before. It is a huge change for us here."

Godfrey and Foster were pleased that the section chiefs had bonded over the relational coordination data instead of competing over whose section had done better. But now it was time for the newly trained coaches to feed the data back to their sections, and there were some lingering concerns. Godfrey explained:

> There's language that we use in the microsystem world. We talk about strengths and opportunities, and it's really important. Because the words we use shape the work we do.[9] We talk about that all the time in the coaching program—and then we point out, "Notice how we model strengths and opportunities." And then we'll talk about [it] when we evaluate the meeting skills, what went well and what could be improved. And we'll run [up] against people who'll say, "What are the positives and the negatives?" And so, at some point, we end up pointing out, "In case you didn't notice, this is the positive spin that we put on everything because there are always opportunities for improvement."

This approach, focusing on the positive and on opportunities for improvement, is supported by findings from psychology and neuroscience suggesting that people tend to become rigid in the face of a threat, which constricts their perceived range of response options. With positive framing, the range of responses broadens, leading to creative solutions that people are more energized to implement.[10]

The newly trained coaches also struggled with the notion that the group itself—not they, not Freeman, and not "the organization"—would decide what improvements were needed. "This group of leaders have all been trained to think 'project' and to be told by the organization what to work on," Godfrey explained,

> so they're really struggling with the fact that we will use the RC data and the assessment of the microsystem to inform what they choose to work on within their section. They're struggling with it and they kept saying again and again, "Do I tell them what they're going to improve? Who's going to tell us about the improvements? How will I know what to work on?" It's just an inbred behavior that they've come to expect to be told what to do. We've tried to tell them, "You've got to trust this process. It's the whole group that will decide what to work on within the targets the organization has set forth."

FEEDING RESULTS BACK TO THE FRONTLINE TEAMS

About a month after the survey closed, the coaches met with their frontline teams to share the results, equipped with a one-page summary of results that had been prepared for their particular sections. The "One-Page RC Booklet" started with a definition of relational coordination, presented an overview of RC results across the eleven sections, and then showed how each section was performing on the seven dimensions as well as a relational coordination map showing identifying the weak ties and the strong ties in each section. Basic principles of relational coordination were summarized at the end, such as "RC is a measure of the process, not of us as individuals"—with some references to the underlying research. Figures 9.1 to 9.3 show the graphics included in the "One-Page RC Booklet."

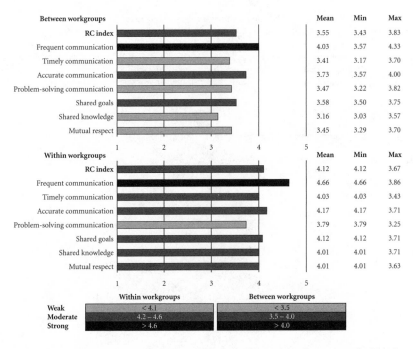

Between workgroups	Mean	Min	Max
RC index	3.55	3.43	3.83
Frequent communication	4.03	3.57	4.33
Timely communication	3.41	3.17	3.70
Accurate communication	3.73	3.57	4.00
Problem-solving communication	3.47	3.22	3.82
Shared goals	3.58	3.50	3.75
Shared knowledge	3.16	3.03	3.57
Mutual respect	3.45	3.29	3.70

Within workgroups	Mean	Min	Max
RC index	4.12	4.12	3.67
Frequent communication	4.66	4.66	3.86
Timely communication	4.03	4.03	3.43
Accurate communication	4.17	4.17	3.71
Problem-solving communication	3.79	3.79	3.25
Shared goals	4.12	4.12	3.71
Shared knowledge	4.01	4.01	3.71
Mutual respect	4.01	4.01	3.63

	Within workgroups	Between workgroups
Weak	< 4.1	< 3.5
Moderate	4.2 – 4.6	3.5 – 4.0
Strong	> 4.6	> 4.0

FIGURE 9.1   Relational coordination and its seven dimensions for one surgical section

SOURCE: Dartmouth-Hitchcock Surgical Department, adapted from Relational Coordination Analytics.
NOTE: This figure shows scores for relational coordination and each of its seven dimensions, between workgroups (top) and within workgroups (bottom) as rated by members of each workgroup. Scores are typically higher within workgroups because members tend to meet their internal needs better than they meet the needs of other workgroups.

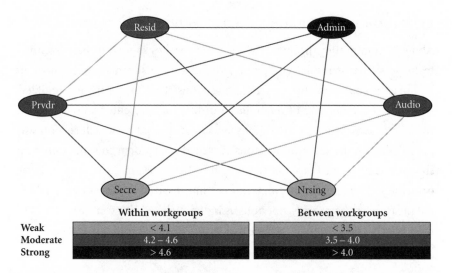

	Within workgroups	Between workgroups
Weak	< 4.1	< 3.5
Moderate	4.2 – 4.6	3.5 – 4.0
Strong	> 4.6	> 4.0

FIGURE 9.2   Relational coordination map for one surgical section

SOURCE: Dartmouth-Hitchcock Surgical Department, adapted from Relational Coordination Analytics.
NOTE: This map displays the strength of relational coordination within and between workgroups as rated by members of each workgroup. It provides a bird's-eye view of RC within and between workgroups. The shading of each circle indicates the strength of RC ties within that workgroup. The shading of each line indicates the strength of the RC tie between the two workgroups connected by the line.

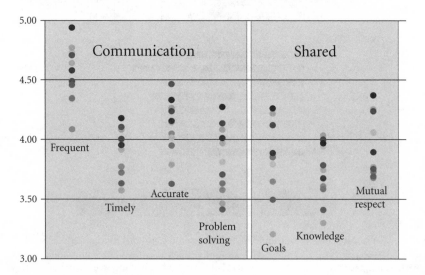

FIGURE 9.3   Summary of relational coordination results across sections

SOURCE: Dartmouth-Hitchcock Surgical Department.

Afterward, the coaches reported that the discussion and dialogue with the frontline teams had been "really constructive and positive for the most part." One key success factor was the timeliness of feeding back the RC survey results. This assuaged fears that it was "just another survey," the results of which would never be shared with them.

In some ways, these coaches were carrying out a typical improvement process, involving structured problem solving around quality and efficiency issues. What was strikingly different was the feedback participants were receiving about the quality of communicating and relating across all of the workgroups on the unit, from the surgeons to the secretaries. It remained to be seen what participants would do with these data and how the coaches would lead that process.

NEW WAYS OF LEADING

As Godfrey and Foster had hoped, the microsystem coaching program was helping participants to develop new ways of leading that seemed a lot like relational leadership—bidirectional and informed by humble inquiry. Teri Walsh, a nurse clinician and coach for the vascular surgery unit, shared her experience:

> I use what I learned with everything I do. Like, people will come to me and say, Did you know this, this, and this? And all I do is, I ask questions about it. I've learned so much from listening. I used to be the type of person—well, nurses want to solve everything, you know. And I work for nine vascular surgeons, who are busy, and they make a decision and crawl up the ladder of inference; so I do that, too, because that's where they all are, and that's how you talk to them.
>
> And so it's very interesting to me that I don't do that anymore, that I'm much more willing to sit back and listen to people more. I've learned more from listening to people, and then I'll ask them, "Well, what do you think would make that perfect, how could we change that, what would make that better, what are you willing to do?" And it makes them feel like they have a little more ownership of the process. And often they end up solving their own problem.

Section chiefs learned new leadership behaviors as well, supported by both the coaching program and the 360-degree leadership feedback they had received. According to Ashley Luurtsema, a practice manager and coach for the dermatology section, "Shane [Chapman, section chief and co-coach] has been very active in the work. And he's definitely been influenced by this process. He has taken meeting skills *very* seriously, and he uses them all the time." The improvement focus for this group was scheduling and patient access.

> We've been working on new patient scheduling and access issues—it's been an ongoing issue for years. Our challenge is how to meet incoming referrals and follow up with patients more quickly after we receive the referral. One of our solutions has been to hire associate providers to help with patient volume. Another solution we've implemented is daily huddles around patient scheduling. We've had one-hour lunch meetings every Tuesday at noon. We've made the improvements we were looking for, and we will continue after our celebration today, then choose a new area of focus.

One section chief stepped down from the coaching role once he realized the ongoing time commitment needed to lead improvement efforts. Others remained in their roles but disengaged once it was clear they were just one voice in the group and didn't have the final say they were accustomed to having. Clearly there was a difference between intellectually understanding the benefits of relational coordination, and the ability to change behaviors accordingly.

IMPLEMENTING RELATIONAL COORDINATION IN TWO SECTIONS: SIMILARITIES AND DIFFERENCES

Though the coaches had all been trained to engage in both relational and work process interventions, implementation varied from coach to coach. As I listened to them report back at a coaches meeting in July 2014, it seemed to me that most of them had not focused a great deal of attention on the relational coordination data or made any concerted effort to coach people in the relational behaviors those data had revealed. Rather, they had done the process improvement work, using the microsystem tools and, often, their lean training, as well. Many of these efforts were to good avail, but in some cases the coaches had given insufficient attention to the relational challenges that would ultimately hold back progress if not addressed.

As coach for the vascular surgery section, Walsh followed a strategy of reminding colleagues from time to time about their baseline relational coordination scores as a way to talk about behaviors that in the past could not be discussed openly. She explained, "One of the really effective things is to be able to say, 'You have to understand that communication and respect were our lowest scores and you have to understand how that affects patient care.' We still struggle with some of our physicians who think nurses are here for them rather than for our patients."

The vascular surgery team was working on the After Visit Summary, and after a slow start had become quite energized.

> It took a while to get everyone up to speed. It has been rewarding to see the group take ownership. We are in a good position now. CHAMP—Committee for Higher Achievement of Medical Practice—is the team name we chose. We keep generating a lot of new ideas so we have a parking lot for future ideas. We chose to work on meaningful use of the After Visit Summary given that starting July 1 the organizational mandate was that we needed to get it done within twenty-four hours. First we had a 90 percent score for submitting within seventy-two hours, then we reached a 90 percent score within twenty-four hours.
>
> It's good. But it's not enough to submit the form. Now we are focusing on the accuracy and completeness of the information. We want to make sure the medications were right, and that something about vascular care is added to the problem list for other providers and the patient to see. We have weekly Friday meetings to plan and monitor our progress.

However, this team faced one relatively major problem, according to Walsh, "We are very excited but the surgeons are not present at this point. They don't look at the After Visit Summary as being about good patient care." The "we" and "they" dichotomy that had arisen here was a flag that warranted further attention.

While the After Visit Summary seemed unimportant to some, it was potentially a key form of coordination with patients and their families, providing them with timely and accurate information and potentially impacting their satisfaction, clinical outcomes, and even safety. The After Visit Summary was also used for coordination among providers in other parts of the system.

Even within the team, the After Visit Summary could provide the secretaries with accurate and timely information they needed to schedule follow-ups and make the necessary referrals. To hand the information to a secretary on a sticky note instead of entering it clearly and completely into the online form felt highly disrespectful to some.

Consider the experience of the otolaryngology section, which also chose to focus on the After Visit Summary. Annette Tietz, practice manager and coach, explained how the process unfolded:

> We decided to work on the After Visit Summary, the summary that goes to the patient, generated through our electronic health record. It's mandated by meaningful use. But often it is incomplete or not understandable. The After Visit Summary is the number one dissatisfier for our secretaries. Our first step was education: Why is it important? Why do we need to do it? Our baseline assessment asked: Was it completed within twenty-four hours? Within seventy-two hours? Was it understandable? Was it executed? What we achieved was accountability for the different parties—what they needed to provide and when. It became more clear. We did a baseline audit, then a secondary audit.
>
> We did group exercises with the RC data. Not just with the improvement team but with everyone in the section. I developed some scenarios based on what I hear people talking about in the halls, outside my office. The scenarios were between-group, like between physicians and other groups. Like role plays. Some of them were about communication issues. Some of them were simulations, like "here's your RC data and here's your budgetary data. What would you do?" The scenarios involved everyone, including the practice manager; our section chief, Dr. Paydarfar; and our nurse manager.
>
> We also shared the detailed baseline RC data with people. The surgeons were surprised by the RC results! Their ratings of others were pretty high, but the ratings of them were not as high. It was an eye-opener for them. I also did one-on-ones with all the surgeons to show them what we need from them with the AVS. Everybody's AVSs have improved. In October, we'll have a celebration meeting, and we'll share the results.

In the otolaryngology section, sharing the detailed RC data on asymmetric relationships between surgeons and the other workgroups, then engaging participants in role plays around relational coordination issues created an opportunity for transforming relationship that work process improvement efforts by themselves may not be able to achieve.

Cronenwett was curious about the opportunity to do more with the RC data to inform behavior change, "Are we taking full advantage of the data from the survey? It's there in the background but we aren't really using it for the intervention. Couldn't we look at the ties that are the most problematic, say among the surgeons in a section, or between the surgeons and the secretaries? Then really hone in on improving that relationship?"

From Freeman's perspective, some key lessons were already beginning to emerge about the contribution of relational coordination to positive organizational change, "RC is like a catalyst to inform us where are the opportunities for change and what are the barriers we need to address to be successful going forward." CEO Jim Weinstein was also supportive of the initiative and hopeful it would foster a different way of thinking:

> I like what's being done with Rich Freeman and his team. I hope it takes good hold and gels so they can move forward, because I think a lot of people are struggling with pretty similar issues. People can get stuck in the past and what they're used to doing and don't utilize resources as effectively. It's a different time now, and it requires different leadership and different skill sets. So I hope this work will really have some long-term impact.

LEADERSHIP DEVELOPMENT GOING FORWARD

What were the lessons for leadership development going forward? Just as Freeman was launching the Department of Surgery initiative, Stephanie Goode had arrived at Dartmouth-Hitchcock as director of learning and organizational development. Coming from a career that spanned multiple industries, Goode saw tremendous opportunities for leadership development. Her primary goal was to design an integrated leadership development approach for the organization that would connect people across their silos and promote systems thinking.

> The Joint Commission [a major accrediting body for US health systems] is reinforcing the silos by measuring us on discrete tasks. Relational coordination,

in my understanding, is very congruent with the systems model of organizational learning. It helps people to realize that I can be good at my thing, but it only helps to the extent that I am attentive to and aware of what you're doing.

From Goode's perspective, the Joint Commission and its metrics for certification tend to push health systems in the opposite direction, reinforcing sub-goal optimization rather than systems thinking.

> It's a highly fragmented approach. We tell people what their specific goals should be. We tell them in what time period. And we expect that this is motivating, when 100 years ago, we already knew that it was not. Nor is it efficient because we are not building Model Ts. Care is complex, and we need systems thinking. A lot of our leadership development currently is focusing around individual behaviors and on how people get along. Relationships do matter, but it's not just about, do I get along with you? It's do I understand your role, do you understand mine, and is this understanding built into our roles?

CEO Weinstein shared the belief that effective leaders have the capacity to engage in systems thinking, though he wondered how such leaders could be created:

> I think you can teach leadership, but I don't think you can create leaders. We have lots of leadership courses and curricula, whether it's at the Tuck School or the Medical School or here at Dartmouth-Hitchcock. I'm not sure that we could actually show we've created leaders and by what measure. So that's kind of a double-edged sword.
>
> I think there are just people who are dedicated to making the world a better place, and there are people who are still kind of dedicated to "me." Smart people will learn skills, and they'll say, because they've learned those skills, they're a leader. Leaders will just lead naturally because they are thinking about the whole.

Whether natural or trained, this ability to engage in systems thinking was indeed a critical capability for leaders. To support the development of relational coordination, leadership training at all levels of the organization would have to support systems thinking, by building shared knowledge across the system.

A BROADER VISION: BEYOND OUR WALLS
TO THE BROADER COMMUNITY

Building relational coordination and improving internal performance in the surgical clinics was a critical step. But it was far from sufficient. From the start, Freeman and his colleagues had viewed the transformation effort as part of a broader vision. To respond to changes in how healthcare is paid for, the change effort would have to go broader. Freeman explained:

> Jim [Weinstein] is emphasizing risk-sharing contracts. The question is, are we going to deliver high-value care under capitation and make enough margin to support our mission? People will still need knee replacements and surgical care. We can still do a little more with productivity, but it's really going to be on the sticky ends of the specialty care we provide . . . in identifying up front which way is going to be the best way. But you've got to set up those pathways so they're efficient.
>
> Fundamentally, the most efficient care across the system will be the most coordinated care, and coordination requires positive and productive relationships along with robust process improvement, and you want relational coordination to be at the level of the patient. You want the whole team functioning at that level, as opposed to the patients being the hub of a bunch of silos that don't connect with each other. What we've got now is still basically uncoordinated care.

While Freeman and colleagues would continue to improve coordination in the eleven surgical sections, a strategy to achieve coordination with other key players was still in its early stages. Many moving parts that were critical to achieving the desired outcome for the patient were not under Freeman's control, so to speak. Even within the Medical Center, anesthesiology and pre-op and intensive care all reported to different leaders. Coordination between surgery and anesthesiology was not within the scope of this initial change effort, despite the fact that anesthesiologists were key players in the operating room and as such had the potential to directly influence the quality and efficiency of surgical care. Beyond the walls of the Medical Center were many additional players with whom coordination had yet to be achieved—primary care and specialty care providers and post-acute facilities and home care agencies—not to mention the insurance companies.

Dartmouth-Hitchcock had recently launched a community-based approach, called Partners in Community Wellness, which represented CEO Weinstein's deepest ambitions for the future. In his view:

> I think keeping the community well and away from the health system is really the goal, by managing care in their homes and in their communities. Partners in Community Wellness is really taking off. We're trying to manage drug abuse, obesity, smoking in communities, teenage pregnancy—the real issues of healthcare. Everybody here in the Medical Center gets hung up on the delivery of healthcare. Of course; that's what they do. But I want to mobilize a whole other health system outside of here.

This broader vision was reminiscent of the efforts in Varde Municipality and other Danish municipalities, as we saw in Chapter 8.

SUMMING UP

The change effort in the Department of Surgery would potentially provide a foundation for accomplishing Weinstein's broader vision. Already, Freeman felt that the change effort had accomplished several things. It had drawn a clear and direct connection between leaders, their perceptions and styles, and better understanding of how these attributes can directly affect the efficiency and well-being of the people who work in their microsystems. Second, it significantly raised awareness of how the multiple relationships participants are engaged in can and do impact how effective and efficient they are in carrying out their work. The effort to date had also defined in a more concrete way the fact that these relationships must be taken into account and nurtured in order to do process improvement work, and that where there are challenges, they must be addressed if the improvement work has any chance of succeeding. Finally, as Freeman pointed out, "we have demonstrated that we can do this work," raising relatively sensitive issues and working together to resolve them.

Meanwhile, the coaches were working to find the balance between work process improvement and relationship improvement. Some surgical sections were integrating these tools in a relatively comprehensive way, while other sections focused on process improvement with less attention to relationships. We also saw variation in the extent to which the coaches were able to engage surgeons in a sustained way, building on their initial enthusiasm for a data-driven effort to improve relationships, work processes, and performance. These variations posed a tremendous opportunity for learning.

Now let's visit Billings Clinic, an organization that was bringing together the three dynamics of relational coordination, coproduction, and leadership, in a relatively comprehensive—and highly inspiring—way.

10 BRINGING IT ALL TOGETHER AT BILLINGS CLINIC

What would it look like to build relational coordination among your coworkers, relational coproduction with your customers, supported by relational leadership throughout your organization? While no one organization can perfectly exemplify this synergistic approach, Billings Clinic has been moving steadily in that direction.

Billings Clinic is an innovative community-owned healthcare organization based in Billings, Montana, and serving patients in Montana, Wyoming, South Dakota, and North Dakota. Consisting of a multispecialty physician group practice, a hospital, and a skilled nursing and assisted-living facility, Billings is a Magnet-designated health system, indicating the central and respected role of nurses there,[1] and a member of the Mayo Clinic Network. In addition to the hospital, Billings' downtown campus consists of a family birth center, a neonatal intensive care unit, a transitional care unit, an emergency and trauma center, an inpatient cancer care unit, and a surgery center. Billings also operates numerous clinics and collaborates with rural hospitals throughout the region. Billings is governed by a twelve-member board consisting of nine community members, two physicians, and longtime CEO Nick Wolter, a physician by training.

THE VISION AND THE CHALLENGE

Billings' vision is to be a national leader in providing the best clinical outcomes, patient safety, service, and value, by working together across professional boundaries. The organization had much to be proud of. Like most healthcare organizations, however, Billings had inherited the professional silos that separate physicians, nurses, and other workgroups from each other in ways that are not conducive to high performance. As CEO Wolter reflected, "Frequently in organizations, hierarchy can inhibit innovation and stifle appropriate conversations. Maybe that's especially true in the world of physicians historically. Hopefully, we are slowly changing that at Billings."

Beyond Billings' own boundaries, Wolter noted, there were other critically important frontiers to be spanned. Bundled payment reforms were being rolled out as part of the effort to achieve accountable care by rewarding systemwide quality and efficiency of care. Crossing these boundaries would require a whole new level of relational coordination, including the ability to negotiate new contracts and to form new relationships with outside organizations. In effect, bundled payments—which the US government initially offered in summer 2013 for Medicare patients with eighteen distinct conditions—were creating the opportunity for healthcare systems to share costs and rewards with payers, moving beyond a fee-for-service payment structure in which each provider charges separately for his or her service. In a bundled payments system, a set of care providers for a particular condition, such as a joint replacement, pregnancy, or hip fracture, can contract together with multiple organizations to provide their services for a flat rate while agreeing to meet certain quality standards. So Billings, like other healthcare organizations, was learning how to coordinate with external partners, even as they were still learning how to coordinate across their internal boundaries.[2]

For more than a decade Billings had been on a journey toward a adopting a more relational approach to achieving quality and efficiency performance outcomes. As CEO, Wolter took seriously the importance of relationships. He had been influenced by his own experiences and by his colleague Curt Lindberg, who served as director of the Partnership for Complex Systems and Healthcare Innovation. Lindberg was a complexity scientist and an organizational development specialist and who had worked with Billings Clinic and other organizations for more than a decade, teaching the concepts of complexity to frontline staff and leaders and supporting their change efforts.

Lindberg saw organizations as complex, highly interdependent systems in which small changes could be amplified to have a big impact. If this is true, then leadership can in principle be exercised in any part of the organization, from the frontline to top management. As Lindberg argued, the complexity view of leadership is consistent with seeing leadership as informal, distributed, and relational (see Chapter 4).[3]

POSITIVE DEVIANCE AS AN
IMPROVEMENT METHODOLOGY

Lindberg and others had introduced an improvement methodology called *positive deviance* to Billings Clinic about eight years earlier. According to the Positive Deviance Initiative:

> Positive deviance is based on the observation that in every community there are certain individuals or groups whose uncommon behaviors and strategies enable them to find better solutions to problems than their peers, while having access to the same resources and facing similar or worse challenges. The positive deviance approach is an asset-based, problem-solving, and community-driven approach that enables the community to discover these successful behaviors and strategies and develop a plan of action to promote their adoption by all concerned.[4]

Together, positive deviance and complexity have powerful implications for healthcare systems, in part because both approaches recognize that power can be exercised usefully anywhere in a system, calling into question the status hierarchies that permeate many healthcare systems. As Lindberg and Schneider wrote:

> Leaders must learn to appreciate that organizational processes are characterized by uncertainty, that is, it is OK not to know how best to proceed. The process is grounded on several beliefs: the wisdom needed for change exists in the organization; change efforts are best led from within the institution by people with firsthand knowledge of its work, history and norms; and expertise within an organization is widely distributed . . . While understanding that self-organization cannot be controlled, the positive deviance movement assumes, and its success suggests, that positive deviance affects the parameters shaping self-organization in human systems: namely, the flow of new information; the number and quality of connections; the degree of diversity in perspectives; and power differentials.

In short, positive deviance is an improvement methodology based on identifying high performers, and then learning from their strengths. Positive deviance disrupts hierarchy in part by recognizing that high performance is driven by the behavior of participants throughout societies and organizations, including those whose roles tend to be invisible or underappreciated. We can already see the resonance between positive deviance and relational coordination, and why Lindberg wanted to bring them together.

LAUNCHING RELATIONAL COORDINATION CHANGE EFFORTS IN THE INTENSIVE CARE UNIT

Relational coordination change efforts first took off in the intensive care unit (ICU), building on earlier efforts to reduce MRSA infections using positive deviance principles.[5] However, in those early days there was some resistance in the ICU to adopting new approaches. Chief learning officer Carlos Arce recalled, "The ICU rebellion occurred midway through the effort. But if it wasn't for the ICU's initial resistance, I don't know how much passion we would have really unleashed in the process. In the long run they became the greatest advocates, and their story was probably one of the more impactful ones."

Once the ICU staff had worked through their various concerns and issues, they embraced complexity science and positive deviance as part of what became highly successful change initiative to reduce MRSA infections.[6] Hoping to build on their capacity and energy, Robert Merchant, a pulmonary critical care specialist and a leader of Billings' Complexity and Healthcare Learning Network, introduced relational coordination to the ICU in 2013. This time, the ICU team was eager to take the lead. Lindberg explained, "We started our RC efforts in the intensive care unit because the staff were highly respected, skilled at teamwork, and constantly looking to improve. Introducing RC was easy—they grabbed onto it very quickly."

Local leadership in the ICU was strong. Merchant, who was the ICU director at the time, soon to become the chief medical officer, was joined by Dania Block, the ICU clinical coordinator. Together, they led a measurement of baseline relational coordination in spring 2013 among twelve distinct workgroups whose roles had been identified as interdependent. The workgroups comprised ICU physicians (intensivists), nurses, social workers, respiratory therapists, physical therapists, occupational therapists, radiologists, dieticians, pharmacists, and chaplains. Response rates to the baseline survey were quite high in part because participants had already developed a high level of understanding of relational coordination prior to the survey launch.

These scores were shared, first in the aggregate for the ICU team, during newly established monthly meetings, at which the team discussed and reflected on their improvement efforts along each of the seven dimensions of relational coordination. Once people were comfortable with the numbers, the results were further broken down by workgroups as shown in Table 10.1.

One finding was that the rehabilitation (physical and occupational) therapists were the lowest-scoring workgroup. Although they played a key role in the care of ICU patients, they also served patients in other units of the clinic, preventing them from being consistently present in the ICU. Timely communication between the rehabilitation therapists and nurses was therefore a major issue flagged by the survey, along with opportunities to improve their shared goals, shared knowledge, and mutual respect. Block explained:

> There were several improvement ideas that just emerged spontaneously in these meetings. Timely communication was one of the challenges we saw in the data. The nurses and therapists started to ask each other "What is timely communication for you?" and soon realized that, if the therapists would visit the ICU in the mornings they could better address patient needs *and* reduce discharge delays. Just one example, and it was not a top-down solution.

Another low-scoring group was patients and families. The ICU staff rated communication from patients and families as sufficiently frequent but relatively low in quality—not particularly timely, and with a tendency toward inaccuracy and blaming rather than problem solving. When patients and families were surveyed to get their perspective, the results were quite similar: they experienced many of the same dynamics with the ICU staff that the ICU staff experienced with them. The scores were sobering for the ICU staff to reflect on; it was also a wakeup call underscoring the need to improve the patient-family-provider partnership in the ICU.

The group with the highest baseline relational coordination ratings was the intensivist physician group. The ICU physicians had requested individual scores to see how each was doing. Among them were three whose scores were particularly high. One longtime ICU physician—Jim Rollins—was a positive

TABLE 10.1 Results from the intensive care unit baseline relational coordination survey

RC dimension	Patients and families	Respiratory therapists	Rehabilitation therapists	ICU nurses	Cardio nurses	Cardio surgery	Cardiologists	Neurologists	Infectious disease specialists	Dieticians	Case managers	SLPs	Pharmacists	Intensivists	All
Frequent	4.35	3.73	3.52	4.82	4.51	3.99	3.92	4.01	4.04	4.24	4.39	4.06	4.55	4.54	4.29
Timely	3.32	3.24	2.87	4.18	4.01	3.23	3.14	3.34	3.30	3.22	3.47	3.03	3.75	4.04	3.58
Accurate	3.20	3.70	3.45	4.20	4.14	3.77	3.79	3.90	3.90	3.55	3.78	3.62	4.05	4.38	3.95
Problem-solving	3.05	3.71	3.47	4.12	4.17	3.51	3.81	3.77	3.82	3.69	3.91	3.69	4.04	4.23	3.89
Shared goals	3.62	3.80	3.61	4.24	4.21	3.71	3.73	3.88	3.95	3.59	4.04	3.66	4.04	4.22	3.96
Shared knowledge	2.76	3.44	3.05	4.08	4.30	3.42	3.39	3.40	3.54	2.99	3.62	3.03	3.59	4.29	3.69
Mutual respect	3.43	3.45	3.33	4.02	4.19	3.31	3.40	3.39	3.51	3.29	3.88	3.38	3.75	4.19	3.75
Relational coordination	3.39	3.58	3.33	4.24	4.22	3.56	3.60	3.67	3.72	3.51	3.87	3.50	3.97	4.28	3.87

SOURCE: Billings Clinic.
NOTE: RC for each workgroup, rated by all other workgroups. ICU, intensive care unit; SLP, speech language pathologist.

outlier, and he began to get questions from others about what he was doing differently. Rollins was reported by staff to have a matter-of-fact yet respectful way of interacting with all members of the team, regardless of their role or formal status. One of his core practices was to make a point of connecting with the patient and the family as soon as possible after admission. "When you do that," he explained, "you get them engaged in a helpful way from the start and that tends to ripple through the whole episode within the ICU, and wherever they go next."

ICU CONNECTIONS AND ICU BINGO

To provide ongoing leadership, a steering group called ICU Connections was formed by volunteers from multiple workgroups. One of their first initiatives was to create a game they called ICU Bingo. ICU care manager Sandra Gritz explained:

> One of the docs in the steering group wanted to make it fun. He proposed a game of bingo, with each of the workgroups competing to see who could get recognized first for demonstrating all seven dimensions. On one axis of the board are the seven dimensions; on the other axis are the various ICU workgroups. The first workgroup to have their column filled in with cards written by members of other workgroups gets a pizza party courtesy of Bob Merchant. The bingo board is displayed on one of the main corridors in the ICU.

The *ICU Connections Newsletter* reported: "We encourage ICU healthcare team members to submit cards for examples of behaviors we want to encourage in the ICU—shared goals, shared knowledge, mutual respect, communication that's timely, frequent, accurate, and focused on problem-solving." As in all games, there were rules. Each submission had to be accompanied by a story describing the positive behavior. Block explained, "Another rule was that you could only write up a recognition for someone outside your own workgroup—for example, nurses could not recognize other nurses but had to recognize people in the other workgroups. It was amazing to see the energy!" The submission form and examples of the submissions are shown in Figure 10.1 and Table 10.2.

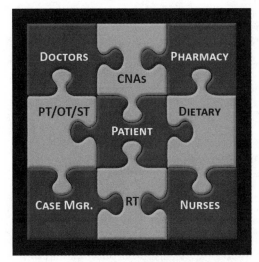

ICU
Connections

Relational Coordination
In The ICU

Tell us about your ICU Connections experience.

Relationships
☐ Shared Goals
☐ Shared Knowledge
☐ Mutual Respect

Communication
☐ Frequent
☐ Timely
☐ Accurate
☐ Problem Solving

Your name/position/unit:_____

The names/positions/units of others involved: _____

Which practice impressed you most: _____

Please tell us the details of your story on the inside of this card:

FIGURE 10.1   ICU Bingo submission form
SOURCE: Billings Clinic.

INTRODUCING RELATIONAL COORDINATION TO TOP MANAGEMENT

Once relational coordination began to take off in the ICU, CEO Wolter decided it was time to introduce the relational coordination principles to his senior executive team. He invited me and my healthcare economist colleague Stan

TABLE 10.2   Examples from ICU Bingo: recognition for relational coordination practices

- Jen Potts, occupational therapist, recognized Ted, ICU nurse, for shared goals, mutual respect, and problem-solving communication.
- Dr. Davis recognized Andy and Troy from radiology for mutual respect, shared goals, and timely communication.
- Jamie Humphrey, ICU nurse, recognized Reina, respiratory therapist, for shared goals and problem-solving communication.
- Amber Hellekson, ICU nurse, recognized Dr. Yandell, cardiovascular specialist, for shared knowledge.
- Jen Potts, occupational therapist, recognized Kristi Nelson, dietician, for timely and accurate communication.
- Dr. Davis recognized Chaplain Doug Johnson for shared goals, mutual respect, and timely communication.

"When Dr. Yandell (cardiovascular specialist) overheard nursing staff discussing a procedure a patient had, he took the time to find an anatomical picture and explain, in depth, what took place. Amber Hellekson (nurse) wrote, 'This was not even his patient or his service … he just took the time to offer his knowledge.'"

"In making discharge recommendations, Jen (occupational therapist) needs as much information as possible about any changes in routines the patient will experience and new knowledge the patient must take in. Kristi (dietician) discussed the new knowledge the patient had to acquire as well as changes in diet and how that would alter the patient's daily routine. Kristi sharing her expertise helped Jen make a safe discharge recommendation."

"When a patient is in a code situation, doctors, nurses, pharmacists, and other team members are focused on working with the patient. Fortunately, we have pastoral care to provide comfort and support to family members. Despite heroic efforts the patient died. Chaplain Doug was present and supportive to the family. Moreover, he offered his compassionate support to the ICU staff, nurses, and MDs."

SOURCE: Billings Clinic.

Wallack to participate as guests in a meeting of his top management team to explain the principles of relational coordination and their relevance for meeting the challenges of accountable care. Following our presentation, chief medical officer Bob Merchant described how relational coordination was working in the ICU thus far.

Wolter then opened up the floor to questions and ideas. After a few awkward moments, questions flowed easily, including (1) What's the best place to start? (2) Are there people who just can't do relational coordination? and (3) How can we learn more? Even though the meeting was already behind schedule that morning, the questions and ideas continued to flow after we had left the room.

RELATIONAL COORDINATION SUMMIT TO ADVANCE
THE LEARNING

The ICU Connections steering group organized a Relational Coordination Summit to share what the ICU team had learned. CEO Wolter attended, along with sixty-five other participants, many from the ICU and some from other parts of Billings Clinic who were curious about what was going on in the ICU. The summit started with conversations of interdependence between pairs of co-workers who were invited to ask each other: What do you find most meaningful about your work? What is it about how I do my work that helps you do yours? What could I do differently that would help you even more?

A highlight of the summit was the use of the fishbowl process to learn from peers about effective relational coordination practices. Physicians, a respiratory therapist, nurses, a rehabilitation therapist, and a care manager sat in the center of a circle and took questions from colleagues about their effective relational coordination practices. "We asked people to tell stories about practices that they saw employed by high-scoring ICU doctors as well as other staff members who were RC stars," Lindberg explained. "We focused on what's working well already and what we can learn from this."

Some of the questions in the fishbowl concerned Dr. Rollins and his effective use of interdisciplinary rounds to coordinate care with the patient, family, and broader team. At the time of the summit not all the ICU physicians were conducting interdisciplinary rounds, and of those who did, not all conducted them in a way that gave voice to others on the team. Gritz recalled:

> Afterward, one of the physicians actually went to a nurse and said, "What do you think about the way that I communicate in the rounds?" She said, "It's bad. It's really bad." "Why?" "Well, because you're not organized. Everything's all over the place. We never know where you're going to be. Everything is inconsistent, and you don't talk to us until after the fact." At least he asked. And now he is doing better.

Lindberg observed some changes, as well:

> The following week, one of the physicians asked an experienced ICU nurse what she found so effective in the ways that Dr. Rollins and others facilitated rounds.

Another influential member of the ICU had been somewhat skeptical about the value of rounds. At the summit she was impressed by the benefits of rounds articulated by many staff members. Now she is one of the biggest supporters.

That individual was Dr. Catherine Stephens, intensivist and department chair of Pulmonary and Critical Care Medicine. She had been involved in the relational coordination efforts only peripherally; then, at the ICU Summit she publicly announced that she would conduct regular rounds. Stephens reflected:

> Before, people were in their own little silos and there wasn't a lot of interaction across them. Everyone in this private practice environment has to see a certain number of patients. Therapists have their own schedules, and we have ours. Now people are doing a lot more rounding. I don't know what has happened but now the dietician is showing up, and the OTs, and the PTs, and the nurses. Even pharmacy. It's good. It's been a bit of a sea change in the past two or three months. It's the relational work Bob and Curt are doing. I think that really got people fired up.
>
>   Before, if someone did rounds, it was just the staff following the doctor around. Now the rounds are more integrated, which is great. Jason, one of our pharmacists, is committed to rounding with us to discuss medications. It's very helpful. Staff are more interactive now. I'm sure care is more coordinated now. It really makes a difference, especially for the more complex patients.

Interaction was not confined to the rounds. "They'll grab you all day," Stephens noted. "It's a little disconcerting, but there's no way around it. Sometimes you need information in a timely way."

COMPLETING YEAR ONE WITH RECOGNITION
AND RESOLUTIONS

Just before Christmas, the first bingo game came to a dramatic close with simultaneous submissions for the rehab (physical, occupational, and speech language pathology) therapists and the ICU nurses. "It could have been either group being the winner," Block reported. "It was just a matter of which envelope I opened first. Dr. Merchant threw a pizza party for the winning group, as promised, on the Thursday before Christmas. And in recognition of their neck-and-neck race, the rehab therapists invited the ICU nurses to share in the pizza party." The outcome was publicized in the *ICU Connections Newsletter*. Interestingly, the workgroup with the lowest baseline RC scores at the start had won the game. According to Lindberg, "It shows there was already a desire to improve and that leadership was already present in that group."

The bingo game had in effect created a new reward structure for teamwork in the Billings ICU. Both those who were recognized and those who gave recognition had become more attentive to cross-functional behaviors, behaviors that are often invisible and undervalued.[7] At the same time, participants were learning more about the interdependence of their roles, and how their behavior could make a difference in other team members' ability to effectively perform their jobs and meet the needs of patients and families. The game reminded me of a practice at Southwest Airlines, called LUV Notes, in which a flight attendant, for example, could recognize a ramp agent for particularly helpful actions taken during a flight departure.

As year one of the relational coordination initiative came to a close, the ICU team developed and posted a set of resolutions for the New Year, shown in Figure 10.2, in effect formalizing a set of behavioral standards that had evolved over the course of the year.

SHARED ACCOUNTABILITY AND SHARED REWARDS

In addition to the bingo mechanism for rewarding relational coordination, physicians in the Billings ICU had implemented a shared rewards system over a decade earlier, a move that may have helped to support the relational coordination effort. Chief medical officer Merchant spoke about the impact of shared rewards on behavior:

> Our salary structure in the Billings ICU is designed collectively. All our earnings
> from all sources—clinical and administrative—are put into one pool and split
> evenly amongst us. This is not new. We have been doing this since I came here in
> 1991, and it started a couple of years earlier. Then, about ten years ago, we put
> a portion of our payments at risk based on performance and quality markers
> in the ICU. From early on our goal in ICU design has been to encourage a team
> mentality.

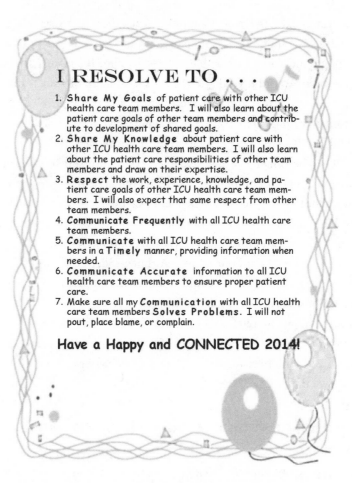

FIGURE 10.2   New Year's resolutions for the Billings intensive care unit
SOURCE: Billings Clinic.

Merchant noted that even the productivity of hens has been found to be driven by collective rewards more than by individual rewards. While this shared reward structure was helpful, however, it was not sufficient. According to Merchant, "Our relational coordination initiative has been key in helping us move from envisioning a shared goal to understanding the essential dimensions to achieve that shared goal."

TRANSFORMING INFORMATION SYSTEMS

The ICU Connections steering group began to wonder if the electronic health record (EHR) could be improved to support relational coordination in the ICU. They proposed to meet with the Billings information systems (IS) staff and with representatives from Cerner, the EHR vendor, to brainstorm potential improvements. The EHR Relational Coordination Workshop was attended by twenty participants from six disciplines who generated a series of ideas, many of which were implemented within a month of the meeting.

With electronic health records, you often hear a great deal of blame accompanied by a kind of resignation that, while we can complain about it, there is no way the situation is going to change. According to Lindberg, the meeting was "all about problem solving"—and the IS people took notice: "The folks from Cerner and the IS department at Billings who were there all told me afterward, 'Boy, it's so refreshing to be in a meeting like this when a diverse group of people are talking about how we can advance the capabilities of information systems for the benefit of patients.'"

IT people do not have a reputation for being good collaborators with non-IT people. So how were the IT people in this meeting able to engage so effectively with the clinical ICU staff around a topic that often resulted in unproductive conflict? Arce explained what he saw:

> It was a well-designed meeting. But what made it really interesting is the level of sophistication of the ICU staff. They now have a true sense of ownership of the concept that improving their coordination is mission-based. You can feel it. They own that piece. And because they own it so well, the attitude around everything—from the patients to the IS folks, the discussions, the tone—all was very appreciative, very supportive. So it became very evident that it was a safe place. That it was an open place. That we're on the same page. They were able to not only appreciate the fact that they were meeting with a key partner, but their interactions were all done with that sense of appreciation for the timeliness of the communication. The frequency of that communication. How they respect what each other does.
>
> The ICU seemed to have had this really magical way of reducing some of that conflict, that confrontational reaction or response. It was like you know, the classic Eastern philosophy, of two groups pushing against each other, and then all of a

sudden one decides, "You know what? I'm no longer going to resist. Here, let me take you to me. Come toward me instead of me pushing you away." It's like, doing that, the folks from IS for a second just kind of fell happily and went with the dance and said, "Yeah, I like this better, too. Let's not push. Let's just kind of hang out together."

A couple of immediate solutions emerged from this process, for example, creating a new IT interface that made it possible for the different workgroups to see each patient more holistically. Lindberg explained:

> One of the main ideas they talked about was displaying a timeline or a schedule for the patient day. You know, the patient is going to be here, then they're going to be there, then they're getting this test. Or they are on what they call their "sedation holiday" between one and two o'clock. So, with this timeline, people would be able to kind of look at the day and see where they could contribute, and see times where they should avoid visiting or doing their work with the patients. They talked about everybody being able to see the individual daily goals for each of the professions. You know, for each patient. So they could see if they're in sync. They could see where there are potential conflicts and then work to resolve those. They asked how you can pull those daily goals and information that's already in the record to a screen that pulls them all together and is very evident.

While the interface redesign sounds straightforward, it was transformative from a coordination perspective. EHRs—including those offered by the major industry vendors Cerner and Epic—are not typically designed to provide visibility around a given patient. To use the EHR to create cross-functional visibility around each patient on a day-to-day basis is intuitive, once you think about it from the patient's point of view rather than the point of view of each silo.

In the workshop, participants also identified many clinical issues as requiring both electronic *and* verbal communication. Occupational therapist Jessica Coffman noted:

> People appreciated being able to acknowledge that the system can't take care of everything, because everybody is skeptical about how far they can go in a person-oriented situation with static information on a system. So there seemed to be a lot of appreciation for acknowledging that there are times when face to face is the way it has to be. For the majority of items we said, "We also need that verbal signal, whether it's face to face or phone. It can't just be electronic." We don't trust that

people are looking electronic. I mean, we're not. I know I'm not. I look at the EHR in the morning. I don't look at it again until the next morning. And most people don't have time to be looking at it constantly.

Gritz explained further:

If you do your chart reviews in the morning, and two hours later PT and OT come along, and they find that there's an activity intolerance that's very significant, they can write it in their chart all day, but nobody's going to have a chance to follow up on that until that night, when the next shift does their chart review. Then they say, "Oh, we've had six hours where somebody was trying to increase activity" which is usually a good thing, but in this case they shouldn't have.

Another plan coming out of the workshop was to use the EHR to communicate to everyone quickly when a decision had been made to give up aggressive treatments and move a patient to what is known as "comfort care," because he or she might be in the last hours of life. At the time, the staff often found out about this only by seeing a cart outside the patient's room containing refreshments for the family members. From the point of view of relational coordination, ICU staff felt the cart was not the best way to find out, particularly for the chaplain who could be helpful in these final hours. Participants agreed there would be an immediate page sent to the chaplain on duty when the comfort care decision was made. Chaplain consults for comfort care to patients and their families increased immediately from three or four per month to twenty-eight per month as a result of this simple change.

TAKING ROUNDS TO A NEW LEVEL

Starting with the ICU Summit the previous fall, there had been a new commitment to conducting daily interdisciplinary rounds with full staff involvement due to growing realization of their value. Still, the uptake was uneven, and if the physician on duty was off the floor, rounds didn't happen. Gritz had been a strong advocate of daily interdisciplinary rounds over the years and now, armed with input from the EHR Relational Coordination Workshop, she was ready to take her leadership on this issue to the next level. "People are starting to do the rounds much more," she explained. "We're definitely seeing some baby steps. So now I'm going to throw a wrench in it by suggesting that we highly structure the rounds."

Gritz developed a protocol to clarify the roles and information needed from each workgroup to make the rounds more participatory and less centered on the physician, building on existing protocols she had found in the literature.

> With this protocol, anyone can lead the rounds. I think one of the things we need to structure is that rounds will occur even if the doctor isn't there. If the doctor is in the ED with an emergency case, then it doesn't happen. Well, we have all these other disciplines that still need this information. If the doctor isn't able to be there on Wednesdays because they have staff meetings, then anybody could lead it.
>
> I have it broken down by discipline, so each discipline can address the issues that they need to address, and then we can also include quality statements: "Do they [patients] have a Foley, and do they need a Foley? When did they get their central line in? What is their pain and how are we dealing with it?"

One selling point was that this protocol could replace the need for additional charting in the EHR, particularly regarding daily goals for the patient. "If the nurses have to spend more time charting, it will not work," Gritz argued. "They already feel like they spend more time with the computer than they do with the patients, so this is just a very quick tool. I'm proposing that we include daily goals in our daily rounds, rather than entering them into the EHR."

> Now, on our rounds, instead of just saying, "This is Joe Smith. He's here with respiratory failure. He's on this antibiotic and he's intubated," now somebody could say, "Well, what is the goal for the day?" Well, for respiratory therapy, they want to wean him. For physical therapy, they'll do some range of motion. For nursing, they want to wean his vasopressors.

Gritz introduced the new protocol at the ICU Connections meeting and explained why the ICU should try it, emphasizing that it was a work in process with a separate field for all users to share ideas for improving it. Coffman expressed her hopes that over time the protocol would "become so engrained that it's just how rounds work. Our verbal communication will be such that we can respect each discipline to adjust their plans to each other's for the sake of the patient." After some discussion, there was unanimous agreement among the participants to test it out.

LEADING CHANGE AT BILLINGS: SPREADING RELATIONAL COORDINATION BEYOND THE ICU

The changes we have seen in this chapter were occurring not through top-down mandates, but rather through direct peer-to-peer influence. As Block explained:

> The way change happens here is by contagion. People hear about what you are doing and they want to learn more. Like when we had the RC Summit back in the fall—people came from the ICU but also from other parts of Billings to find out what we were doing. The same thing happened with positive deviance and complexity. It's great to have support from the CEO like we do—but it's important to have the frontline leading the change.

Lindberg agreed, "That's a core principle of complexity—in a complex system leadership should come from everywhere. That's the beauty of what we are seeing at Billings." Here, we are confronted with the paradox of an organization that enjoys top leadership support for fundamental change, but whose top leader was not *driving* the change process. CEO Wolter was providing moral and financial support, but with a light touch.

Still, some strategic planning was involved. In discussions with senior executive team members the previous fall, Wolter had identified several areas where increased relational coordination could support strategic priorities for Billings. Discussions led by Lindberg with the Complexity and Clinical Care Network and the Relational Coordination Learning Network had identified several emergent opportunities for relational coordination. The resulting plan for the spread of relational coordination contained a mix of emergent opportunities and strategic priorities.

EMERGENT OPPORTUNITY: CARE TRANSITIONS BETWEEN ICU AND HOSPITALISTS

As an occupational therapist, Jen Potts worked with patients in many units at Billings, not just the ICU. But through her experiences in the ICU and as a member of ICU Connections, she began to see opportunities to use relational coordination to improve patient care on other units. She reached out to others to start conversations; one of these conversations was with Jennifer Pflug, hospitalist physician and chair of the Hospitalist Program. According to Pflug, "Jen [Potts] actually connected with me because she, being the very thoughtful person she is, was trying to see if there are ways to improve communication between our groups because we work together a lot, and I just think that we don't know each other very well. We're like ships passing in the night." Potts agreed, "Both of our roles can be like islands. We know people wherever we go, but we're all over the hospital, so trying to connect is really hard. I think that, coming out of this, we're going to have a lot better communication."

Before reaching out to Pflug, Potts did some research to understand what hospitalist physicians do.

> I found out that hospitalists are relational coordinators. Hospitalists spend so much time coordinating with everyone—with people's outside physicians, families look to you, and all the specialists are supposed to be coordinated with you. There's a lot of demand for your role, so how can we make our communications more efficient for you? And vice versa. I thought, "Gosh, wouldn't this be really good?"[8]

Pflug felt that there were other roles—in addition to the occupational therapists—that she and her fellow hospitalist physicians needed to coordinate with better. "Respiratory therapy is another one. Pharmacy is one, too, although that has gotten a little better now that the medicine reconciliation pharmacists are there. We know them and work with them. I think it would be great for our care managers to have some increase in relational coordination too."

Pflug felt the time was right to get started with relational coordination in the Billings hospitalist service and wanted advice about what the next steps would be. Potts advised, "The conversations of interdependence I think are a nice starting point, and there's a handout with four different questions." Pflug responded gratefully:

> I'd like that because I'd have to say, we as the hospitalist group probably have not a ton of knowledge about this. I had to talk to my group about what it meant. It was all kind of new to them. But I want to introduce it because I think it's important, and it would be helpful . . . I think this would be a good time to start trying to improve our communication. I think it would be really helpful if you could come to our next meeting and just talk.

Potts wondered how she and her colleagues could contribute to the learning process, "We have some unique ways to spread relational coordination if we can understand what each group does. If we can have some of those conversations of interdependence on a daily basis so that people recognize that we're interested in what they're doing, and that we do work together as a team, then I think they're going to buy into it more. It just comes down to better patient care."

STRATEGIC PRIORITY: ORTHOPEDIC SURGERY

Some frontline leaders in orthopedic surgery were eager to learn more about relational coordination in preparation for the bundled payment contract Billings had recently negotiated with outside payers for joint-replacement patients. The director of research explained, "We are considering an RC intervention with those providers and patients to support the bundled payment contract because it will be key in terms of both cost and quality to be well coordinated." Lindberg saw an additional bonus, "One of the reasons that the joint-replacement project appealed to us was because it involves several organizations—orthopedics, as well as outside organizations that provide home care and rehabilitation care. This will be our first relational coordination effort involving other organizations."

The launch meeting for the orthopedics initiative was framed as an introduction to relational coordination, to end with a "go/no go" decision by participants. Lindberg set up the room carefully, placing about twenty chairs in a circle, with handouts and two flip charts. Chad Miller, director of the Orthopedics, Sports Medicine, Neuroscience, Occupational Health, Rheumatology, and Rehabilitation Services, began by explaining why he had organized this meeting, saying he believed it would "be good to enhance even more what we are doing with joint replacements, given the process improvement work we have already done, bringing length of stay down to under three days."

There was good turnout from nurses, therapists, and care managers who worked in the orthopedics area and were interested in learning more. Four participants from the ICU had also been invited to share their stories. Two nurses attended from post-acute organizations, including a new home healthcare organization that would care for Billings' total joint-replacement patients. Arce attended as chief learning officer.

Lindberg invited everyone to participate in a relational mapping exercise. He asked participants to split into two teams, and to "get with at least some people they did not already work with on a regular basis." He asked each team to "identify the groups of people who depend on each other to provide really good care for joint-replacement patients." Each of the two teams, working separately, identified more than twelve workgroups involved, and they wanted to continue listing others. However, Lindberg asked them to simplify down to six workgroups to start, just to get a sense of what was going on. Once each team had drawn bubbles with each workgroup inside, Lindberg asked them to characterize the ties between each of the workgroups as weak, medium, or strong, using any three colored markers they wanted to use.

After initially hesitating to identify weak ties, the teams became more comfortable. Lindberg then asked each of the two teams to present their maps. What had they found? Both teams noted that their maps showed a lot of complexity, and a fair number of weak ties, more than they had expected. Lindberg then led a discussion among the ICU participants. How had they started in the ICU? As an ICU leader, Block pointed out that their relational coordination work had started as a conversation, just like this one:

> The ICU had always prided itself on good outcomes, and we thought we could do it even better. We felt that positive deviance created a good starting point for our work on relational coordination. It helped to make the necessary conversations a little less uncomfortable. It opened up channels to work on things—and you have to look at things that are not working. We decided this is what we need but at a higher level.

Block explained that they had formed the ICU Connections steering group, which met monthly, and included representatives from nearly all the workgroups. Gritz shared their experiences with ICU Bingo and noted that the second round of bingo was about to begin. Gritz, who had turned out to be a good graphic designer, explained that she was going to design a new game board over the weekend, using the colors of the new space the ICU had just moved into.

Several orthopedics participants shared positive reactions and commitments to moving forward, then admissions discharge and transfer nurse Curtis Ferrin shared his reservations: "Why relational coordination? Are there other methods that are just as good? And how do we know this will work?" Arce responded that he knew a lot about teamwork and had been a coach since he was sixteen years old. He found relational coordination useful because it was the best way he had seen to identify the little things that happen between people—the timeliness of communication, the lack of goal alignment or respect—and to show how they add up to make a big deal. Still, it was the ortho group that would have to decide whether to go that route, he pointed out. They would have to own relational coordination. There were good reasons to go forward, but there might also be good reasons not to go forward. A physical therapist pointed out that relational coordination had already helped her to listen to co-workers' concerns about the poor communication they were experiencing and to provide them with a breakdown of the dimensions that could be the issue and how they could be addressed. She also shared that the relational coordination framework had helped her to become more knowledgeable about other people's roles, to respect their work, and to be a more helpful colleague.

Participants were concerned that the orthopedic surgeons were not yet involved and that none had attended this planning meeting. Still, several were optimistic that the surgeons would be interested in measuring their relational coordination because of their interest in numbers and performance improvement. Based on the ICU experience, Coffman argued:

> I think we definitely need a survey to get started in joint replacements. I think we need to send out the RC survey, like we did with the ICU, to provide a preliminary "so this is really what people think of you." Just an honest, anonymous assessment. I think that was an effective tool for us in the ICU, and I feel like we keep on coming back to that preliminary survey—we just keep coming back to it. I think we need that in the total joint program. I think we need data to see where we are at and what we need to work on.

By the end of the discussion, each of the quieter participants had spoken, as Lindberg paused multiple times to ask if anyone else had anything to share.

Each confirmed his or her support and shared the reasons he or she wanted to go forward. Ultimately, Ferrin expressed his support as well, recalling that the culture at Billings used to be much different and noting that change was possible. Chris Manning, responsible for coordinating with post-acute providers, spoke up:

> Curtis, I understand exactly what you are talking about. I am the oldest one here, and I have seen the same changes, and I think we can and should continue on this path. I am completely supportive of going forward, because my job and the success of my job is all about those little things that make up relational coordination. I know that together they add up to a good patient experience.

BRINGING IT ALL TOGETHER: RELATIONAL COORDINATION AS ADAPTIVE CAPACITY

The story of Billings Clinic hints at the potential for relational coordination to become a systemwide framework for collaboration, one that reaches across departments and beyond the walls of a single organization. As CEO Wolter reflected:

> There is quite a number of people now in the physician group, nursing, and other areas that want to participate in leading this forward, being honest about where we don't perform well, but at the same time trying to build on what's been successful. I think the relational coordination approach has captured interest because it builds on things like positive deviance, which, if you think about it, finally became successful in a group of people across many silos spending enough time together, and a kind of cultural belief that we could improve took hold, and allowed us to implement some of the tactics that had been difficult to implement.
>
> It's also creating relationships across different parts of the organization as we tackle improvements that require all sorts of coordinated relationships, because not everything can be done within a single department. So I think this comes at a very good time for us. It's worked because there's a belief by many in our organization that to get true improvement requires activities that are system-based, and we all know now that individual excellence does not by itself create the best safety or quality outcomes.

Without underplaying the role of top management and the quiet but steady support provided by Wolter, we can see that the Billings Clinic story is about the power of frontline leadership, both formal and informal. In particular, the Billings story shows the potential for frontline leaders to use relational coordination as a set of principles and tools to build a high-performance, high-touch culture across a wide array of workers in different silos and at different levels of the traditional professional status hierarchy. We have seen frontline leaders at Billings use relational coordination to break down those silos and status hierarchies by creating a new awareness of interdependence and new ways of talking with one another. Wolter reflected:

> I suppose it's obvious, but it's interesting how difficult it can be. The relationships across the different types of professionals in the organization either foster the culture where that kind of work can be done, or present barriers. We have areas where there are barriers, of course, whether it be in the occasional surgical department, or one operating room area where the staff and the physicians somehow aren't getting along very well, but I think where we see parts of the organization embracing relational coordination, the odds are that there will be some diffusion, and we'll see other parts of the organization embrace it over time.

Gritz summarized the effort thus far from a frontline leader's perspective:

> I think that the most important thing that has resulted from this whole relational coordination effort is awareness and mindfulness, that I am aware of what your job is, what your contribution is, what your needs are, and I am aware that I have a job that impacts you; and that it's true for every discipline. I think that is what relational coordination teaches everybody. We do not work in a vacuum, though sometimes you can start to feel that way. And so I think we've been successful with every discipline on the unit, every type of provider, with making them mindful that there are other people out there who have contributions and who need something from you.

It seemed likely that relational coordination and relational leadership would continue to diffuse throughout Billings Clinic. Another opportunity going forward would be to engage more deeply with patients and their families, partnering with them to coproduce outcomes as Dr. Rollins had demonstrated in the ICU. Indeed, looking back across all four cases—Group Health, Varde Municipality, Dartmouth-Hitchcock, and Billings Clinic—relational coproduction is probably the biggest untapped frontier that we have seen. If relational coproduction works when supported by relational coordination and relational leadership, as Figure 1.2 illustrated, then these four organizations are on a promising pathway to achieving that critically important goal.

One thing was certain—the environment would continue to change, requiring not just operational capacity but equally high levels of adaptive capacity. From Wolter's perspective:

> There's probably never been so much change so fast in healthcare, certainly not in my career, and the uncertainty of where it's all headed, because all the reforms that are in place continue to evolve. Some of the policy initiatives out there right now may not be sustainable, and yet you have to prepare to deal with fairly rapidly evolving payment reforms, which are connected to quality and safety performance. Although payment reform provides a really good incentive to perform well, getting the work done can be very difficult in an environment that's evolving so rapidly.
>
> So I connect it back to relational coordination—if you do have an organization where the relationships are strong enough that there's some resiliency and some basic underlying trust that together we'll find our way through this as we try new approaches, and maybe succeed with some and don't do so well with others, I think this will be very beneficial. Resiliency is going to be pretty important for us over the next five years.

SUMMING UP

The Billings case shows concrete actions that support the growth in adaptive capacity. It shows people who are in the process of learning about RC, applying RC, and finding creative and adaptive ways of doing so. This case also demonstrates how a pilot in a small section of the organization can provide a template the rest of the organization can learn from.

The Billings case also illustrates that the role of CEO cannot be underplayed. Even when change efforts succeed, experience shows that a new CEO can come in and unwittingly destroy the achievements if they do not understand the underlying principles. This suggests the need for a model of change that everyone can understand, and one that helps new CEOs and new employees more generally to understand what is going on and how to support it. The Relational Model of Organizational Change is designed to provide exactly that guidance.

Embedded in these four cases are many useful tools for implementing the Relational Model of Organizational Change. Let's turn now to Part III, which outlines some of these tools in greater detail, to facilitate their use in your organization and the organizations you serve.

PART THREE TOOLS FOR CHANGE

In Group Health, Varde Municipality, the Dartmouth-Hitchcock system, and at Billings Clinic, we have seen four organizations working hard to meet performance pressures by transforming the way co-workers, clients, and leaders relate to one another. Now we move from these real-life stories about how the change process unfolds to explore in more detail the tools that were used to facilitate change. To capture these lessons in the form of practical tools, we return to the Relational Model of Organizational Change and its three types of interventions, shown in the accompanying figure. The tools introduced in the next three chapters are tools that you can use in your own organization and the organizations you work with.

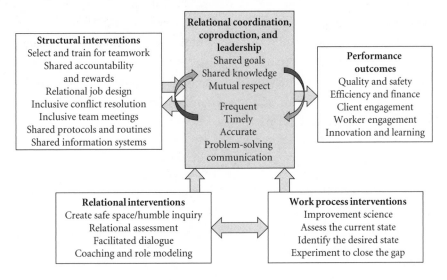

Relational Model of Organizational Change

Relational interventions (Chapter 11) are informed by organizational development and positive organizational psychology, carried out with tools such as relational diagnosis, facilitated dialogue, coaching, and role modeling. These tools enable participants to engage in the process of examining and transforming relational dynamics.

Work process interventions (Chapter 12) are informed by improvement science and carried out with tools from continuous improvement, lean / six sigma, and microsystems.

Structural interventions (Chapter 13) are informed by economics and management science, carried out with human resource management tools, such as payment structures, accountability structures, hiring, training, job design, conflict resolution structures, and with coordinating mechanisms such as meetings, boundary spanners, protocols, and information systems. We will see how these familiar tools can be used in a more relational way, once relational interventions have helped participants to begin developing new ways of communicating and relating.

All three types of interventions are already well-known. So what is different about their use in the Relational Model of Organizational Change? First, all three interventions are informed by the principles of relational coordination. Second, they are used in an integrated way. As change agents, we tend to work in silos, focusing on one type of intervention to the exclusion of the others. By working in these silos, we mirror the silos of the organizations we are seeking to help, and we risk reinforcing those silos. Throughout Part III we will learn how these interventions—relational, work process, and structural—can be informed by the principles of relational coordination, and how they can work together in a synergistic, integrated way.

11 RELATIONAL INTERVENTIONS TO CREATE NEW WAYS OF RELATING

Relational interventions discussed here are informed by process consultation, organizational development, and positive psychology.[1] The underlying philosophy is that participants can be proactive in transforming their role relationships with each other, their clients, and their leaders and that the ultimate responsibility for change rests in their hands. In this chapter, I will show how relational interventions and the tools associated with them can be further informed by the principles of relational coordination, as articulated by Tony Suchman:

> Interventions informed by relational coordination improve participants' capacity to self-manage their interdependence: to understand their common goal, to understand how their individual work fits into the larger work process, and to carry out their work with a mindfulness of how their actions affect the work of others. This requires reciprocal feedback that is frequent, timely, and respectful, provided continuously throughout the work process. Teams achieve their highest level of performance when they have a discipline of ongoing group reflection on how they are working together, supported by adequate communication skills and a systems view of their work. This enables them to align their efforts and to avoid inadvertently making each other's work harder, thus reducing waste, error and interpersonal friction.[2]

In this chapter we explore a set of tools for "doing" relational interventions, tools that we have already seen in action in our four cases. Some of these tools are familiar to organizational development experts, and others are relatively novel—relational mapping, the RC survey, methods for feeding back RC results, and games of positive recognition. We will see how all of them are informed by the principles of relational coordination.

CREATING A SAFE SPACE THROUGH HUMBLE INQUIRY

With organizational change, participants experience both survival anxiety and learning anxiety. With survival anxiety, Ed Schein explained, "you begin to recognize the need to change, the need to give up old habits and ways of thinking and the necessity of learning new habits and ways of thinking."[3] With learning anxiety, however, "you also realize that the new behaviors may be difficult to learn and the new beliefs or values that are implied may be difficult to accept." These new behaviors are particularly difficult to learn when they involve new role relationships—new ways of relating to others—which produces various kinds of identity threat, including fear of loss of power or position, fear of temporary incompetence, fear of being punished for incompetence, fear of loss of personal identity, and fear of loss of group membership. For change to occur, survival anxiety must be greater than learning anxiety. Ideally, this should be achieved by reducing learning anxiety.

To reduce learning anxiety and enable change to occur, such scholars as Chris Argyris, Amy Edmondson, and Ed Schein have identified benefits of creating feelings of psychological safety for participants, also known as safe spaces. The labels for safe spaces differ along with the methodologies for creating them—"cultural islands," "relational spaces," and "safe containers"—but they have in common the goal of creating psychological safety to enable learning and change.

The primary difference when creating safe space informed by principles of relational coordination is to highlight mutual interdependence and to create the conditions for mutual respect, minimizing to the extent possible the impact of power differentials. In the four change efforts we observed in Part II, the change agents had their own approaches to creating a safe space in which learning and change could occur. But there were also commonalities. The change agents often (1) paid careful attention to setting up the room prior to a meeting, typically seating participants in a circle; (2) were highly attentive to who was invited and to the expectations for their participation; and (3) sought to establish a mutually respectful environment by role modeling positive relational behaviors. The change agents would invite the group to articulate its own standards of behavior, for example, by asking people to discuss the question, "What do you need from others in order to be your best self?" first in pairs, and then with another pair, and then with the whole group.

Another common element is the use of humble inquiry by change agents and leaders.[4] Humble inquiry is basically a technique for expressing vulnerability by asking questions to which one does not already know the answer. By admitting publicly that they are dependent on the expertise of others, leaders can make dependence on the expertise of others seem more acceptable, thus helping to lower status barriers that are based on expertise. Through humble inquiry, leaders say, in effect, that while I may know many things, I can't possibly know everything in this complex system, so we must therefore depend on one another to get the full picture. CEO Nick Wolter of Billings Clinic was the epitome of the humble leader, demonstrating his willingness to learn from others by asking them questions and listening carefully to their answers.

RELATIONAL ASSESSMENT OF THE CURRENT STATE THROUGH RELATIONAL MAPPING

Other tools used in the cases helped participants assess and reflect on their current relational patterns, giving particular attention to highly interdependent roles. Participants created relational maps were created in order to visualize the current state of relational coordination across interdependent roles. What are these relational maps and how do they work? I have long illustrated relational coordination as a network of communicating and relating around a work process—drawing a small circle for each workgroup involved, then drawing lines to connect the circles. Each circle indicated relational coordination within a workgroup, and the lines indicated relational coordination between each pair of workgroups.

One day, as I prepared to teach executives from the energy sector, I observed the instructor who preceded me teaching lean/six sigma as an improvement methodology. I watched as he introduced value stream mapping to the executives, in effect providing them with a visual tool for diagnosing the sequence and timing of work process tasks in their organization, and to reflect on possible solutions for improving them. It occurred to me that the network map I had been using might provide a useful exercise for these executives. I tried it that afternoon, while introducing the concept of relational coordination. I was encouraged by the wide range of work processes the executives were able to map, from the financial-planning process to the oil-rig turnaround process to the HR performance-review process. I was even more encouraged by the clarity of the conversations they were able to have with each other regarding the current state reflected in their maps, and about their biggest and most urgent opportunities for improving relational coordination and organizational performance. Figure 11.1 shows an example of relational mapping.

To do relational mapping well, it is important to establish a safe space. I have found it is helpful to remind participants that they are mapping relationships between roles, not particular individuals, that the maps represent a hypothesis about what is going on, and that additional perspectives are needed to create the most accurate picture.[5] Over the years, this relational mapping exercise has proven to be remarkably flexible across types of organization and work processes. It has also proven to be remarkably flexible across cultures, including in the United States, Canada, Denmark, Sweden, Norway, Australia, Japan, and Thailand. I had expected, for example, that Japanese participants would be hesitant to draw red lines—but I found that they, the youngest ones in particular, were eager to indicate where the coordination breakdowns and lack of alignment were happening.

Carsten Hornstrup carries out relational mapping with clients using facilitated dialogue. According to Hornstrup:

> The approach I use is a very focused and very instructive dialogue. What we actually do is we give people the seven questions of RC, and then we just have in front of us a map of the different groups to do the relational mapping exercise. We just ask everyone to look through these questions and based on that, look at each group that's around there, internally and between the groups, assessing whether there is strong relational coordination, medium relational coordination, and low relational coordination. And a quick round, that might be somewhere between six and up to fifteen people. The facilitator interviews one person at a time, giving them the chance to say, "I think as seen from my perspective, as a representative of my functional team, these are the strengths, these are the in-betweens, and these are some of the weaknesses when it comes to relational coordination around this issue."

Two relational maps are shown in Figure 11.2.

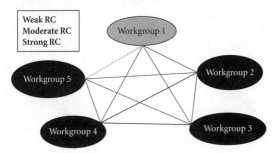

Getting started

◦ Form a team of 3 to 6 people
◦ Identify a work process in need of
  coordination—e.g., "back surgery"
◦ Which workgroups are involved? Consider
  including the customers…
◦ Draw a circle for each workgroup and lines
  connecting between them
• Weak RC = red
• Moderate RC = blue
• Strong RC = green

Drawing your map

Weak RC
Moderate RC
Strong RC

Workgroup 1

Workgroup 2

Workgroup 3

Workgroup 4

Workgroup 5

RC = Shared goals, shared knowledge, mutual respect,
       supported by frequent, timely, accurate,
       problem-solving communication

Reporting back

◇ Where does relational coordination currently
  work well? Where does it work poorly?
◇ How does it impact performance outcomes?
◇ What are the causes?
◇ What are some potential solutions?
◇ Where are your biggest opportunities for
  change?

FIGURE 11.1   Relational diagnosis using RC mapping

Relational mapping has the capacity to reflect the state of teamwork across all the roles in a work process, including those that tend to be overlooked because of their relative low status; roles that work in different locations or for different organizations; and roles that exist outside work organizations, such as clients and their families, neighbors, and friends. Sometimes the process of relational mapping makes visible workgroups that tend to be overlooked

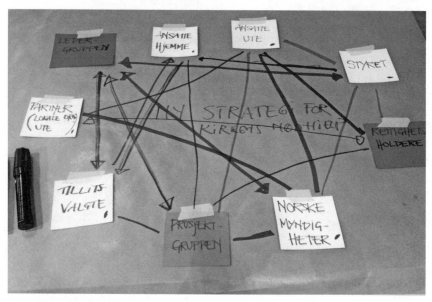

FIGURE 11.2 Relational maps

despite their critical interdependencies with others—like front-desk receptionists or transport workers. Sometimes the process makes visible the interdependencies that exist between well-recognized workgroups that were previously seen as operating independently. When participants report back about their maps, they often note new insights, such as "we realized the aides need to be on this map—they spend more time with the patient than anyone else, and we don't even think about them."

RELATIONAL ASSESSMENT USING THE RC SURVEY

Going beyond the impressionistic mapping of relational coordination ties, the relational coordination survey can be used as a next step to engage more participants and allow participants' private assessments of their own ties with the other roles to be aggregated into a overall map.

But why take this step? Why use a survey? I originally created the relational coordination survey for research purposes to assess the relational coordination of flight departures between different airline sites and to test the association of relational coordination with an array of organizational structures and with performance outcomes of interest to airlines. Measurement is not just a tool for research, however. Measurement is also a tool for change.

Measurement is a common way for participants to assess the current state and to assess their progress over time. Indeed, measurement is considered by many management scholars and practitioners to be an essential component of an improvement process.[6] As Deming suggested several decades ago in his analysis of industry performance challenges, the *way* we measure and *what* we measure can strongly influence behavior in organizations and should be designed to do so in an intentional way. Deming was particularly attentive to the need to "drive fear out" and "measure the process, not the person" in order to create the potential for improvement rather than finger-pointing and blaming.[7] The RC survey should therefore be used to measure the quality of communicating and relating across the interdependent roles in a work process, and used for the purpose of learning rather than punishment.

As we saw at Group Health, Varde, Dartmouth, and Billings, the RC survey generates diagnostic information regarding the current state of teamwork, thereby providing feedback and helping to launch conversations that can produce insight and improvement. Measuring relational coordination has the potential to focus attention on the less visible elements of how work gets done, just as relational mapping does. But the survey can reflect a wider array of voices, in a more protected way, than is possible with relational mapping. In effect, the survey takes qualitative relational processes and asks people to assign numerical values to them, producing quantitative measures that enable rankings, network analyses, and statistical analyses. By doing so, the survey creates the opportunity for new dialogues between participants who are more qualitatively oriented and those who are more quantitatively oriented. In organizations and industries in which many powerful participants are geared to value quantitative results—heads of finance, engineers, physicians, chief operating officers, and so on—this characteristic of the survey can be very useful for creating useful new dialogues.

The relational coordination survey includes just seven questions, shown in Table 11.1. It was recognized in a recent meta-analysis as one of only two teamwork measures in the healthcare context that are both fully validated and "unbounded" in the sense of having the ability to measure teamwork beyond the scope of well-defined teams.[8] It is able to measure teamwork beyond the scope of well-defined teams because it is a network measure, and because it is geared to measuring teamwork between roles rather than specific individuals. Each of the seven questions is asked about each workgroup involved in the target work process, resulting in a larger number of questions (7 ∗ number of workgroups = total survey questions). The survey assesses these seven dimensions among each of the work process roles, in both directions, for example assessing perceptions of respect between surgeons and secretaries in both directions. The survey therefore reveals whether the ties are reciprocal (experienced in the same way) or nonreciprocal (experienced in different ways).

Though we call it the relational coordination survey, it is also used in adapted forms to measure relational coproduction and relational leadership.[9] The workgroups that we ask about in the survey can represent co-worker roles, but they can also represent customers, their families, external suppliers, and leadership.

TABLE 11.1   RC survey questions

RC dimension	Survey question
1. Frequent communication	How *frequently* do people in each of these groups communicate with you about [focal work process]?
2. Timely communication	How *timely* is their communication with you about [focal work process]?
3. Accurate communication	How *accurate* is their communication with you about [focal work process]?
4. Problem-solving communication	When there is a problem in [focal work process], do people in these groups blame others or try to *solve the problem*?
5. Shared goals	Do people in these groups *share your goals* for [focal work process]?
6. Shared knowledge	Do people in these groups *know* about the work you do with [focal work process]?
7. Mutual respect	Do people in these groups *respect* the work you do with [focal work process]?

REFLECTING ON SURVEY RESULTS

When participants have finished responding and the survey results are tabulated, change agents have an opportunity to review the results and develop some initial interpretations to guide their next steps. Change agents have different approaches for what they look for to guide their next steps. One common approach is to assess up front the extent to which respect is an issue. Hornstrup explained:

> Before I go into choosing the path and what that will open up, I first have a look at two things. One, which of the dimensions of the RC survey seems to be the lowest scoring? Because if it's some of the communication dimensions, that is often relatively simple. You could sort of head off in any direction. But if it's a lack of mutual respect, then I start by looking at who more specifically might have an experience of low respect. And then I start with those specific groups before I enter into working with the whole system.
>
> When I start looking at the numbers like that, what I also have a look at what I call an asymmetrical understanding of relational coordination. In these organizations it seems like the more privileged ones in the hierarchy assess relational coordination higher than the others. Or if there are any leaders in the survey, they often assess relational coordination higher than the staff.

These nonreciprocal ties are common between roles with substantial power or status differences and yet are often invisible to those in the positions of higher power.

RC survey results are displayed graphically, in three different formats (Figure 11.3). First, the seven dimensions of relational coordination are shown using bar charts. Here they are shown aggregated across all the workgroups involved. Change agents often begin by sharing the overall results, asking participants to reflect on strengths and opportunities and how the results compare to their own experiences. The same results can be shown for each individual workgroup, giving participants in that workgroup feedback from all the other workgroups on the quality of their communicating and relating.

The RC index shown in Figure 11.3 is simply an average of the seven dimensions of relational coordination, the same validated index that has been used for research purposes and associated with a wide array of performance outcomes across many industries and many countries, as summarized in Chapter 2.[10] While the evidence suggests that higher relational coordination is associated with higher performance, the low, medium, and high distinctions indicated by the shading are approximate cut-offs based on the distribution of RC scores observed over the years.

More detailed results can be seen in the matrix, which shows each workgroup's ratings of each other workgroup, for all seven dimensions of RC taken

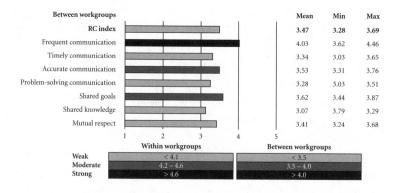

Between workgroups	Mean	Min	Max
RC index	3.47	3.28	3.69
Frequent communication	4.03	3.62	4.46
Timely communication	3.34	3.03	3.65
Accurate communication	3.53	3.31	3.76
Problem-solving communication	3.28	3.03	3.51
Shared goals	3.62	3.44	3.87
Shared knowledge	3.07	3.79	3.29
Mutual respect	3.41	3.24	3.68

	Within workgroups	Between workgroups
Weak	< 4.1	< 3.5
Moderate	4.2 – 4.6	3.5 – 4.0
Strong	> 4.6	> 4.0

FIGURE 11.3   RC survey results: the seven dimensions
SOURCE: Relational Coordination Analytics, Inc.

TABLE 11.2   RC survey results: matrix

					Ratings of					
		Case managers	Clerical	EHR admins	Lab	LPNs	MDs	RNs	Social workers	Therapists	PAs
Ratings by	Case managers	—	4.00	4.86	4.43	4.00	4.57	4.43	4.29	4.43	4.57
	Clerical	3.43	—	3.00	3.14	3.86	3.71	4.29	4.71	3.14	3.71
	EHR admins	4.00	3.57	—	3.71	4.71	4.00	4.00	3.86	3.71	4.00
	Lab	4.29	4.00	4.57	—	4.43	4.43	4.43	4.00	4.29	4.00
	LPNs	4.00	4.00	4.43	3.86	—	3.71	4.00	4.00	3.86	3.71
	MDs	4.86	3.86	5.00	4.71	4.57	—	4.43	4.86	4.71	4.00
	RNs	4.43	3.14	4.00	4.00	3.57	3.71	—	4.00	4.00	3.71
	Social workers	4.86	4.00	4.71	3.57	3.43	4.71	3.43	—	3.57	4.71
	Therapists	4.00	4.00	4.43	3.86	3.86	3.71	4.00	4.00	—	3.71
	PAs	3.43	3.14	3.00	3.14	3.86	3.71	4.29	4.71	3.14	—

SOURCE: Relational Coordination Analytics, Inc.

NOTE: EHR admin, electronic health record administrator; LPN, licensed practical nurse; MD, medical doctor; PA, physician assistant; RN, registered nurse.

together (Table 11.2). You can also dive deeper and look at the matrix specifically for timely communication, or for shared knowledge, or for mutual respect.

Relational coordination maps (Figure 11.4) are produced, using the data in the matrix, to enable participants to visualize the overall strength of ties both within and between groups. An additional map is available to highlight all nonreciprocal ties between workgroups, which can be eye-opening to see, particularly for those who have a more positive experience of a working relationship than their colleagues in the other role.

FACILITATED DIALOGUE TO FEEDBACK RESULTS

According to practitioners, sharing relational coordination measures with participants is like giving them a mirror to look into, or "like putting the elephant on the table"—it allows them to see what is there and to talk about it together, generating solutions based on their understanding. Sharing the metrics with participants can bring attention to areas of teamwork strength, as

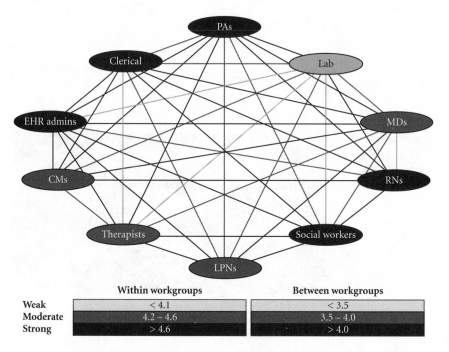

	Within workgroups	Between workgroups
Weak	< 4.1	< 3.5
Moderate	4.2 – 4.6	3.5 – 4.0
Strong	> 4.6	> 4.0

FIGURE 11.4   RC survey results: map
SOURCE: Relational Coordination Analytics, Inc.
NOTE: CM, case manager; EHR admin, electronic health record administrator; LPN, licensed practical nurse; MD, medical doctor; PA, physician assistant; RN, registered nurse.

well as identify areas of opportunity for improvement, such as timelier communication, greater goal alignment, greater knowledge of each other's work, or more respectful interactions—either team-wide or in specific role relationships. Sharing relational coordination measures with participants helps to make important work dynamics visible. One of the early intervention leaders, Claire Kenwood, psychiatric leader from the National Health Service in Scotland, noted, "One benefit of the relational coordination measure is that it provides information about organizational aspects that staff members often feel are overlooked—the perceptions and quality of the relationships between individuals, between groups, and between organizations."

As Joan Resnick, an organizational effectiveness expert in the Kaiser-Permanente Northwest region, explained, "We're finding RC to be an efficient diagnostic tool. It helps us to understand the culture of primary care and how it relates to specialty care. We're feeding back baseline RC survey results to the four medical offices in our region now. People get the seven dimensions, and they're learning quickly." Clearly, the results can be sensitive. Therefore, change agents who have used the RC survey for interventional purposes advise that skilled coaching is needed to help participants to make sense of the measures in a way that fosters productive conversations and maximizes the potential to unfreeze current relationship patterns rather than simply make bad relationships worse. The following advice for change agents who are about to embark on a change process involving interventional uses of the RC survey was drafted in 2011, with input from Ed Schein and Tony Suchman:

> While the RC survey is well established as an observational research tool, its use as an intervention is still at relatively early stages of development. It would be easy to underestimate the complexity of this work. Overly simplistic interventions can cause harm. Reviewing RC scores can elicit shame, defensiveness, projection, triangulation, and scapegoating; it can exacerbate conflict and compromise performance. The lower the level of relational coordination (and thus the greater the need for an intervention), the greater the likelihood of a dysfunctional response to the scores.
>
> As elegant and straightforward as the RC survey is as a measure, it is not a magic bullet for improving team performance or organizational culture. It needs to be used as one part of a broader intervention that includes longitudinal individual and team coaching, trustworthy processes for relational learning and accountability, and leadership development to assure consistent parallel process across levels of the team or organization. Such work requires the involvement of skilled coaches/consultants with deep experience in group dynamics, systems work, conflict resolution, and the teaching of emotional self-management. For all these reasons, we urge you not to tread lightly or naively into the realm of interventions. Be prepared to invest the necessary time and resources and be sure you have access to the skills and experience that the work requires.[11]

As we saw in our cases, change agents often took very different approaches when sharing relational coordination data with participants. Some were cautious, as advised by Schein and Suchman. Concerned about the risk of scapegoating, personalizing, and misinterpreting—for example, failing to recognize the structural causes of low scores—some change agents preferred to share with the whole team only the aggregate team results along the seven dimensions and to let each workgroup within the team see its own results privately, offering it help interpreting and making sense of them.

Others took another path, sharing even the more fine-grained results with everybody on the team, including the matrices and the network maps showing the strength of relational coordination as rated by each of the workgroups. This greater transparency carries risks, but these may be balanced or offset by the benefits. As Hornstrup noted in Chapter 8, he was more concerned about lack of transparency:

> Maybe I'm not a sensitive guy, but this survey is not asking, "Do you love me?"—it's just asking, "Do people respect each other's contribution to how we do our job?" I mean, it's the voices of people, so I would probably turn it the other way around. I think not to use the data rather openly would not be sensitive to the people who answered this survey. And of course, I've had separate discussions with those groups that have really low numbers. But they are not surprised. Because they know. The ones who are going to get the lowest score, they know before they get them. That's often why they're a bit defensive.

Hornstrup was careful to share the data with frontline leaders first, however, before sharing with top leadership or the frontline employees: "That's where I'm very careful. Who to share the data with first. Don't go senior. Don't go to the employees. Instead, go to the people who are pointed at, who are accountable for results, who have all the pressures—the frontline leaders. We need to talk to them first."

Hornstrup was also careful to share the data separately with the workgroups that had less power and who did not seem to have a secure voice, as signaled by their low scores on respect or asymmetric ties: "It seems like sometimes you have to go in there and have the ones who are less privileged in the system, to help them find themselves on their own terms before you bring them into the room with others. Because otherwise, sometimes they're simply silenced there."

Others, for example, Curt Lindberg at Billings, started by sharing the scores on all seven dimensions with the whole team and then shared each workgroup's scores on each dimension separately with that workgroup. These change agents shared the more detailed cross-workgroup ratings in the matrices and network maps only when the participants were ready to address more sensitive issues, and as a sufficiently safe space opened up to enable that dialogue to happen productively. The bottom line is that flexibility, judgment, and an understanding of the organizational context are key in sharing the assessments with participants. Relational assessments are expected to work best when they are used dialogically rather than prescriptively, not as a report card but rather as a way to open up new conversations.

DETERMINING NEXT STEPS: EMERGENT DESIGN

After interpreting and making sense of their results, the participants are typically put in charge of determining next steps, and given the opportunity to put the feedback fairly quickly into action. Hornstrup shared:

> These cross-functional teams can actually meet and use this map afterward to guide their work. Maybe they have wide gaps they can identify and they can say these are the targets, these are some of the initiatives that we need to take, then have status meetings to check on their progress . . . And then we use that also as a way of prioritizing the most obvious areas for improvement, and prioritizing next steps and who will do what.

The idea is that the participants take responsibility for identifying areas for improvement and for creating and implementing plans to achieve improvement. The lead change agents may have ideas, but they do not provide a complete plan for approaching an improvement effort. Lindberg described his approach:

> We use emergent design for strengthening relational coordination, given the desire to enhance how people interact. We try to interact with interested volunteers in a manner that displays the RC dimensions and then we use the results of these interactions to determine next steps. To help people build relationships and relate in effective ways that stimulate creativity, we use a variety of tools, such as 1-2-4-all, Appreciative Interviews, Open Space, Fishbowl, et cetera. These tools are called Liberating Structures and they are very much aligned with the principles of RC.[12] They encourage listening; they welcome and respect diverse perspectives; they help people build new relationships; they focus on problem solving; and they feature abundant interaction. As an initial set of plans unfold, there are multiple

opportunities to make sense of what happened, which then informs next steps, and so on.

A key feature of this approach is voluntarism. This means handing the decision to staff, asking whether they want to pursue an improvement effort around something they care about using an RC-informed approach, then relying on volunteers to guide the effort with some nurturing leadership support. The emergent design approach therefore relies heavily on a coach-the-coach model with encouragement and mentoring for the formal frontline leaders or the informal frontline leaders who inevitably emerge.

Voluntarism is also relevant when designing interventions to engage clients in relational coproduction. Interventions like self-management for patients with chronic conditions can fail when the voice of the customer is not considered.

FACILITATED DIALOGUE: CONVERSATIONS OF INTERDEPENDENCE

Conversations of interdependence are one of the simplest and most powerful tools I have seen for conducting relational interventions. We saw them in action at Group Health and the Billings Clinic. Suchman developed this tool to foster shared knowledge among participants in a work process who don't know enough about each other's work to be able to coordinate well. Lack of shared knowledge, for example, makes it difficult to engage in timely communication and can undermine respect for each other's work. According to Suchman:

> By learning to have regular conversations about how we are impacting each other's work, we can improve the performance of our team, achieve better results, enjoy our work more. These conversations of interdependence allow people to understand how their work fits into the larger whole and become more mindful of the needs and roles of other team members, and how we affect each other's ability to achieve good outcomes.[13]

A coach simply invites participants who play different roles in an interdependent work process to take turns interviewing each other one on one, using the following questions:

- What are your primary responsibilities?
- What do you find most meaningful about your work?
- What is it about how I do my work that helps you do yours?
- What could I do differently that would help you even more?
- When does our work seem to be well aligned, and when do we seem to be at cross-purposes?

These conversations occur in pairs, often within the context of a meeting or workshop. Participants can be given a homework assignment to carry out additional conversations of interdependence with people in the other work-groups before the next meeting.

PERSPECTIVE TAKING THROUGH IMPROVISATION

Other change agents have used improvisation as a tool to jumpstart new patterns of relational coordination. Carlos Arce, chief learning officer at Billings, explained how improvisation works:

> No one is safe from improv. You are brought into the activity, and that's been part of the fun—bringing people in and having them play a role, or even just being in the live audience. The cool thing is that it exposes some dynamics and subtleties that end up leading the change. The context is one of self-discovery, enjoyment, pleasure, and playful interaction that actually lends itself to folks relaxing, dropping their guard, sharing, and exposing things in a way that might be helpful for other people.

In the same spirit, Marjorie Godfrey and her colleagues used improvisation as a tool to break down barriers when they began working with the Dartmouth-Hitchcock surgical units. When the coaches were going through their initial training in relational coordination and microsystems, Godfrey tried an improvisation exercise in which some of the surgeons ended up dancing. Godfrey recalled this as a turning point because it broke some of the stereotypes and rigidities associated with the role of surgeon. Role play was used later by Annette Tietz, one the Dartmouth-Hitchcock coaches, to play out some challenging scenarios among her colleagues in the otolaryngology department, and to test out new patterns of communicating and relating, informed by the baseline relational coordination data (Chapter 9).

Leslie Owen at Blue Shield California used improvisation in a similar way. She and her colleagues had already measured baseline relational coordination and were a few months into the intervention phase. As she described it:

> The group performed a skit where relational coordination was very poor, and it was a comedy routine. And then we talked about improvements and how it relates to the domains, the RC domains, and what we could do in our everyday work to be aware of that and to improve those. And that's about where we are at this point at Blue Shield. Actually Marcus [physician leader and vice president] was in the skit. Bless his heart. He was our certified nursing assistant. It was great. And it was really helpful. I mean we all have seen things go badly, and you know, we've all seen poor relational coordination. But just to see it and then talk about each domain, and what happened, was really valuable.

Owen's colleague Florence Nerby served as creative director. In Nerby's humble opinion, "We should get an Oscar. Seriously though, it was a lot of fun. And being in nursing for decades, I have seen poor relational coordination my whole career, so it's very exciting to see this work."

As a lead change agent at both Billings and Blue Shield California, Lindberg reflected on why improvisation works:

> In improv, people get to see the work and roles of others, and even step into the roles of others, developing their shared knowledge: What did you notice? What might you have done differently? What have you seen others do that is particularly effective? Information flows, diverse perspectives are honored, and the impact of good and bad everyday patterns of interaction are observed for participants to evaluate.

Professor Michele Williams has identified through her research the power of perspective taking for enhanced interpersonal understanding and strengthened social bonds. Perspective taking is a skill that can be learned by anyone, she argues.[14] Perhaps improvisation, and role playing more generally, is a way to learn perspective taking in a way that enhances our role relationships.

GAMES OF POSITIVE RECOGNITION: RC BINGO, RC TREE, HIGH FIVES

Positive deviance means looking for individuals or groups who have already figured out innovative solutions and then recognizing, celebrating, and disseminating those solutions, as we learned in earlier chapters. I have seen the growing use of games of positive recognition to foster new patterns of relational coordination. The practice at Southwest called LUV Notes (Chapter 10) was, in effect, a game of positive recognition across different workgroups. Another game of positive recognition was ICU Bingo in the Billings intensive care unit (Chapter 10). Another was the RC Tree created by frontline leaders in the primary care clinics at Group Health (Chapter 7). These games are about building a new culture, where people begin noticing different things, and recognizing them publicly.

APPRECIATIVE INQUIRY: STORYTELLING TO IDENTIFY STRENGTHS

Appreciative inquiry elicits stories about moments of success, looking for the core themes or factors, and then developing a shared vision of what a future could look like if those core factors were present in abundance. In a workshop with Swedish leaders and change agents, for example, participants were invited to tell stories about times they had experienced high levels of relational coordination and then identify some of the underlying factors that made it possible. Four of the seven groups presented stories of "magical moments" or "magical meetings" that turned a negative dynamic into a positive one by bringing the parties into dialogue in ways that had seemed unlikely or even impossible given their previous experience.

COACHING AND ROLE MODELING

The tools shown in this chapter, informed by principles of relational coordination, have one primary purpose—to create new conversations among participants in interdependent roles and enable them to practice new patterns of behaviors in order to achieve high performance outcomes. Change agents and other leaders play a critical supporting role here, offering their own actions as a way to role model the desired behaviors. Desired behaviors may include treating participants in high- and low-status roles in an equally respectful way, as well as admitting what one does not know and asking others for help. As noted earlier, change agents may engage in humble inquiry, for example, making clear that it is safe to admit not knowing everything and safe to ask others for help.

Role modeling is powerful and can be captured more generally in the principle of parallel process. In his workshop "Improving Work Processes with Relational Coordination," Tony Suchman begins with the principle of parallel process.[15] He advises participants to carry out all of their work in the spirit of relational coordination in order to role model the principles they are seeking to foster. This simple advice brings to mind Gandhi's advice to "be the change you wish to see in the world."

Marjorie Godfrey at Dartmouth has taken the idea of coaching to a new level. Building on her practical and scholarly expertise, she has developed a coach-the-coach model to embed change capacity in organizations by training a group of internal leaders to lead relational and work process interventions, as we saw at Dartmouth-Hitchcock. This approach has the potential to produce more scalable, rapid, and sustainable change. Godfrey points out that an additional benefit is that leaders are supported in learning a new way to lead, "When a leader wants to turn from being a command and control leader who is just responsible and accountable for finances and operations to a leader who is developing, lifting up and helping everyone be the best they can be in a collective way to achieve team goals, this is how they can learn to do it."[16]

Coaching is often a critical component of interventions designed to build relational coproduction with customers. When this personal contact is not considered, otherwise well-designed interventions can fail. According to the project leader of a coaching intervention for patients with chronic conditions:

> The most important reason why these self-management interventions failed is that patients wanted to stay in personal contact with the diabetes nurse. More is happening at these consultation hours than just having your checkup. Patients can ask the diabetes nurse questions about anything related to their disease that they are dealing with and share their concerns. Diabetes nurses have the time available

during these checkups for these additional questions and talk about things patients are concerned about. We have a very pleasant and skilled diabetes nurse with whom they feel free to exchange personal information. I think they might want to do the checkups themselves, but don't want to lose the personal contact with the nurse.

Another project leader concurred:

Self-management means that patients have to deal with their condition in a proactive manner. But disease management goes even further than that. Motivational interviewing, for example, provides professionals with techniques to change thinking and behaviors among patients beyond just empowering and coaching them. It is not just a coaching role of asking patients what they need, how you can help them, and letting them decide what's best. It is even more than that: it's about talking about the dilemmas they are experiencing, what they think is important, and changing their thought and behavior patterns in order to really motivate them to work on changing their lives.[17]

Anyone can engage in coaching and role modeling simply by being intentional about using their own behavior to create change in others. Coaching and role modeling are therefore powerful tools for frontline leadership. In my early research in the airline industry, there was a phrase I heard from time to time at Southwest Airlines. Workers there occasionally explained to me that part of their job was to "turn people around." In effect, they had been trained to see their jobs as transforming adverse relationships into collaborative relationships through their own actions and by role modeling, reminiscent of the biblical parable in which we are advised, when struck, to turn the other cheek.

As I understand it, this parable is not about playing the role of victim; it is about the power we have to reverse negative cycles—whether long-standing or momentary—by reacting in an unexpected way. By doing so, we invite the other into a new way of being. This is one interpretation of what Billings' staff did, for example, in meetings with their information systems department (Chapter 10). Informed by their own relational coordination work, they modeled a new behavior—problem solving rather than blaming—that invited their IT colleagues to reciprocate, thus transforming the relationship and creating improvements in the information system for the purpose of better patient care.

SUMMING UP

Each of the tools for carrying out relational interventions described in this chapter has a common purpose—to enable participants to create and practice new patterns of communicating and relating across interdependent roles. These tools for relational interventions are informed by the principles of relational coordination. Many of the tools are also informed by positive psychology, which highlights the power of positive framing to overcome the threat-rigidity effect that is associated with purely critical approaches to change, helping to unleash creative energy.[18]

Relational interventions by themselves are not likely to be sufficient, however. As Schein pointed out:

> The projects that I am familiar with that have really made changes all started with a model that integrated relational coordination kinds of issues with work process redesign, done correctly in a leadership climate and culture ready for change. The bad uses of lean failed precisely because they ignored relational coordination at the beginning. Relational coordination could fall into the same trap.[19]

Using the RC survey or any tool as an isolated initiative is precisely what the Relational Model of Organizational Change is intended to avoid. In our live case studies, participants found relational interventions useful precisely because they were *not* used as an isolated initiative but rather were used to help them carry out their improvement work more effectively.

In the next chapter, we will consider tools for carrying out work process interventions. In particular, we will see the relational interventions we explored in this chapter can increase the effectiveness of work process interventions, interventions to redesign and improve the work itself.

12 WORK PROCESS INTERVENTIONS TO CREATE NEW WAYS OF WORKING

On the face of it, work process interventions appear to be the polar opposite of relational interventions. While relational interventions are focused on transforming relationships among the people who doing the work, work process interventions are focused on transforming the work itself. Process improvement and relational coordination come from distinct silos of expertise. They have distinct languages and distinct methodologies, driven by distinct "inquiry preferences"—in particular, one appears to be more technical and measurement driven, while the other appears to be softer and more relationally driven.[1] At times, they are seen as competing paradigms. People who identify with one of these paradigms can feel threatened when confronted with the other one.

One day, I was out walking with a colleague who is an organizational development practitioner skilled in relational interventions. We ran into a leader of one of the local hospitals that she works with. Tension emerged as they discussed the design of an upcoming meeting and whether to include an internal consultant who uses lean tools to improve performance. "Are we going to bring him to that meeting? If we do, then it's going to be defined as an OE [operational excellence] problem." For them, it seemed to be an either/or choice about which approach would be used to define the problem and therefore the solution. It did not seem realistic that the two approaches could be used in a complementary and synergistic way. The very silos that we are working to overcome in organizations can also limit our collective impact as change agents.

This competition between social and technical approaches to organizational change is not simply a US phenomenon. For the first couple of years that I was invited to Denmark, it seemed that the organizational development practitioners did not talk to the lean practitioners, and vice versa. Now, more and more, they are talking. Still, of the twenty-five change projects we identified and analyzed in "The Interventional Uses of Relational Coordination: Early Evidence from Four Countries," we found that while all used relational interventions, such as creating a safe space, feeding back relational coordination data to participants, and engaging in coaching and role modeling, only 44 percent used work process interventions. One possible explanation for this finding is that many of the practitioners and change agents who were initially drawn to the relational coordination framework had training that was conducive to relational interventions—such as organizational development—and few had been trained in work process interventions.[2]

For decades, sociotechnical systems designers have seen relational and work process interventions as complementary approaches to organizational change.[3] In this chapter, I introduce tools for carrying out work process interventions, showing how they can be informed by the principles of relational coordination. Once change agents have used relational interventions to begin changing the way participants communicate with and relate to one another, they can use work process interventions more effectively to transform the work itself.

PROCESS IMPROVEMENT AND RELATIONAL COORDINATION AS COMPETING PARADIGMS?

The benefits of integrating process improvement and relational coordination first arose for me in conversations with colleagues Ed Schein and Amy Edmondson. We were meeting regularly to develop what became the Relational Model of Organizational Change. At the time, Schein was in conversations with the CEO of Virginia Mason, a health system in Seattle, Washington, known for its deep implementation of lean methods.[4] He had been influenced by those conversations to see process improvement as far more central to organizational change than he had previously thought.

It was Earl Murman, astronautics and aeronautics physicist at the MIT Lean Advancement Initiative, who first referred to relational coordination as "the soft side of lean." In Murman's experience, shared goals, shared knowledge, and mutual respect, as well as timely, accurate, problem-solving communication, helped to drive effective process improvement. Some observers object to calling relational coordination "the soft side of lean," seeing the label as somehow minimizing the real challenges of building high-functioning relationships and the importance of these relationships for successful change efforts. Both Dale Collins Vidal, surgeon leader at Dartmouth-Hitchcock, and Marjorie Godfrey, co-director of the Dartmouth Institute Microsystem Academy, have pointed out that relational coordination is actually quite hard in the sense of being both measurable and challenging to achieve.

Regardless of the term we choose, the relational side of lean may indeed be important to its success. One central finding of Godfrey's research was that in the absence of skilled coaching with attention to relational as well as technical dimensions, lean does not work well.[5] Another study found that process improvement in hospitals was associated with an *increase* in clinical quality but a *decrease* in the quality of the patient experience.[6] This outcome seems likely when work process improvement is carried out using technical tools with little attention to the relationships with the customer or between the roles that work with the customer.

Indeed, process improvement is about connecting across silos. To drive out waste and engage in just-in-time production, people must connect with each other horizontally instead of referring all problems up the chain of command to be resolved at a higher level. In the traditional bureaucratic model, buffers in the form of excess inventory or wait time for customers exist between the steps in the process, minimizing the need for workers to communicate directly with each other. However, excess inventory is wasteful because of storage and inventory costs, and negatively impacts quality by increasing customer wait times. More fundamentally, inventory reduces transparency and, therefore, the ability to identify and address performance issues in a timely way. A negative feedback loop is set up that demoralizes staff and frustrates managers. In sum, lean is all about seeking to deliver products and services just in time, in response to customer demand. To do so requires communicating on the fly in a timely, problem-solving way with each other and with the customer.

Microsystems is another approach to process improvement that addresses both relational and technical aspects of systems. Defined as "the smallest replicable units" of production or value creation, microsystems are the places where workers meet each other, and where workers meet their customers. According to Godfrey and her colleagues Paul Batalden and Eugene Nelson, microsystems are effective or ineffective, producing high or low levels of performance, depending on their design. As Batalden famously said, "Every system is perfectly designed to produce the outcomes it produces." One of the distinguishing factors is the quality of interrelating among workers who carry out interdependent tasks. "Microsystems that work as high reliability organizations, similar to those described by Weick and colleagues, are [those in which participants are] 'mindful' of their interdependent interactions."[7]

TOOLS FOR CHANGE AT THREE STAGES OF WORK PROCESS IMPROVEMENT

Now let's consider tools for change at three stages of work process improvement: (1) *assess the current state*, (2) *envision the desired state*, and (3) *experiment to close the gap*.

Assess the Current State

Work process improvement typically starts with an assessment of the current state. One tool for assessing the current state is simply "going and seeing." There is no substitute for observing the work itself, in real time. In lean parlance, this is known as "going to the *gemba* (a Japanese term meaning "the real place"). Practitioners have discovered that it is extremely useful for participants to then step back from immediate observation and visualize the "system" or the "process" they are part of. In a sense, they are creating a boundary object that represents the system. Tools for developing a visual representation of the current state include process mapping, value stream mapping, or flow charts that trace the customer journey. These tools produce insights into the current state that are not available from the perspective of any one workgroup, given each workgroup's unique line of sight. They can therefore be used to highlight connections between the tasks carried out by the different workgroups, including customers, making interdependencies more evident.

The "5 Ps" tool is used to assess the current state of the microsystem. What is the *purpose* of the microsystem? Who are the *patients* or the *customers*, and what are their characteristics? Who are the *professionals* or *workers*, and what are their distinct roles? What are the *processes* through which work is carried out? And what are the *patterns* of interrelating through which these processes are carried out? The microsystem and the larger system in which it is embedded is seen as a complex adaptive system that evolves over time. In particular, the fifth P—patterns—is key to the adaptive capacity of the microsystem. "Patterns are the consistent behaviors, sentiments and results that emerge from the relationships of the parts involved in a complex adaptive system."[8] The 5 Ps tool is illustrated in Figure 12.1.

To assess the current state, participants must go beyond the microsystem to understand the broader context. This broader context is made up of the *mesosystem*, which is simply a set of interdependent microsystems, and the *macrosystem*, which is the regulatory, cultural, social and political environment within which the microsystem is situated. These "3 Ms" help participants to assess the current state more broadly by helping them to see the system at multiple levels. Context diagrams are a tool for mapping and assessing this broader context.

Identify the Desired State

Attention to the current state is a powerful way to begin a journey of improvement. Whenever we represent the current state visually and analyze it, it becomes clear that there are flaws in it. But identifying flaws is not sufficient. Rather, we must identify a desired state. The second core element of work process interventions, therefore, is envisioning the desired state. The desired state is perhaps the least-well-developed stage of work process improvement. Some argue that practitioners tend to focus instead on identifying the flaws in the current state, and then allow those flaws to drive the improvement process. Recall system thinker Ackoff's critique in Chapter 6: "Most applications of

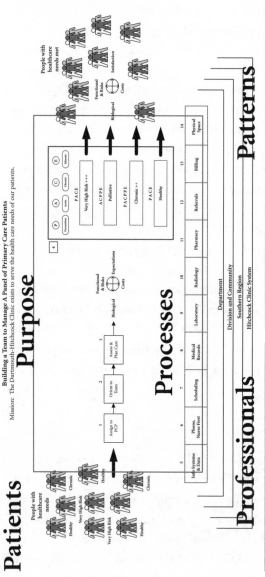

FIGURE 12.1   The 5 Ps template for assessing the current state

SOURCE: E. C. Nelson, P. B. Batalden, and M. M. Godfrey, *Quality by Design: A Clinical Microsystems Approach* (San Francisco: Jossey-Bass, 2007).

improvement science are directed at improving the parts, but not at improving the whole . . . [As a result] the parts don't form a system because they don't fit together."[9] To improve the whole rather than simply the parts, Ackoff noted, "improvement programs have to be directed at what you want—not at what you don't want."

This means that a fundamental step in work process improvement is achieving clarity about the shared purpose or shared goal, and to get relevant stakeholders together in the room to envision the desired state. Attention to this step can prevent wasteful solutions, such as building emergency department capacity when the real need is for primary care capacity to keep people *out* of the emergency department, or even overbuilding primary care capacity when the real need may be public investment in healthy communities, including in childcare, sidewalks, bike lanes, safe neighborhoods, healthy food, job placement, or a cleaner environment.

The lean approach to identifying the desired state is to identify the *customers* and find out what they value. After all, it is the customers—not the workers—who ultimately define what is value added and what is not value added. A tool for identifying customers and hearing their voices is the customer stakeholder analysis. "Taking a customer perspective, lean determines the value of any given process by distinguishing value adding activities from non-value adding activities."[10] The microsystems methodology further envisions the desired state by articulating the purpose of the microsystem and identifying its desired outcomes, using the 5 Ps template (see Figure 12.1).

Positive deviance offers a unique approach to identifying the desired state. Positive deviance starts by inviting participants to notice when things work particularly well, to recognize that success, and to use that success as a way to build an understanding of the desired state and how to get there. In effect, positive deviance meets Ackoff's criteria for an improvement program that is "directed at what you want—not at what you don't want." Although we saw positive deviance and appreciative inquiry in Chapter 11 as tools for relational interventions, both also have the potential to be used for work process interventions. Indeed, organizational scholars Marguerite Schneider and Curt Lindberg argue that positive deviance is an alternative improvement methodology that avoids a focus on gaps and deficits, providing instead a strength-based approach with the potential to build high-functioning rela-tionships and unleash creative energy.[11] One study found that high-quality working relationships enabled the success of work process improvement ef-forts by providing participants with the "psychological capital" to frame resource constraints as a positive challenge rather than a deficit, in effect sup-porting the positive deviance approach.[12]

Experiment to Close the Gap

Once the current state and the desired state are identified, it is then possible to identify the gap between them, identify solutions or "countermeasures" that might close the gap, and to test those countermeasures to discover their effectiveness. One tool for pulling together these pieces into a single coher-ent picture to inform the experimental process is the A3. The A3 is a stan-dardized communication tool intended to make it easier for participants in improvement efforts to understand each other. What is important is not the format itself, but rather the process and thinking behind it and the conversa-tions it facilitates. It is intended to foster effective and efficient dialogue among participants, to foster problem-solving communication, encourage frontline initiative, and clarify who is responsible for problems or solutions. A3 helps participants to clarify links between problems, their root causes, and proposed countermeasures.[13]

The A3 asks developers to articulate why a problem they have identified is important to the organization and how it impacts the customer in a negative way. There is relatively brief attention given to envisioning the desired state, in the form of articulating goals. Finally, the A3 asks developers to propose solutions to the deficits that have been identified. Ground rules for present-ing an A3 aim at creating a respectful environment for communication—with no interruptions, only clarifying questions permitted, and plenty of time al-lowed for postpresentation feedback; any needed refinements to be made on the spot. After an A3 has been developed, the experimental cycle Plan/Do/Check/Adjust is used to test and continuously refine the proposed solutions, assessing their impact on closing the gap between the current state and the desired state.

COMBINING WORK PROCESS INTERVENTIONS
WITH RELATIONAL INTERVENTIONS

As we review these tools for work process interventions, it is apparent that relational interventions play a critical role in their effective use. Relational interventions can help participants to develop *shared knowledge* or systems thinking, enabling them to better assess the *current state* and even helping them to know who should be involved in assessing the current state. Relational interventions can help to develop *shared goals* among multiple participants including both workers and clients, enabling them to better identify the *desired state*. Relational interventions can also help participants to develop *mutual respect* and *problem-solving communication,* enabling them to identify and test potential solutions through experimentation, to close the gap between the current state and the desired state.

Let's take a closer look at how some change agents have innovated to combine relational and work process interventions in a synergistic way.

Combining Work Process and Relational Interventions at Salus Global

One of the earliest attempts I observed to combine relational and work process interventions emerged in obstetrics. An obstetrician and an obstetrics nurse in Canada—Ken Milne and Nancy Whitelaw—discovered through their work together that relational approaches between care providers and with patients seemed to result in fewer errors, better quality outcomes, less waste, and fewer liability claims. With support from a Canadian insurance association, they formed a consulting practice, called Salus Global, to teach their methods to obstetrics staff throughout Canada. Together with their colleague Margaret Nish, Milne and Whitelaw designed a process to facilitate experimentation and learning by organizations that were seeking to change their dynamics and improve their performance. Milne explained, "At the beginning we didn't know what to call what we were doing, but after reading organizational theory in the late 1990s, I realized we were doing relational coordination."

In the change process they designed, interprofessional improvement teams are formed at the start to take stock and gain insight into how their relationships and communication impact their performance. Participants identify common themes of shared experiences through narrative, then they use the RC survey to measure their relational coordination. Once they understand the current state of relational and communication dynamics across roles, they set goals and strategize ways to improve their performance that can be tested through a rapid-cycle improvement process in the work place. Next, the successfully tested strategies are implemented by the interprofessional improvement team, and their impact is assessed by re-measuring relational coordination and evaluating the achievement of performance goals. Finally, performance goals at the unit level are linked back to organizational goals.

In one recent engagement, the identified goals for improvement were to establish effective problem-solving communication; to value, understand, and respect each other's role and scope of practice; and to improve the patient-flow process for elective cesarean sections. Multiple strategies were developed by participants, with positive outcomes. Delays in elective cesarean sections were dramatically reduced, and on-time starts improved from 28 percent to 89 percent for obstetricians, from 66 percent to 75 percent for anesthesiologists, and from 38 percent to 75 percent for nurses. Results from a standardized patient satisfaction survey showed an increase in patient satisfaction from 46 percent to 67 percent; and overall RC scores improved on all seven dimensions of relational coordination. Consistent with the Salus approach, senior leadership support had been negotiated as a precondition for this engagement, and the program director was able to lend her credibility, integrity, and mentoring leadership to the process.[14]

Introducing RC as the Soft Side of Lean in the Maine State Government

Another early effort I observed was in the Maine Department of Health and Human Services, where pioneering work was carried out by Walter Lowell and Kelly Grenier through the Office of Lean. Their job was to respond to the many requests for help from employees throughout the department to improve the quality and efficiency of service delivery. According to Lowell, "It was a blame/shame environment when we started. During the training, we started to see the goal alignment, the shared knowledge, and the respect they were developing for each other. We saw it but didn't know what it was. We realized that when the lean training works, it's because they are changing their relationships in really important ways."

Given its importance to the success of their efforts, Lowell and Grenier wanted to ensure that this relational transformation would happen on a regular basis. They looked to others for insights and, in the summer of 2011, found material that Earl Murman had posted online referring to relational coordination as "the soft side of lean." They learned more by reading *The Southwest Airlines Way.*[15] According to Lowell, "Once we saw relational coordination, we realized it was an integral part of organizational transformation and the lean work we were doing." Figure 12.2 shows how these principles were adapted for Maine state government.

Grenier led the development of a training program for coaches. Coaches learned to use value stream mapping to help participants create shared knowledge, gaining insight into each other's tasks and how those tasks intersected with each other's in the work process. Coaches learned to help participants

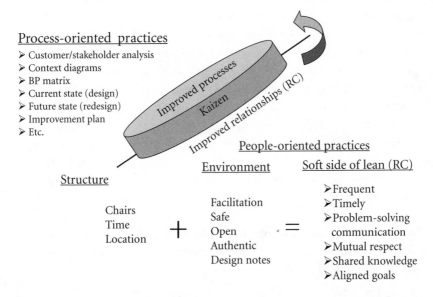

FIGURE 12.2   Introducing relational coordination as the soft side of lean in Maine state government
SOURCE: Walter Lowell.

identify shared goals by asking, "What are we really trying to accomplish here?" Coaches learned how to create a safe space in which respectful interaction and problem-solving communication could occur, without fear of blame or shame. Lowell explained the Office of Lean's overall improvement approach:

> We start all our improvement work with a charter which is developed with the sponsor of the improvement work. The charter is very specific about intent and purpose for the improvement work to be done along with establishing boundaries for the work and targeted outcomes. This is designed to ensure the improvement team has consensus on what the problem is. From an RC perspective, the intent is to establish shared knowledge of the current situation.
>
> The team is then brought together to work on establishing a consensus on the current state of the process we are working on. This usually is the first time an intact work team has ever been ask to document what they actually do. It is during these sessions [that] we see all the RC unfolding—what we called the "soft side of lean." The focal point for the improvement session includes developing the value stream map and teaching the team some new concepts about how work works (i.e., process, flow, waste, value added time, etc.). We use a whole day to develop a value stream map because we want to give the participants tools to be able continue the work once the event is completed.
>
> The RC dynamics are quite obvious during these sessions. It is common for [participants] to say things like "now I know why we can't get things done" or "all this time I thought the problem was me." We emphasize throughout the session that they work in systems/processes, and when these are broken no one can be successful. We want to fix the process, not the people. This is very comforting thought for many because few have ever thought of work from this perspective.
>
> Our lean lab provided a safe place for these discussions, since it was not at their work site. We had them sit in a semicircle so there were no barriers between them, a very deliberate strategy that some initially find uncomfortable but they get over this pretty quickly.

Lowell and Grenier observed transformations in the interactions of those who went through lean training in conjunction with relational coordination training. The combination of relational and work process interventions appeared to be a powerful way to achieve improvements in the work as well as improvement in the ongoing work relationships. Despite the thoughtfulness of their integrated approach and their attentiveness to creating a safe space, however, Lowell and Grenier did not measure relational coordination or do relational mapping or use other tools to "make visible" the current patterns in a way that could help participants to understand and take responsibility for those patterns. Of greater concern, Lowell and Grenier were not able to engage the leadership of state government in a meaningful way. These challenges ultimately limited the impact and sustainability of their work. Grenier explained, "People can get really discouraged when they go back to work—some say, 'It was a great training'; but within a couple of months, they are back in their old boxes. Nothing has changed to support their new ways of working together.'"

The major flaw appeared to be quite simple. In addition to lacking some aspects of the relational interventions we learned about in the previous chapter, the change strategy designed by Lowell and Grenier also lacked the structural interventions needed to support sustainability. The structures for how people were hired, trained, rewarded, and measured, and even local structures, such as meetings, conflict resolution, and so on, continued to reinforce the old silos.

For these structural transformations to be possible in the broader context of the Maine state government would ultimately require the support of state leadership. Lowell scheduled meetings with key officials from the governor's office and, at certain points, was optimistic about the potential to win that support. Yet the governor, who had originally supported the Office of Lean, lost an election against a tough and ultimately successful challenger, whose platform called for deep cuts in state government without any investments in process improvement. As Lowell moved on to build similar training programs elsewhere, he reflected on how the early efforts in Maine had fallen short:

> We were never able to engage our senior leaders in this work. Even though they did see us as a useful tool to solve some of their problems, we could not communicate to them the potential larger cultural change that we were seeing in the small groups we worked with. Art Byrne in his recent book *The Lean Turnaround* advocates including the CEO in as many of these improvement events as possible, which I think is the right idea given all the RC dynamics that are taking place and quite visible for them to see. Despite what senior leaders say, most are clueless about what lean means, and RC really does have to be seen to be believed.[16]

Integrating Relational Coordination and
Lean at Group Health Cooperative

Now let's consider Group Health's efforts to integrate work process and relational interventions. As we know from Chapter 7, Group Health decided to combine relational coordination with the lean methods they had already introduced. Despite the clear successes Group Health had with lean, its leaders came to see the lack of attention to relationships, including insufficient development of shared knowledge, shared goals, and mutual respect across roles, as limiting lean's impact. They decided to "layer RC on top of lean" by introducing relational coordination methodologies to teams that were already well-trained and experienced in lean methodologies. As they ventured into this experiment, the Group Health leaders thought deeply about and debated and how the primary care teams could use RC and lean together. Internal lean consultant Lindsay Pappas explained:

> One of the things that we've been pondering and thinking about is about the Relational Model of Organizational Change, and what comes first, and how everything's weighted in terms of focusing on relational skill development, or on process development and improving process. And how to fit all those things in. I don't know that they're untangle-able. We've been talking about relational and process interventions in terms of foreground and background, and asking what comes to the foreground at different points and what goes to the background.

To generate ideas, Group Health leaders conducted a brainstorming session to determine how to link the new relational tools to the more familiar lean tools. A broad and diverse group spent two days building an integrated RC/lean toolkit. The leaders who participated represented a spectrum, including clinical leaders, administrative leaders, human resource management leaders, and research leaders from the Group Health Research Institute. Nearly all had participated in the Relational Coordination Intervention Training in the previous two months, and about half had participated in the Relational Coordination Research Roundtable at University of California, Berkeley.

The two-day workshop was led by Pappas and Diane Rawlins, an external organizational development consultant who had worked with Group Health for many years. Unlike the arm's length, quasi-suspicious relationship that was often observed at the time between organizational development and lean practitioners both in the United States and Europe, Pappas and Rawlins from the start articulated a desire to establish a respectful collaborative relationship. Day One of the RC/Lean Brainstorming Workshop was aimed at building a shared knowledge base within the group. According to Claire Trescott, then the director of primary care, Day One resulted in "more clarity on the common underlying principles of relational coordination and lean—for example, systems thinking and problem-solving rather than blaming communication—and respect for people."

On Day Two the task was to combine relational tools and lean tools. By the end of the day, the flip charts on the walls around the room were filled with multicolor Post-it notes indicating tools—both relational and technical—participants had used previously that had the potential to help interdependent teams build shared goals, shared knowledge, and mutual respect, as well as timely, accurate, and problem-solving communication. The resulting RC/lean toolkit was summarized as follows:

Shared Knowledge

- What it means: the degree to which participants perceive that their work in the focal work process is understood by other workgroups
- Methods:
  - Write and share your own job description with other team members.
    - Step 1: This is what I do.
    - Step 2: This is how what I do relates to what other team members do.
  - What does each person do?
    - Scope of practice
    - Core activities
    - Write down 3 things others don't know I do (invisible work).
  - Role play the work process. Physically simulate.
  - Role clarity. Use RACI (responsible, accountable, consulted, informed) diagrams. Conversation of interdependence. Create a conversation that

helps people know how they affect each other: What is it about how I do my work that helps you do yours? What about how I do my work gets in your way? How could I do my work differently that would help you more?

- Relational mapping
- Work process mapping
- Work shadowing. Go-see, work observation, gemba observation
- Multidisciplinary education events on specific new issues, e.g., opioid exchange
- Cross training. Flexibility to span across boundaries
- Group presentation about how group works as a unit. Act out
- Proof in the pudding. Engage in improvement/innovation work to solve shared problems
- Standard work. Simple, organic, around process, include all roles, don't functionally separate
- Epic electronic health record. Establish norms for interoffice communication, take a week "fast" from Epic communication, determine appropriate medium for different kinds of communication
- Regular measurement and feedback
- Task board in lunch room for people to list their tasks

Shared Goals

- What it means: the degree to which participants perceive that other workgroups share their goals for the focal work process
- Methods:
  - Process for team to establish goals together
    - Have dedicated time as a team to develop goals together
    - Be clear. What are we trying to achieve here? Is there one main goal? Subgoals underneath? Which of the subgoals are shared, and which are unique to certain groups?

- Team discussion. What are the times when our goals are aligned? When do we seem to be working at cross-purposes?
- Sticky notes. What are my top 3 goals? What is our team goal?
- Establish patient-centric goals.
  - Set long term goals, reflect on past long term goals
  - Visioning exercise
  - Start with already shared goals (e.g., patient safety) to build mutual respect and shared knowledge.
  - Link goals to triple aim: access/quality/affordability.
  - Time-based goals. Reduce lead time (time from scheduled to seen); reduce non-value-added time (wait time; time lost due to scrap, rework, errors).
  - Make goal/target explicit and visual.
  - Shadow patient through entire visit, spend time in the waiting room listening.
  - Interview patients by phone and in the waiting room.
  - Use existing data to understand patient experience: Yelp comments, Patient Experience Survey comments, Press Ganey
  - Find a way to remember or discover patient goals.
  - Develop common understanding of the patient/customer.
  - Focus groups with specific types of patients, to discover their needs—e.g., single moms or patients over age 75 living at home alone
  - Patient focus groups to identify areas for improvement, shared goals from patient perspective
  - Expanded huddle weekly to discuss complex patients.
  - Team-based patient care conference. Agree on patient goals.
  - Establish self-care/team wellness goals.
  - Design constructive conversations to make these goals explicit.

Mutual Respect

- What it means: the degree to which participants perceive that their work in the focal work process is respected by other workgroups
- Methods:
  - Establish a system of behavioral accountability. Team norms
    - What understandings do you need to have with each other to show up fully, to do your best work, to feel respected?
    - How do we speak up when we see each other violating one of our norms?
    - "Spirit of Improvement" guidelines from Lean
    - Ground Rules / Code of Conduct: What are the trust breakers?
    - "The Pledge"
    - Include participation and listening.
  - Recognize and reward
    - Kudos
    - Formal recognition at team meetings
  - Build on strengths
    - Stories about times when you have felt respected
    - Paint the picture: this is what respect looks and feels like to me.
  - Have interdisciplinary staff meetings.
    - Connect on a personal level.
- Share stories of personal life.
- Spend time together in a morale event.
- Understand each other's personal views.
- Hoopla—guided personal storytelling
- Storytelling, stepping stones
- Conversations about origins: motivators/passion/success
  - Highs/lows. What were the highs and lows for the day/week around patient care?

- Team-defined meeting format, good listening
- Role-specific storytelling, best practices

Timely Communication

- What it means: the degree to which participants perceive that other workgroups communicate in a timely way about the focal work process
- Methods:
  - Conversation of interdependence. What is timely to you? What do you need to know, and when?
  - Norming. What are our agreements about method and urgency of communication?

Accurate Communication

- What it means: the degree to which participants perceive that other workgroups communicate in an accurate way about the focal work process
- Methods:
  - Templated documentation. After establishing what accurate means in a work process establish templated/standard.
  - Communication models:
    - Cone in the box
    - Ladder of inference
    - Heedful interrelating
    - Intention/impact
    - Humble inquiry

Problem-Solving Communication

- What it means: the degree to which participants perceive that other workgroups communicate in a problem-solving rather than a blaming way about the focal work process
- Methods:
  - Establish a method for delivering feedback.

- Agree upon and learn a conflict resolution method—then *use* it.
- End use of electronic health record for avoiding direct conflict
- Peer coaching
- Action/decision logs
- Idea boxes
- Structured team huddles
- Dedicated time for team problem solving
- Use language around RC communication dimensions/challenges in value stream mapping for continuous improvement
- Understand conflict behavior styles and strategies/tools for adapting to people with other styles
- Interest-based negotiation
- PDCA (Plan/Do/Study/Act) problem-solving methodology
- A3 problem-solving methodology

PUTTING THE TOOLS INTO ACTION

At Group Health, lean and RC were relatively easy to combine in practice. The teams in each clinic used lean tools to analyze and improve relational co-ordination, and then used their newly improved relational coordination to advance, extend, and deepen their process improvement efforts. As the coaches finished their training and took leadership of the improvement work, Pappas moved on to work with teams throughout Group Health and found herself using the lean/RC approach:

> I'm now very attentive to relational coordination when I work with a group where there's a basic lack of mutual respect, for example. But it can be helpful in any improvement project. Here's one example, from Urgent Care and the lab, where we used lean and RC together.
>
> The workshop participants represented frontline staff in Urgent Care as well as the lab. Local leaders of both departments attended as well as the lean coaches. What were our shared goals? Technically, it was "improve throughput" but we talked about it in terms of patient and staff experience and qualitatively

and quantitatively described both the current state—confusing, room for error, unpredictable—and the future state—simple, smooth, clear. To develop shared knowledge, we went to observe work at the frontline. The Urgent Care staff—RNs, unit clerks, techs—walked the lab staff through the Urgent Care department and their methods for sample collection and ordering through result retrieval and action. Then we went to the lab, and the techs walked the Urgent Care staff through their process.

Immediately, improvement ideas started flowing. "You mean if we send you a sample without an order it just sits here?" "Wow, you have to throw out how much blood at the end of the day because it hemolyzed or you never got an order?!" It was low hanging fruit!

We simulated their process using a pen as a stand-in for the sample and a sticky note as a stand in for an order, and used the lean concepts of pull, flow, and take time to question their process. We also brought in a discussion of reciprocity from relational coordination. It turns out this concept is very much in line with pull and flow. If the downstream process does not have what it needs to proceed when it is needed, or if a mistake has been passed on, the outcome of the process is not only at risk but relational aspects are as risk, as well (blaming, trust, lack of respect). After getting clear on the target (shared goals) and the current state (shared knowledge)—the group spent two days "try-storming" some countermeasures. The result was new agreements on standard work that ensured process quality.

At the end, I asked questions I don't typically ask related to sustainability: "Over the past three days, this group, who didn't know each other before, has formed a team and has come to understand each other's work, which set you up to improve your shared processes. The rest of your department did not have that opportunity. How will you bring this back to your teams?" Finally, I asked, "How do you sustain the improvements you just made? What can you do to keep Urgent Care and lab connected despite your departmental divide?" The result they came up with was to have a lab representative attend the Urgent Care huddles on a regular basis and have airtime to share information, give updates, and be seen as part of the team.

In effect, Pappas, Rawlins, and their colleagues had discovered how to combine work process and relational interventions in a fairly seamless way. But they took two additional steps to foster sustainability. First, they coached frontline participants to design and implement their own structural interventions to sustain the improvements they had made. Secondly, from the start, they engaged frontline and mid-level leadership to gain their understanding and support. There was little mention of top leadership, however, creating concerns about sustainability.

SUMMING UP

These experiences help us to better understand the tools that are available to carry out work process interventions in the Relational Model of Organizational Change. In particular, we can see the potential synergies between relational and work process interventions, how one can support the other, and how one without the other could lead to an unbalanced approach that is either excessively relational (touchy-feely with inadequate connection to the work) or excessively technical (focused on the work but ignoring the relationships through which the work is carried out).

The stories from Maine state government and Group Health raise the issue of how to sustain these new patterns of interaction once they do take hold. In the following chapter, we will consider how structural interventions like shared accountability and rewards, shared protocols, team meetings, boundary spanners, and shared information technology can be used to support and sustain the new relational dynamics. But we will also see that implementing these structures is feasible only once the new relational dynamics have begun to emerge—perhaps the most fundamental insight suggested by the Relational Model of Organizational Change.

13 STRUCTURAL INTERVENTIONS TO SUPPORT AND SUSTAIN THE NEW DYNAMICS

Structural interventions are the third type of intervention in the Relational Model of Organizational Change. These are new structures introduced to support and sustain shared goals, shared knowledge, and mutual respect among co-workers, clients, and leaders. Some structural interventions can be introduced locally with the support of frontline leaders, such as new types of team meetings, new protocols to clarify roles and the connections between them, or boundary spanners whose role is to coordinate the work of others. Other structural interventions can be introduced by middle managers in HR or IT, such as hiring and training for teamwork; revising accountability and reward structures; or designing new supervisory roles, shared conflict-resolution practices, and shared information systems. Each intervention may be supported, or even mandated, by internal stakeholders, such as top management or the board of directors, or by external stakeholders, such as suppliers, investors, customers, industry associations, regulators, or policy makers. An intervention may also be *undermined* by internal or external stakeholders if it is seen as threatening or is simply misunderstood.

Some of these structures are familiar from Chapter 5, where they were first introduced. We saw how structures can be designed to support new relational dynamics and key performance outcomes, but we did not explore how they were implemented. It was as though a magic wand had simply called them into existence. We know from the Relational Model of Organizational Change that although these structures can *support* new relational dynamics, they cannot, by themselves, *create* new relational dynamics. When participants' sense of self is defined by the old relational dynamics, new structures will feel unfamiliar, unwelcome, and awkward. These new structures will often "fall flat" or be rejected, like new shoes that do not fit, and are likely to add problems rather than resolve them. These new structures can be implemented successfully only when participants themselves see the need for them and participate in their design and implementation, having understood the principles of relational coordination, relational coproduction, and relational leadership through their own direct experience.

In this chapter, we explore five structural interventions—shared accountability and rewards, relational job design for boundary spanners, inclusive team meetings, shared protocols, and shared information systems—paying particular attention to how they are designed and implemented by participants who have already begun building shared goals, shared knowledge, and mutual respect among themselves and with their customers and leaders using the relational and work process interventions we learned about in the previous two chapters, thus avoiding the top-down phenomenon of forcing the adoption of new structures that do not fit.

SHARED ACCOUNTABILITY AND REWARDS

One of the most powerful structural interventions in the Relational Model of Organizational Change is shared accountability and rewards. In many industries, accountability and reward structures were traditionally designed to achieve command and control, reinforcing silos by holding managers accountable for key performance indicators specific to their functions, and by failing to counterbalance these functional forms of accountability with broader forms of shared accountability and rewards. Siloed accountability and reward structures have the advantage of enabling top leaders to control subordinates by asking, in effect, "Who's the best here?" People in different parts of the same organization can make each other look good or bad, and siloed accountability and reward structures favor making each other look bad.

As organizations face increasingly complex environments, it has become clear that workers and leaders need to cross internal organizational boundaries to achieve the desired outcomes for customers. But when workers' accountability is to their own functional leaders, they may not feel safe going beyond their silos. Doing so might jeopardize their careers by making a leader who is in competition with their leader "look good" and their own leader "look bad." I have heard co-workers from United States to Denmark to Japan discuss this challenge and conclude that, to achieve relational coordination, "We need to have the courage to do the right thing," clearly recognizing the risks for their careers. When existing structures of accountability and rewards are siloed, they must be redesigned so that it is not only permissible to connect directly with colleagues in other departments—it's actually valued and rewarded.

In our Part II stories of change, we saw that shared rewards can support efforts to change behaviors. For example, we saw our colleagues in Varde Municipality respond to a new national payment model in which they would be responsible for paying 20 percent of the costs of hospital or physician visits for their citizens. This new reward structure, stemming from the Danish healthcare revolution, was intended to motivate municipalities across Denmark to engage in more proactive efforts to achieve health and wellness in their communities. It worked. But one of the most important steps Varde and other municipalities took was to address fragmented relational dynamics across their agencies. Without those relational interventions, the new reward structure mandated by national policy makers would have been highly divisive, giving rise to blame rather than problem solving.

We saw participants at Dartmouth-Hitchcock and Billings Clinic working to create accountable care organizations in response to a new payment model that stemmed from the Affordable Care Act—a reward structure in which organizations assume responsibility for the cost and quality of care for patient populations in place of the traditional piece-rate payment model. This new shared reward structure was one of the key motivations for the change efforts we observed in Dartmouth's surgical units (Chapter 9). As one of the surgical leaders pointed out, the new reward structure initially created something of an identity crisis for surgeons: "Within surgery, some of the sections are particularly troubled because for the first time ever they're having trouble making budgets. Normally, surgeons are the ones who bring in the bulk of the money for institutions—sort of prized and highly valued and right now they're just expensive." To respond successfully required them to engage in interventions to begin changing surgeons' relational dynamics with their colleagues, patients and leaders.

I observed the same tension at the University of Washington Regional Heart Center as its leaders began to implement an at-risk contract with the Boeing Company for the heart care needs of Boeing employees and their families. Surgeons who had learned to work successfully within the previous piece-rate reward structure by keeping the operating rooms at full capacity and building new ones when needed, were now hearing about the need to promote population health upstream and prevent readmissions downstream. Some were frustrated with the mixed messages they were receiving during this historic transition to accountable care, and understandably so. Within a relatively short period, however, they transitioned from arguing that there was no point in learning to coordinate better—what they really needed was additional operating-room capacity—to expressing interest in the process of building shared goals and shared knowledge across their healthcare system to respond more effectively to the new reward structure.

At Billings, the orthopedic surgery department had negotiated a payment contract under which they would be paid a "flat fee" by the federal government for the overall care of each patient receiving a joint replacement, covering both hospital and post-hospital costs. The arrangement would reward them for achieving greater coordination not only internally, within the clinic, but also externally, with rehabilitation and home care providers and with patients and their families as well. Surgeons at Billings understood that going forward, they could succeed only by achieving better quality outcomes for the overall patient recovery, at lower costs. They had already streamlined and standardized their internal workflows through a work process intervention based on lean principles, and had already begun to build a relationship with a home care agency that was eager and willing to partner with them. However, they had not yet adequately transformed their internal working relationships, according to orthopedics staff; nor had they fully developed the partnership with the new home care agency or with other external providers. Frontline workers in orthopedics, including nurses, physical therapists, and case managers, then began launching a relational intervention, receiving advice from their colleagues in the Billings intensive care unit—hoping to bring the orthopedic surgeons on board.

As health systems like Dartmouth-Hitchcock, University of Washington, and Billings moved to adopt shared reward structures, other health systems, such as Group Health and Kaiser Permanente, were already organized around shared rewards. Like all vertically integrated companies, however, these integrated health systems still suffered from some fragmentation among their different components. Kaiser Permanente, for example, was organized regionally, and each region—Southern California, Northern California, Hawaii, the Northwest, Colorado, Georgia, and the Mid-Atlantic states—was responsible for optimizing the quality and minimizing the cost of care for its own members. Relative to other organizations, Kaiser Permanente had achieved a high level of shared accountability and rewards, but the leadership felt they could do better. One frontline leader reported, "At the level of the regions, there was this sense that, 'Well, as long as I make my numbers, I will get my performance bonuses or recognition or whatever.' Then our new CEO determined that 'each of the regional leaders is not going to get his or her rewards unless every region achieves its targets.'" The new shared reward structure was intended to reinforce shared accountability across the regions: "They wanted to promote the notion that we're all here to help each other and not just feel good because we made our own targets." The CEO of Kaiser Permanente was clearly willing to give up the traditional divide and conquer model in favor of shared accountability and shared rewards across the regions in order to meet the demands of the environment.

But some traditional accountability and reward structures still remained in place *within* the Kaiser regions. Ellie Godfrey, a vice president in the Northwest region, realized that the old structures were still influencing the behavior of frontline workers when she began leading efforts to improve the coordination between inpatient and outpatient care.

> When I realized that we had a problem, it was when I was trying to explain to employees why they need to talk each other when they're taking care of the same patient, and one of them said, "But why would I talk to them? They report to a completely different person." So their idea was, given the way the organization

chart is, Why would you talk to somebody who has a different leader? People are thinking, "I'm accountable for what happens within the purview of my leader." And they are not making this up—they are getting these signals from us as leaders. It's not good for the organization or the patient, but we have to realize we are responsible.

The good news was that through efforts to build relational coordination at the frontline, leaders like Godfrey became aware of the impediments that the existing accountability structures created for coordinated care, and were ready to take responsibility for making the needed changes. According to Godfrey, "We now have staff and physicians from different parts of the delivery system working together and with patients to develop patient centered care plans, agree to main point of contact for the patients, and clarify roles and responsibilities across the system as it relates to coordinated care."

In Varde Municipality (Chapter 8) we heard similar conversations. As municipal leaders reviewed baseline relational coordination survey results in the form of a network map that showed weak ties among many of the workgroups serving the citizens of Varde, the CEO of the municipality reflected:

> This map and the weak ties we see here just reflect the way we have told our employees to work. We are telling them, "You have to go and work and do your job." We think we have told them they should work together, and we think it's the way we do our work as leaders, but if those employees closest to the citizens are still asking, "Does that mean we can call for help from somebody else if we need it?" then we haven't said it enough.

Changing accountability and reward structures feels risky. But it is fairly straightforward. In Varde, leaders began to create shared budgets to strengthen shared goals between areas that needed to coordinate better. At Blue Shield California, chief health officer Marcus Thygeson began to hold his leaders accountable for the level of relational coordination in their teams, in addition to other key outcomes. According to director of training and support Steve Freund, "Leaders used to see relationships as a positive spillover. Now they are starting to see relationships as having positive spillovers." Note, however, that the new accountability structures were not implemented on their own—they were preceded by relational interventions that changed the way leaders understood the work and their role in supporting it.

RELATIONAL JOB DESIGN FOR BOUNDARY SPANNERS

Boundary spanners can also support the three dynamics of relational coordination, coproduction, and leadership. Boundary spanners have the task of creating relational coordination among professionals and at the same time creating relational coproduction with clients—pulling the whole team together to solve the needs of a particular client population and engaging clients as members of the team. We find this boundary spanner role in airlines, in the form of operations agents; in banking, in the form of customer service managers; and in hospitals, in the form of case managers.

In the Windsor Regional Health System, case manager and clinical nurse specialist Alissa Howe Poisson serves as boundary spanner to bring the professions together and ensure that they are "on the same page" regarding the patient's path of care, to avoid confusion and missed signals. One of her key roles is to engage in conflict resolution.

> People do consult with me a lot about conflicts on the unit. Sometimes I coach. And often I will say, "Have you called so-and-so? Have you asked him to help you understand?" I get called several times a day for stuff like that. I think it's about talking to each other in a respectful way. I mean nobody really likes to be questioned about why they're doing the things that they are doing. But when it involves a team, we need to know so that we're on that same page. I can help people solve these conflicts by giving them some resources, but I can't come and solve every problem. When all else fails, then I need to intervene, but I don't need to have those conversations for you. I need to help you learn how to have those conversations.

Going beyond airlines, banks, and hospitals, boundary spanners have been emerging as a critical component in initiatives to build health and wellness in the community, where they are sometimes called "wellness coaches," "health coaches," or "navigators." Our colleagues at Partners Healthcare in Boston, for example, created a new boundary spanner role as a key component of their community-based health and wellness model. "It was incredibly important to convert to a team-based care model," physician leader Sree Chaguturu explained. "[To do this,] we were simultaneously implementing lean operations and cultural transformation."[1] Thus the new boundary spanner role was created in the context of lean and culture change efforts. In the primary care clinics, experienced nurses were hired and deployed as care managers to work side by side with other primary care professionals and to lead team-based coordination. Each care manager's principal task was to develop a one-on-one relationship with 180 to 200 high-risk patients. They worked with each patient to develop a customized treatment plan and then coordinated the patient's care team. The care team included traditional care providers, such as the primary care provider and the pharmacist. To go upstream and influence the social determinants of health, the team also included nontraditional service providers, such as a mental-health service provider, a social worker, a financial counselor, and a community resource specialist to assist with housing and other social issues. Care managers conducted both home and office visits, educated patients about their treatment and service options, facilitated patient access to services, and helped to train patients in self-management.

At Group Health (Chapter 7) we found medical assistants who were training to become health coaches for patients with obesity. We also saw this role emerging in Varde Municipality as part of an effort to keep citizens healthy and out of the hospital. For these new boundary spanner roles, motivational interviewing has become a critical tool for engaging customers or citizens in the change toward healthier behaviors. As Varde health director Margit Thomsen explained, "It's not enough to say 'do it because I'm a nurse.' It has to connect to something the citizen cares about."

Regardless of the industry, boundary spanner roles tend to be counterproductive when they are added as new structure in a context that lacks the basic relational coordination dynamics. According to Carsten Hornstrup:

> What they do now, when relational coordination is lacking, a lot of organizations put in what we would call boundary spanners, but to me it seems like that just becomes yet another unit. What I find is if relational coordination already works relatively well, boundary spanners can do boundary spanning, but if relational coordination is poor, the others say, "Okay, it's a boundary spanner. Hand off." So you have six of them involved, but only one is taking actual responsibility. The other five take less responsibility. So at a system level, responsibility for boundary spanning deteriorates.

Indeed, we have seen mixed findings in the research on boundary spanning.[2] If relational coordination is at least moderately strong, participants can make good use of boundary spanners who are well-staffed and skilled to facilitate conversations and shared understandings. If relational coordination is too weak, adding boundary spanners can make it worse because participants may use it as a crutch. Starting with relational and work process interventions enables participants to develop a basic level of shared goals and shared knowledge so that they can make effective use of the new boundary spanner role.

INCLUSIVE TEAM MEETINGS

Although team meetings seem to be a relatively straightforward intervention, they are often challenging to implement and sustain. The initial enthusiasm can fade, leaving participants cynical and resistant to further change efforts. According to a physician leader in an East Coast health system, "We implemented bedside rounds, we came up with clear protocols and roles. When everyone was there, it worked well. The issue is getting everyone there at same time. You can't really schedule it. It's been hard to sustain—now it's falling apart and people are feeling cynical."

Why did this effort fail? It appeared that the meetings were introduced in a context that suffered from low levels of relational coordination. The meetings on their own were not capable of creating new relational dynamics. There had been no relational interventions preparing the way to enable participants to use this new structure effectively.

At Windsor Regional Medical Center, by contrast, team meetings were initiated by frontline staff as part of their efforts to improve relational coordination and their work processes, facilitated by Ken Milne and Nancy Whitelaw of Salus Global. Poisson, a case manager and clinical nurse specialist, explained how the team meetings worked:

> Say we have a high-risk patient, where there's a number of specialists involved in their care, and not everybody is communicating as well as they should. We're not really sure initially which direction we are all headed with this patient and what the plan of care should be. It's very upsetting to the patient when their care team

is giving different messages. What are our priorities and which way are we going with this patient because there seems to be a difference of opinion at that time.

I'll usually talk to the physicians and ask, "Can we get a team meeting together?" We then plan a date and time as soon as possible to have a discussion about the care of the patient and get everyone on the same page. Most of the time, nobody is wrong in their ideas for the patient, but they're all coming from a different specialty. It's important to bring all required specialties to the table so they can share their expertise and plan the safest possible care for the patient. So we say, "Everybody, let's bring all of your expertise to the table."

And we have that conversation so that we are giving the same message and not confusing the patient by having different ideas, but we're also providing the best care because we know what each of your perspectives is and why we're moving in that direction, why she's on this medication, why she needs this test.

Although it was part of her role as a boundary spanner to convene and facilitate team meetings, Poisson's strategy suggested that some traditional power dynamics remained. She noted, "I typically like to get the most re-sponsible physician to facilitate that meeting. They're the experts. And to be honest with you, the physicians often take some of those questions and discussions better from one of their physician colleagues than from a nurse colleague."

Nurses typically had valuable input to offer, so a key role for Poisson as boundary spanner was to work through the existing relational dynamics to get the right people to the table and to ensure they understood the value of their contribution. As she explained:

Sometimes the charge nurse is a great resource because she'll ask, "How is this actually going to work on the floor? It sounds like a good idea, but how are we going to make this work?" Sometimes other clinical practice managers will come when the care of the patient crosses their specialty—it's another set of ears, another brain to brainstorm.

So it's just trying to get everybody's expertise to the table to provide the best care for the patient. Sometimes, maybe some of the specialists don't always want to come. I'll just say, "This is what you're doing for the patient. Surely you have some expertise that you can bring to the table because we'd really like to hear it." If that doesn't work I just say, "Look, you do have expertise and we do need you." After that, they don't usually refuse.

It was soon understood that anyone who identified the need for a team meeting could call one. As Poisson's colleagues began to see the usefulness of the meetings, they were more likely to initiate them on their own:

> Sometimes it's the physician who will call and say, "Can you set up this team meeting for this case?" Sometimes it's been one of our charge nurses that says, "Hey, look, this is the situation. Here is what everybody is saying. There seems to be a difference of opinion. Maybe we need to have one of those team meetings again." So the more we have them, the more that kind of happens. People are starting to see that they're useful.

Our colleagues in Varde Municipality described a similar experience. Karin Viuff's job was to initiate and host team meetings when a patient's situation was sufficiently complex that the most efficient solution was to get family members, the citizen, and members of the care team around the same table to share their multiple perspectives—so necessary in order to identify and effectively implement creative solutions. When I first met Viuff, she described the difficulty of persuading colleagues to participate in the meetings. Once baseline relational coordination data had been shared, however, and frontline leaders began engaging in relational coordination and relational leadership training, Viuff observed a change in her colleagues' attitudes. "Now people are calling me up and saying 'we need to meet about Mrs. So-and-So—can you help us to set it up?' Now I can respond to the needs that they see for themselves, and I'm not dragging them to the table so much anymore."

Likewise, at Billings Clinic (Chapter 10), we observed the spread of daily rounds in the intensive care unit. Not all physicians had been holding rounds, and not all physicians who had been holding rounds were leading them effectively from the standpoint of other team members. And yet there was no real avenue for addressing the inadequacy of this structure. Mandates were not believed to be the answer, based on a widespread understanding of the limitations of mandates. Certainly, people might comply and "go through the motions," but that was not seen as sufficient.

Once relational interventions to measure and assess baseline RC data were launched, with conversations about these data in a space that felt safe for learning and experimentation, participants soon began to address daily rounds. In Chapter 10 we saw physicians asking nurses and other colleagues, "How are my rounds?" and how sometimes the responses were, "Well, not great—they are pretty bad." Recall that the ICU Connections steering committee sponsored an ICU Summit meeting including a fishbowl featuring the physicians who had received the highest ratings from colleagues on the baseline RC survey, who were interviewed publicly about how they conducted their rounds. Recall that physicians who had not previously conducted rounds were able to see the value of rounds from the perspective of their nonphysician colleagues. The relational interventions leveled the playing field and opened up conversations for learning and improvement that had not existed previously, despite the ICU having already been "pretty good at teamwork." And recall the use of positive deviance and contagion rather than top-down authority to foster the redesign of team meetings. As a result of relational interventions that laid the groundwork, participants at Billings redesigned their team meetings, not driven by compliance or fear of reprisal, but driven instead by shared goals, shared knowledge, and mutual respect.

SHARED PROTOCOLS AND ROUTINES

Shared protocols take many forms. At their most effective, they are ways to visualize how the tasks or perspectives or insights of multiple participants are interconnected. At their most effective, they include clear roles for customers as well as workers, and they are used by leaders to support and coach participants in carrying out their interdependent roles.

As we saw at Billings, shared protocols can be useful to guide team meetings and to help ensure that distinct perspectives are heard and incorporated into action. Particularly when traditional patterns of interaction have been dominated by one or two groups, shared protocols can help to reinforce new patterns of interaction. As part of the effort to improve the use of family-centered rounds in the Billings intensive care unit, care manager Sandra Gritz designed the protocol shown in Table 13.1. To welcome continuous feedback and input from users of the protocol, she included a column to the right to invite feedback and suggestions for refinement. Inviting constant input

TABLE 13.1   New protocol for interdisciplinary rounds

ICU Connections
Relational Coordination In The ICU

Billings Clinic Intensive Care Unit
Multidisciplinary Rounds Checklist

	Item	Comments	Orders/Plans
MD	Patient's Daily Goal(s) Plan of Care Disposition/Code Status Specific MD Concerns		

RN	Patient's Daily Goal(s)
	Specific Concerns
	Quality & Safety:
	  Foley
	  Central Line
	  DVT Prophylaxis
	  Skin Integrity
	  Delirium
	  Pain Control
	  Sedation Holiday		

RT	Ventilator
	  Vent Settings
	  HOB ≥ 30
	  VAE Prevention
	  Weaning Protocol
	O2 Needs (NRB/NC/SM)
	Breathing Treatments
	Specific RT Concerns		

PT/OT/SLP	Patient's Daily Goal(s) Orders Activity Level Anticipated Discharge Needs Specific Therapy Concerns		
Dietician	Diet Ordered TF Access/Type of TF Residuals TPN Specific Dietary Concerns Nutrition/Diet Education Needs		
Pharmacy	Electrolyte Management Glucose Control IVABX Appropriate Sedation/Analgesia/Paralytics Transition to PO Meds Specific Pharmacy Concerns		
Case Mgt.	Ready for Transfer out of ICU Anticipated Discharge Needs Barriers to Discharge Plans Specific Case Mgt. Concerns		
Family Issues	Family Up to Date Family Conference Social Issues Pastoral Care Palliative Care/Comfort Care Specific Family Concerns Family Journal		

SOURCE: Billings Clinic.

makes the protocol a "living document" and avoids what is often the downfall of protocols—that they are used mindlessly and robotically, rather than as a guide and "jumping off point" for mindful improvisation as the situation emerges.

The Billings Clinic's shared protocol for daily rounds has many features in common with surgical checklists and clinical pathways, including the goal of ensuring that multiple voices have the opportunity to speak up and offer input, and to ensure that key issues are addressed. However, researchers have found contradictory evidence regarding the usefulness of surgical checklists and clinical pathways in fostering relational coordination and improving performance.[3] Why? As we learned at Dartmouth-Hitchcock, some errors, including wrong-site surgeries, had occurred "despite compliance with the checklist and timeout. The issue was a rote completion of the checklist, and there wasn't any communication and feedback." These examples—and the research evidence—suggest that checklists, clinical pathways, and other shared protocols are more effective when there is a baseline level of relational coordination to support their effective use. Just mandating their adoption without first developing new relational dynamics to support their use is a recipe for disappointment.

SHARED INFORMATION SYSTEMS

Finally, information systems are another structure that can be designed to support relational coordination—but often are not. As a physician leader at Indiana University Health noted:

> Our new information systems have made coordination worse, not better. In the past at least we had to wait around for someone to hand us the paper chart, so we might have a little conversation about the patient. Now we're all sitting in front of our screens and we are not talking. And the way it's set up, it's reinforcing our silos, not breaking them down.

Similarly, a leader at Dartmouth-Hitchcock recalled a time when her colleagues were carrying out conflicts via the electronic health record—one would comment negatively on the orders entered by the other, and sometimes reverse them. "After a while I said, 'You need to talk to each other. Just walk down the hall and have a conversation!'"

Just as we saw with other structural interventions, information systems cannot create positive relational dynamics from scratch. Ann O'Brien, national director for clinical informatics at Kaiser Permanente, pointed out that, in her experience, "Information systems cannot create relational coordination. If you don't have relational coordination, a good information system will not create it. It could make it worse." Emily Barey, director of nursing informatics for Epic Systems, agreed and pointed out that in her experience information systems work better when they are implemented in organizations that have already begun to achieve a level of relational coordination.

In other words, there is a bootstrapping dynamic. You need to be already engaged in building relational coordination in order to know *how* to use a shared information system well. If your relational dynamics are weak, even a well-designed system will likely make them worse, becoming a weapon in the local turf wars rather than a tool for achieving high performance. Moreover, the system is unlikely to be well-designed if it has not been informed by the shared knowledge and shared goals of the participants.

For example, we learned about a workshop that the ICU clinical staff at Billings had organized with their internal information systems experts and an external IT vendor, after working on relational coordination for about a year. According to Curt Lindberg:

> The folks from Cerner [IT vendor] and the IS department at Billings who were there, all told me afterward, "Boy, it's so refreshing to be in a meeting like this when people are actually talking about how we can advance the capabilities for the benefit of patients." Because many times, of course, they're at odds. And sometimes IT and IS are trying to push something that people don't understand. There are some real battles fought out on this turf.

Chief learning officer Carlos Arce noted:

> The ICU staff have done all the work amongst themselves to understand the relational coordination concepts, but that's not what this was about. The workshop was about the electronic medical record. A very practical, real issue. So they were able to not only appreciate the fact that they were meeting with a key

partner, but their interactions were all done with that sense of appreciation for the timeliness of their communication. The frequency of that communication. How they respect what each other does. All those pieces were in there, but it was all applied and very specific to a real tangible need.

Also key to this change process was the inclusiveness of the workshop and its careful design. The bottom line was that the desired changes were identified with relative ease—as shown in Table 13.2—and largely implemented within a month.

Leadership at the top management level was essential as well. In order to invest time and effort in working with frontline workers, given the constant demands for their time, IT people need to know that coordination and co-production is a strategic priority for the organization and that information-system redesigns will be supported by the accountability structure. As Fred Brodsky at Group Health pointed out in Chapter 7, efforts that lack this clear leadership support end up being wasted investments, in his experience.

> "Garbage in, garbage out" is a common saying about information systems, meaning that the system is only as valuable as the data that people put into it. What we are seeing here is that this is also true from a relational perspective. The relationships that underlie the information that is entered will drive its usefulness. So we need to ask not only whether people understand what is in the information system, but how do they make sense of what's in there and how do they see the value of what's in there? If nurses don't value what physical therapists have to say, or if doctors don't value what nurses have to say, it doesn't matter how well those data are captured or presented in the information system.

Ina Sebastian, of the MIT Center for Information Systems Research, analyzed the use of an information system in a Hawaiian health organization. She created a conceptual mapping between different aspects of the information system and the seven dimensions of relational coordination. She found that

> how people use information systems reflects and maybe even reinforces high or low levels of relationships. The information system I observed offered several potentials for coordination. But clinicians acted on these potentials differently, depending partly on their relationships. For example, the information system provides users with the potential for sharing information with others in a way

TABLE 13.2 Electronic medical record relational coordination workshop

Inputs to workshop

Participating

Chief learning officer	Hospitalist physician
Cerner information systems	Intensivist physician
Billings information systems	Emergency physician
RN, care manager	Pharmacist
RN, information systems	Occupational therapist
Nurse practitioner	Physical therapists
Human resources	Respiratory therapist
Partnership for complex systems	Speech and language therapist
Chaplain	Chief medical officer

Guiding questions

In pairs and then small groups, attendees asked:

- What information does each discipline need from other disciplines to provide superior care of ICU patients, that they are not routinely receiving in a timely manner?
- What information can my discipline offer to the other disciplines to enable them to provide superb care of ICU patients?
- When is this information needed?
- What vehicles can best support these information needs—EMR, personal interaction, or both?

Output of workshop

Unmet information needs	When needed	EMR, personal interaction, or both
Input on patients and plans from additional specialties (i.e., neurosurgery, cardiovascular surgery, neurology, hospitalists, trauma surgeons) during ICU rounds. It was noted that nurse practitioners and physician assistants could assist in meeting this need. It was also observed that for this to be practical, rounds would need to happen on a more consistent basis.	Daily at set time	Personal interaction
Awareness of each discipline's daily goals for each patient—so goals of all members of ICU team are readily available to everyone.	Every day—as early as possible	Both
Consistent nursing documentation of common elements—easily accessible by all ICU team members.	Daily	EMR
Information on timing of daily schedule of key activities (i.e., surgery, sedation holiday, colonoscopy) for each patient. Also, a process for working through conflicts in schedule.	Ongoing	Both
Order for speaking valve to be communicated to nursing, respiratory therapy, and speech therapy.	As order is placed	EMR

(*continued*)

TABLE 13.2   (*continued*)

Unmet information needs	When needed	EMR, personal interaction, or both
Clarify expectations about participation by various disciplines (core and optional) daily work rounds and interdisciplinary rounds and daily alerts when rounds are to start.		
Essential information about patients coming from the ED.	Upon transfer	EMR
Essential information from ICU about patients transferred to other units.	Upon transfer	EMR
Knowledge of when sedation holiday will take place and what happens during holiday.	In the morning	Both
Knowledge about when decision is made to move patient to comfort care status—communicated to all disciplines.	When decision is made	Both
Process for identifying and resolving conflicting activity orders (i.e., between nursing and rehab).	When apparent	Both
Accurate height and weight on patients. Is it possible to use standing scales instead of bed scales?	Admission and daily	EMR
Sharing information with patients and family members.	Daily	White board

SOURCE: Billings Clinic.
NOTE: ED, emergency department; EMR, electronic medical record; ICU, intensive care unit; RN, registered nurse.

that is understandable and includes all necessary details through progress notes. If relationships are on a high level, team members will likely take advantage of these potentials and write a great note. They care if other team members understand how they arrived at their assessment or what exactly happened during the shift. If relationships are on a low level, clinicians may not care to elaborate and really communicate their thought processes to others in a note.[4]

In effect, existing relationships could either enhance or limit users' ability to make use of the information system. Shared goals played a role in how clearly and elaborately participants wrote progress notes. Shared knowledge enabled participants to communicate in a way that would make sense to other disciplines. With high mutual respect, the notes were more likely to be read.

Another colleague found that spatial redesign created conversations that facilitated the success of a new information system. In one unit of the health system, computer terminals were all placed in the same room.

> They're all sitting at different terminals, but they go into the same room to input their data, and so they would have conversations and say, "Well, what do you think about this?" and "What do you think about that?" So they'd be having a conversation as they input their data, and that really made a difference for the quality of what went in because they had already kind of figured out how to put it in.
>
> It helped them use a language in putting in the data that could be understood by others because they already—just by having that little back-and-forth conversation—figured out how to say it in a way that the person gets it. And then you can put it in the system that way rather than just using your own professional language and your own acronyms, all the little things that you do that are just for other physical therapists. If you don't have these conversations, you don't even know how to write it in a way that makes sense to the others. And just being in that same room gives you the feeling that, "Oh, that's a person who actually should be able to read what I'm doing right now, so I've probably not said that very clearly."

People often do not think of entering data in an information system as being an act of communication with other professions. They may think of it as communicating with themselves or with an administrator who has to track data for payment purposes. But they are not thinking, "I'm actually communicating with other professionals working with this client." Being in the same room with the other professionals to enter the data can change their frame of reference. Another way to create this reframing is requiring the notes entered into the information system to be captured as e-mails sent by professionals to one another, clarifying for themselves who is the recipient of their communication. However, these techniques are not likely to work if participants are connected by very low levels of relational coordination, with little sense of shared goals and little understanding of each other's work

Information systems can also transform the client/professional relationship, thus supporting relational coproduction. Client-centered IT solutions are common in the aviation, banking, finance, and other service-sector industries. Efforts to create patient portals are now common, and there are high hopes for fostering relational coproduction between patients and care teams, as we saw at Group Health.[5] Structural solutions are insufficient to move this work forward. Even well-designed structural interventions are not likely to succeed until relational and work process interventions have built a baseline level of shared goals, shared knowledge, and mutual respect among participants.

SUMMING UP

In the structural interventions explored in this chapter—shared rewards and accountability, boundary spanner roles, team meetings, and shared information systems—we have seen an interesting bootstrapping phenomenon. It appears that these structural interventions can successfully support the new relational dynamics only when introduced into a context when these dynamics have already begun to emerge and take hold, transforming the way people see themselves and their role in the organization. It is not sufficient to create them by mandate. Participants need to have some experience of relational coordination in order to use the new structures effectively.

In order to get timely, accurate, problem-solving communication to occur in team meetings, for example, leaders can foster a relational climate of mutual respect and shared knowledge, while helping participants develop shared goals. When these conditions are not met, staff will not attend or will simply go through the motions. When these conditions are met, team meetings and other structural interventions help to support new relational patterns, changing roles and power relations in a way that lifts up the voice of the customer and distributes information and authority more evenly among the professionals who are there to meet their needs.

As I introduced relational coordination and coproduction to organizational leaders recently, one of them asked, "Doesn't this require not just new structures but also a different way of leading?" The answer is yes. If leaders are not connected among themselves, it is hard for them to role model the need to be bigger than one's own job and the need to think about the whole customer experience. It is difficult to do cross-functional conflict resolution everyday if top leaders do not reinforce its importance, and if frontline leaders are not rewarded for bringing people together.

The message needed from leaders is that each participant has certain tasks to carry out and certain expertise to bring to bear, but that these tasks should be carried out, and expertise should be deployed in the context of shared goals. Each participant should be bigger than his or her own job. Participants are accountable for their own jobs, but their accountability is bigger than any one job. Leaders should ask themselves, "How can we support new structures that allow the necessary connections to happen on a regular basis, not just through heroic effort?" As Diane Rawlins pointed out in the context of her change work at Group Health, "Normal conversations go a long way—and also the structures that enable those normal conversations. Not just relying on heroism. It can be exhausting if you're trying to work against the structure every day. We're too busy to be asking people to be working uphill every day."

The Relational Model of Organizational Change shown in Figure 6.1 illustrates how the three types of interventions are expected to work together synergistically to support changes in relational dynamics. While the Relational Model of High Performance in Chapter 5 had a one-way arrow between structures and relational dynamics, the Relational Model of Organizational Change features arrows in both directions, showing that structural interventions do not *create* new relational dynamics, but rather are co-created *with* them, in a kind of bootstrapping process. While structural interventions are critical for embedding the new relational dynamics into the roles of co-workers, clients, and leaders, these structures cannot be expected to create the new relational dynamics from scratch.

The Relational Model of Organizational Change reflects a more nuanced, less linear understanding of the change process. Martha Feldman, Steve Barley, Wanda Orlikowski, Leslie Perlow, and other organizational theorists have explored the co-creation of structures and patterns of interrelating. They call this mutually reinforcing process "structuration." While structures are not capable of creating high-quality patterns of communicating and relating on their own, these structures are needed to sustain those patterns over time by embedding them into our roles and our daily practice, thus preventing the need to continually reinvent the wheel.[6] The Relational Model of Organizational Change simply gives us a more complete picture of how this happens and the essential role that high-quality relationships play in the process.

14 BRINGING IT ALL TOGETHER IN YOUR ORGANIZATION— AND BEYOND

We began this book by arguing for a relational response to the performance pressures that organizations face today. Throughout the chapters, we've seen change agents create new cultures by fostering relational dynamics among participants that include more respectful interactions and broader systems thinking. We've seen interventions that transform relationships—among co-workers, with clients, and with leaders—away from the fragmented dynamics of dysfunctional organizations into the cohesive dynamics of high-performing organizations.

We have found, paradoxically, that the three core dynamics—relational coordination, relational coproduction, and relational leadership—need to be present at some level in order to successfully implement the structures that can effectively support them. New structures that are introduced into a context dominated by negative relational dynamics will feel awkward, like new shoes that do not fit. A kind of bootstrapping is needed. The new relational dynamics must be created by using relational and work process interventions to jumpstart changes in the ways we communicate and relate with one another—before new structures can be successfully introduced to support these dynamics.

The idea of jumpstarting organizational change with relational interventions has been explored in recent years by an emerging cadre of organizational theorists.[1] With the Relational Model of Organizational Change we have taken the next step, identifying three types of interventions that together support positive change: (1) relational interventions to give birth to new patterns of interaction, (2) work process interventions to diagnose and improve the work itself, and (3) structural interventions to reinforce and sustain the new ways of working together. As we learned in Chapters 11through 13, these three types of interventions are quite synergistic. Given that they come from different "thought worlds," however, it is easy for change agents ourselves to become siloed and fail to use the three interventions in a synergistic way.

"BE THE CHANGE" YOU WISH TO SEE IN THE WORLD

Perhaps the most powerful learning from this book is the most obvious—that change agents play a critical role in creating organizational change. We have seen their power to create change through small actions that, taken together, have cumulative and transformative effects. This lesson was reflected by a frontline leader at Billings Clinic, who observed, "Relational coordination is about the little things that add up to make a big difference." This is the lesson of complexity science, and the reason why positive deviance can create powerful change through ripple effects and contagion.

The key is to carry out these "little things" with intention, with awareness of one's power, one's influence, and one's impact on others as well as with deliberate planning with others to create collective impact for positive change. Not being so naive as to think that structures and policies don't matter, but rather realizing that to change those structures and policies requires first enacting or living the changes in a way that helps others to visualize the change that is needed and to see why it is both possible and desirable to create this change.

This leadership can be exercised by virtually anyone who recognizes his or her power as a coach and role model. It's quite simple, according to one teenager:

> Each day allows for a new opportunity to make a difference in the world. Through simple acts of kindness, those differences can be made. The power of a simple act of kindness is truly undervalued. Each kind word or gesture made toward another person has the ability to impact their day, even their lives, tremendously. I do these simple acts of kindness in hopes to improve the culture of our community . . . I make sure I show my appreciation toward the teacher by thanking them each time I leave their classroom. At the beginning of each semester, I find that there is a

minimal number of students who thank the teacher. By the end of the semester, most students are also thanking the teacher. Leadership by action is a powerful thing that leads to a bettered community.[2]

Perhaps all change starts with individual transformation, impacting others who are touched by those individuals through the process of mutual recognition. Indeed, this is the logic behind the ethical and practical imperative to "be the change you wish to see in the world," as Mahatma Gandhi advised, or to "become peace to create peace," as Thich Nhat Hanh tells us.

Individuals exert a powerful influence for better or worse through the examples that they set for treating others. This is the so-called contagion effect. I remember frontline employees at Southwest Airlines telling me that "it's our job to turn you around." This simple statement brought to mind the religious principle of "turning the other cheek"—not for the purpose of masochism but for the purpose of reversing deep-seated negative relational dynamics by responding in an unexpected way, creating space for a new positive relational dynamic.

CREATE CHANGE THROUGH POSITIVE RELATIONAL CONTAGION

Change happens "in relation." Relational interventions are methods for fostering intentional change in the ways people relate to one another. The underlying principle of relational interventions introduced in this book is participation—not manipulating participants into a better state but rather engaging with participants to help them identify and achieve a better way of being together, where they themselves ultimately take responsibility for their actions and the outcomes of their actions. This positive relational contagion can be spread by individuals throughout an organization, as we saw at the Billings Clinic through individuals like Jen Potts, Sandra Gritz, Bob Merchant, and their colleagues in the intensive care unit. This positive relational contagion can extend into the community as well, when individuals take this positive energy from work into their lives as family members, friends, neighbors, and community members.

I recall that after the terrorist attacks of September 11, when Southwest Airlines made the decision not to lay off employees during the sharp downturn in air traffic, and instead asked employees to get through the crisis by working together, sharing the burden, and finding new efficiencies. I conducted a comparative analysis of Southwest's and other airlines' responses to the crisis in "Relationships, Layoffs and Organizational Resilience: Airline Industry Responses to September 11th," comparing Southwest's zero layoff decision to the decisions of other airlines, and finding a significant negative correlation across nine airlines between the extent of their layoffs and the extent of their stock-price recovery twelve months later. CEO James Parker said at the time, "Clearly we can't do this indefinitely. We are losing millions of dollars a day. But we are willing to take a hit, even to our stock price, in order to protect our people." One stock analyst remarked, "Southwest is doing what it does best, which is to shine in the face of adversity."[3]

The positive impact of these actions went beyond the airline and its employees. A minister in one of the cities in Texas where Southwest had a large presence told the press that the Southwest employees and families in his congregation had inspired others during this period of great challenge to the national psyche and collective sense of safety. This positive contagion was not simply a matter of extraordinary individuals, though such individuals certainly played a role. Rather, the positive contagion was supported by structural interventions that Southwest had made prior to the crisis.

In particular, key policy decisions made by Southwest over time had laid the foundation for positive relationships to serve as a source of resilience under pressure. First, Southwest had adopted an operational strategy of quick turnarounds at the gate, requiring high levels of relational coordination, relational coproduction, and relational leadership for its success. Second, as the company grew, its leaders had created a set of organizational structures to maintain connections across employee workgroups and with key supply-chain partners—shared rewards, shared accountability, shared protocols, hiring and training for teamwork, inclusive conflict resolution, boundary spanners, and so on—supporting the three relational dynamics and enabling Southwest to execute consistently on this operational strategy.

Third was the commitment, made decades earlier, to make layoffs a last resort—even in the face of a Wall Street investment culture that celebrated and rewarded the ruthless sacrifice of employees for short-term financial gain. And fourth was a financial structure—a low debt/equity ratio—to back up that commitment and enable resilience in times of adversity, ignoring Wall Street pressure to take on more debt as part of a strategy of "keeping managers on their toes" that, in reality, makes companies more fragile and vulnerable to layoffs.[4]

The lesson is simple, though challenging at times—we need to practice relational coordination to achieve relational coordination. There are no short cuts. Simply put, there can be no organizational transformations—or broader social transformations—without personal transformations. This simple lesson has profound implications for our personal as well as our professional lives, for our colleagues, our families and friends, and our communities.

LEVERAGE THE POWER OF RELATIONSHIPS TO ACHIEVE OUTCOMES FOR ALL

Relationships matter at the most basic level. As human beings, we exist as members of collectives, and we survive only if we are accepted and recognized by others, starting at birth. We are thus interdependent, both emotionally and physically, at the most basic level of survival. The most powerful thing we can do to others is to recognize them as fellow creatures—or not.[5] In *The Socially Embedded Human Subject: A Moral Standpoint for Achieving Social Justice*, I argued that mutual respect is the starting point for human identity. The socially embedded human subject is simply ourselves, as we are created by each other and for each other.[6] Consistent with this philosophical perspective, neuroscientists have found evidence that cooperation is inherent to the human condition. As summarized by Bruce Wexler in *Brain and Culture*, cooperative social interaction is key to survival of the human infant and to subsequent development of the human species.[7]

Abundant research has shown that positive human relationships improve outcomes for individuals, organizations, and communities.[8] For individuals, positive social relationships are associated with higher levels of physical and psychological well-being and lower risk of death.[9] Positive relationships affect the hormonal, cardiovascular, and immune systems of the body, enhancing our health and well-being and further enhancing the relationships themselves.[10] In organizations, social capital facilitates the transfer of knowledge, and relational coordination enables the achievement of coordinated collective action among organizational members. Moreover, friendships among co-workers and the presence of caring and compassionate relationships are significant predictors of organizational outcomes. In communities more broadly, the density and patterns of social connections predict the level of economic vitality. Social capital and the existence of positive social networks also account for community-level outcomes, such as educational attainment, financial well-being, and the reduction of crime.[11]

Finding solutions to these social needs will require more than individual change and workplace transformation. We also need greater political alignment and a greater sense of shared responsibility. In today's divisive political context, it may help to recall conservative thinkers, such as Adam Smith, who argued that a well-functioning public sector is the essential foundation for a well-functioning private market economy. In *The Wealth of Nations*, Smith explained in great detail how a vibrant market economy requires public investment in schools, transportation, legal institutions, and more.[12] During the 1950s and 1960s, the United States made substantial investments of the kind recommended by Smith, which found support across the political spectrum. In turn, we reaped the benefits: economic growth that was broadly shared, creating a large middle class and relatively low levels of poverty. Other developed nations around the world have made similar investments and reaped similar gains.

Many developed nations have continued to invest in the common good; however, other countries have fallen behind. The United States has regressed to levels of inequality that surpass the levels seen on the eve of the Great Depression.[13] Extreme inequality harms economies by fostering an inadequately skilled workforce to meet the needs of business and insufficient wealth to purchase the goods that workers are producing. Extreme inequality also harms democracy by creating breakdowns in social cohesion and political processes that are held hostage to the interests of the wealthiest citizens. In effect, we become stuck in a vicious cycle.[14] Where do we start? Political alignment and a sense of shared responsibility are sorely needed.

NEUROPLASTICITY MEANS THAT WE CAN CHANGE

In the face of these challenges, a promising finding supported by neuroscience is that humans can create deep change through deliberate interventions into the cycle of causality. Consider Jack Shonkoff and colleagues' research demonstrating the impact of early relationships on children's brain development. Growing up in a more connected set of relationships helps to foster a more connected neural network. In a real sense, our brains reflect the relational networks in which we live and develop.[15] Consider Wexler's pioneering work on the impact of culture on brain development. Cultural patterns shape human behavior by shaping our neural networks; and in turn, we replicate the culture in which we were raised by acting out behaviors that are shaped by these neural networks.[16] This process is called *neuroplasticity*, and it refers to the potential to reshape neural patterns in a fairly short time frame by engaging in a new set of experiences. Successful interventions are those that disrupt a mutually reinforcing cycle between neural patterns, behavioral patterns, and culture and introduce a new set of behavioral patterns that give rise to new cultural dynamics and to new neural patterns.

In their integrative synthesis "Evolving the Future: Toward a Science of Intentional Change," David Wilson and colleagues seek to identify a unifying mechanism that underlies the human capacity for intentional change:

> Humans possess great capacity for behavioral and cultural change, but our ability to *manage* change is still limited . . . All species have evolved mechanisms of phenotypic plasticity that enable them to respond adaptively to their environments. Some mechanisms of phenotypic plasticity count as evolutionary processes in their own right. The human capacity for symbolic thought provides an inheritance system with the same kind of combinatorial diversity as genetic recombination and antibody formation. Taking these propositions seriously allows an integration of major traditions within the basic behavioral sciences, such as behaviorism, social constructivism, social psychology, cognitive psychology, and evolutionary psychology, which are often isolated and even conceptualized as opposed to each other.[17]

The applied behavioral sciences include well-validated examples of successfully managing behavioral and cultural change at scales ranging from individuals, to small groups, to large populations. However, these examples are largely unknown beyond their disciplinary boundaries, for lack of a unifying theoretical framework. Viewed from an evolutionary perspective, they are examples of managing evolved mechanisms of phenotypic plasticity, including open-ended processes of variation and selection. Once the many branches of the basic and applied behavioral sciences become conceptually unified, we are closer to a science of intentional change than one might think.

POSITIVE RELATIONSHIPS AS UNIFYING MECHANISM FOR CHANGE ACROSS LEVELS

What is the unifying mechanism across these levels that explains the potential for change? One common element of successful interventional strategies, Wilson and his colleagues found, is the development of high-functioning relationships. Successful relational interventions have been carried out at multiple levels, from individuals to families, schools, communities, and regions. Ross Gittell and Avis Vidal showed that in low-income neighborhoods, this works through relational interventions by community organizers who connect neighborhood residents to financial and other resources outside the community.[18] Nobel laureate Elinor Ostroff showed how relational interventions work in communities and regions challenged by scarce resources by building relationships among key stakeholders, who then develop norms and rules of use that can be relationally enforced.[19] In other words, the principles of shared goals, shared knowledge, and mutual respect are relevant at many levels, including (1) relationships between individuals; (2) relationships between groups; (3) relationships between organizations; and (4) relationships between regions, ethnic groups, and even nations.

THREATS TO POWER AND PRIVILEGE AS OBSTACLE TO POSITIVE RELATIONAL CHANGE

Recall the obstacles to relational coordination, relational coproduction, and relational leadership discussed in Chapter 1. All of these obstacles, at their core, were about the disruption of identities that had been shaped by differential power and privilege. Cooperation threatens power differentials, and, the evidence suggests, power differentials also threaten cooperation. A recent study explored this dynamic:

> We are particularly interested in the effect of power on cooperation, due to its relevance to workplace dynamics in institutions where power hierarchies exist ... Who is the more diligent co-operator? Is it the power-holder, who is ultimately in control of the final outcome? Or is it the subordinate, who has to depend on the power-holder to obtain a share? Do power-holders and subordinates perceive joint losses and gains in the same way?[20]

The researchers found that while both high- and low-power subjects were equally sensitive to early signs of conflict, high-power subjects expended fewer motivational resources on the cooperative activity. They concluded that power differentials tend to prevent people—particularly high-power holders—from engaging in cooperation. But there is an interesting caveat! The researchers deliberately created an experiment *without task interdependence*. Why?

Interdependence is a condition that can overcome differential power as participants become aware of it and embrace it. Under conditions of interdependence, neither party, regardless of its relative power, can fully accomplish its goals without cooperation from the other. Sometimes participants discover their interdependence in the context of heightened performance pressures that require them to coordinate in ways not previously necessary. Change agents can help by creating a relational space in which to experiment with new patterns of interrelating. They can help participants to carry out work process interventions that experiment with new ways of accomplishing the work to achieve desired performance outcomes. And then they can help participants to create new structures to support the new patterns of working together—for example, adopting shared protocols that allocate speaking time to each role—to counteract traditional patterns of domination and subordination, allowing crucial information to be heard.

LEVELING UP RATHER THAN LEVELING DOWN

When we equalize power, however, we need to ensure that we are level *up* rather than *down*. This realization came to me during the Danish Greenhouse for Leadership conference in Copenhagen, where over four hundred leaders from the Danish public sector had gathered, in fall 2011, to generate new solutions for delivering public services—health, education, and criminal justice—to citizens more effectively and more efficiently. After brainstorming in small groups and reporting back to the larger group throughout the day, a union leader and a management leader sat together on stage on a sofa, with a coffee table and candles, reflecting on what they had learned and how they as leaders could help to move the solutions forward. I was struck by the civility of this labor/management dialogue, which was occurring at the same time that public unions were under attack in the state of Wisconsin. I had been invited to give a closing keynote about the power of relational coordination for achieving high performance, an argument that resonated with the audience's belief in the importance of social capital for building a good society. Afterward, as many commentators expressed curiosity about relational coordination, one participant said, "I like what you are saying. But how do you bring the pilot, and the doctor, down to everyone else's level?" Her question confused me. I didn't know how to answer.

Soon after, I realized why. When shared goals, shared knowledge, and mutual respect are well established, it's because those with less power have been *elevated*, not because those with more power have been *lowered*. I realized that power is not a zero-sum game. Power is not a fixed quantity that requires some to have less so that others can have more. This realization shed light on my earlier experiences. I had come away from my interviews at Southwest Airlines with the feeling that power was everywhere in abundance, regardless of one's position in the company. As one of my first interviewees had pointed out, "No one takes the job of another person for granted here. The skycap is *just as* critical as the pilot. You can always count on the next guy standing there." Note that he did not say, "The pilot is *no more* critical than the skycap." Even though both statements suggest equal status, they are very different. By contrast, I came away from interviews at American Airlines with the feeling that power was in short supply and that many if not most people at the company, regardless of position, felt constrained and frustrated by their inability to get things done. Even the pilots, who were clearly at the top of the worker status hierarchy, seemed to feel insecure.

I saw a similar contrast between Billings Clinic and Dartmouth-Hitchcock. At Dartmouth, participants from the frontline through top leadership at times expressed a sense of powerlessness, a frustration at their inability to get things done. At Billings, participants at all levels of the organization tended to express a sense efficacy and a sense of having the power they needed to get things done. Both organizations were engaged in intentional change based on the principles of relational coordination, but Billings was further ahead on this journey. At a dinner event where a surgical leader from Dartmouth first met a frontline nursing leader from Billings, the surgeon listened, impressed, as this relatively young nursing leader described what she and her colleagues were doing to create change at Billings. The surgeon finally asked, in effect, What kind of organization do you work for that enables you to feel so powerful?

When shared goals, shared knowledge and mutual respect are well established, it's because participants have recognized and embraced their interdependence, allowing those with less power to be elevated and those with more power to become comfortable with sharing it. Power is not only equalized; it is expanded for everyone. Eventually, participants' expanded sense of power and efficacy extends beyond their own team and throughout the broader system.

Inspired by the stories of change agents you have met in this book and informed by the Relational Model of Organizational Change, I urge you to go forth and do great things, using relational, work process, and structural interventions in synergistic ways. Above all, "be the change you wish to see" in the organizations you are striving to help, and in the broader community.

NOTES

CHAPTER 1

1. See, for example, J. P. MacDuffie, "Human Resource Bundles and Manufacturing Performance: Organizational Logic and Flexible Production Systems in the World Auto Industry," *Industrial and Labor Relations Review* 48, no. 2 (1995): 173–188; J. T. Dunlop and D. Weil, "Diffusion and Performance of Modular Production in the U.S. Apparel Industry," *Industrial Relations* 35, no. 3 (1996): 334–355; C. Ichniowski, K. Shaw, and G. Prennushi, "The Effects of Human Resource Practices on Manufacturing Performance: A Study of Steel Finishing Lines," *American Economic Review* 87, no. 3 (1997): 291–313; R. Batt, "Work Design, Technology and Performance in Customer Service and Sales," *Industrial and Labor Relations Review* 52, no. 4 (1999): 539–564; E. Appelbaum, T. Bailey, P. Berg, and A. L. Kalleberg, *Manufacturing Advantage: Why High-Performance Work Systems Pay Off* (Ithaca, NY: ILR Press, 1999); M. A. Youndt, S. Snell, J. W. Dean Jr., and D. P. Lepak, "Human Resource Management, Manufacturing Strategy, and Firm Performance," *Academy of Management Journal* 39, no. 4 (1996): 836–866; J. Womack, D. Jones, and D. Roos, *The Machine That Changed the World* (Cambridge, MA: MIT Press, 1990); C. Collins and K. Smith, "Knowledge Exchange and Combination: The Role of Human Resource Practices in the Performance of High-Technology Firms," *Academy of Management Journal* 49, no. 3 (2006): 544–560.

2. See, for example, R. Batt, "Managing Customer Services: Human Resource Practices, Quit Rates, and Sales Growth," *Academy of Management Journal* 45, no. 3 (2002): 587–598; S. Eaton, "Beyond Unloving Care: Linking Human Resource Management and Patient Care Quality in Nursing Homes," *International Journal of Human Resource Management* 11, no. 3 (2000): 591–616; V. H. Fried and R. D. Hisrich, "Toward a Model of Venture Capital Investment Decision-Making," *Financial Management* 23, no. 3 (1994): 28–37; I. C. MacMillan, L. Zemann, and P. N. Subbanarasimha, "Criteria Distinguishing Successful from Unsuccessful Ventures in the Venture Screening Process," *Journal of Business Venturing* 2, no. 2 (1987): 123–138; J. H. Gittell, *The Southwest Airlines Way: Using the Power of Relationships to Achieve High Performance* (New York: McGraw-Hill, 2003); A. P. Bartel, "Human Resource Management and Performance Outcomes: Evidence from Retail Banking," *Industrial and Labor Relations Review* 57, no. 2 (2004): 181–203.

3. J. H. Gittell and G. Bamber, "High and Low Road Strategies for Competing on Costs and Their Implications for Employment Relations: Studies in the Airline Industry," *International Journal of Human Resource Management* 21, no. 2 (2010): 165–179.

4. B. Becker and B. Gerhart, "The Impact of Human Resource Management on Organizational Performance: Progress and Prospects," *Academy of Management Journal* 39, no. 4 (1996): 779–780; T. Bailey, P. Berg, and C. Sandy, "The Effect of High-Performance Work Practices on Employee Earnings in the Steel, Apparel, and Medical Electronics and Imaging Industries," *Industrial and Labor Relations Review* 54, no. 2 (2001): 525–544; H. Ramsey, D. Scholarios, and B. Harley, "Employees and High-Performance Work Systems: Testing Inside the Black Box," *British Journal of Industrial Relations* 38, no. 4 (2000): 501–532; C. Ichniowski, T. Kochan, D. Levine, C. Olsen, and G. Strauss, "What Works at Work: Overview and Assessment," *Industrial Relations* 35, no. 3 (1996): 299–333; J. Horgan and P. Muhlau, "Human Resource Systems and Employee Performance in Ireland and the Netherlands: A Test of the Complementarity Hypothesis," *International Journal of Human Resource Management* 17, no. 3 (2006): 414–439; MacDuffie, "Human Resource Bundles"; Dunlop and Weil, "Diffusion and Performance"; Ichniowski, Shaw, and Prennushi, "Effects of Human Resource Practices"; Batt, "Work Design, Technology and Performance"; Appelbaum et al., *Manufacturing Advantage*; Youndt et al., "Human Resource Management"; M. West, C. Borrill, J. Dawson, J. Scully, M. Carter et al., "The Link Between the Management of Employees and Patient Mortality in Acute Hospitals," *International Journal of Human Resource Management* 13, no. 8 (2002): 1299–1311; M. Huselid, "The Impact of Human Resource Management on Turnover, Productivity and Corporate Financial Performance," *Academy of Management Journal* 38, no. 3 (1995): 635–672; J. E. Delery and D. H. Doty, "Modes of Theorizing in Strategic Human Resource Management: Tests of Universalistic, Contingency, and Configurational Performance Predictions," *Academy of Management Journal* 39, no. 4 (1996): 802–835; Collins and Smith, "Knowledge Exchange and Combination"; Bartel, "Human Resource Management"; P. M. Wright, T. Gardner, and L. Moynihan, "Impact of HR Practices on the Performance of Business Units," *Human Resource Management Journal* 13, no. 3 (2006): 21–36; P. Cappelli and D. Neumark, "Do High Performance Work Practices Improve Establishment Level Outcomes?" *Industrial and Labor Relations Review* 54, no. 4 (2001): 737–775; Gittell, *Southwest Airlines Way*; J. H. Gittell, "Organizing Work to Support Relational Coordination," *International Journal of Human Resource Management* 11, no. 3 (2000): 517–539; O. C. Richard and N. B. Johnson, "High Performance Work Practices and Human Resource Management Effectiveness: Substitutes or Complements?" *Journal of Business Strategy* 21, no. 2 (2004): 133–148; J. H. Gittell, R. Seidner, and J. Wimbush, "A Relational Model of How High Performance Work Systems Work," *Organization Science* 21, no. 2 (2009): 490–506; J. Cutcher-Gershenfeld, "The Impact on Economic Performance of a Transformation in Workplace Relations," *Industrial and Labor Relations Review* 44, no. 2 (1991): 241–260; C. J. Collins and K. Clark, "Strategic Human Resource Practices, Top Management Team Social Networks, and Firm Performance: The Role of Human Resource Practices in Creating Organizational Competitive Advantage," *Academy of Management Journal* 46, no. 6 (2003): 740–751; M. Gibbert, "Generalizing About Uniqueness: An Essay on an Apparent Paradox in the Resource-Based View," *Journal of Management Inquiry* 15, no. 2 (2006): 124–134; Fried and Hisrich, "Toward a Model of Venture Capital"; MacMillan, Zemann, and Subbanarasimha, "Criteria Distinguishing Successful from Unsuccessful Ventures"; S. A. Snell and J. W. Dean, "Integrated Manufacturing and Human Resource Management: A Human Capital Perspective," *Academy of Management Journal* 35, no. 3 (1992): 467–504; Batt, "Managing Customer Services"; Eaton, "Beyond Unloving Care"; P. Osterman, *Employment Futures: Reorganization, Dislocation and Public Policy* (New York: Oxford

University Press, 1988); T. A. Mahoney and M. R. Watson, "Evolving Modes of Workforce Governance: An Evaluation," in *Employee Representation: Alternatives and Future Directions*, ed. B. E. Kaufman and M. M. Kleiner (Madison: Industrial Relations Research Association, University of Wisconsin, 1993), 135–168; A. S. Tsui, J. L. Pearce, L. V. Porter, and J. P. Hite, "Choice of Employee-Organization Relationship: Influence of External and Internal Organizational Factors," in *Research in Personnel and Human Resource Management*, ed. G. R. Ferris (Greenwich, CT: JAI Press, 1995), 13:117–151. For a review of the European evidence, see the *2012 Dortmund/Brussels Position Paper on Workplace Innovation*, supported by the European Commission's General Directorate on Industry and Innovation.

5. The relational requirements for integrative solutions have been explored by M. P. Follett, "Constructive Conflict," in *Dynamic Administration: The Collected Papers of Mary Parker Follett*, ed. E. M. Fox and L. Urwick (London: Pitman, 1973), and later scholars, including R. E. Walton and R. B. McKersie, *A Behavioral Theory of Labor Negotiations: An Analysis of a Social Interaction System* (New York: McGraw-Hill, 1965); R. Fisher and W. Ury, *Getting to Yes: Negotiating an Agreement Without Giving In* (New York: Random House, 2012); R. E. Walton, J. Cutcher-Gershenfeld, and R. B. McKersie, *Strategic Negotiations: A Theory of Change in Labor Management Relations* (Cambridge, MA: Harvard Business Review Press, 1994).

6. Gittell, Seidner, and Wimbush, "Relational Model."

7. Gittell, *Southwest Airlines Way*; J. H. Gittell, *High Performance Healthcare: Using the Power of Relationships to Achieve Quality, Efficiency and Resilience* (New York: McGraw-Hill, 2009).

8. For an analysis of this trend, see V. Ramaswamy and K. Ozcan, *The Co-Creation Paradigm* (Stanford, CA: Stanford University Press, 2014).

9. D. B. Weinberg, *Code Green: Money-Driven Hospitals and the Dismantling of Nursing* (Ithaca, NY: Cornell University Press, 2003).

10. J. H. Gittell, A. von Nordenflycht, and T. A. Kochan, "Mutual Gains or Zero Sum? Labor Relations and Firm Performance in the Airline Industry," *Industrial and Labor Relations Review* 57, no. 2 (2004): 163–179.

11. For more on the relational basis of human identity, see M. P. Follett, "Relating: The Circular Response," in *The Creative Experience* (New York: Longmans and Green, 1924). To learn about how we tend to prefer others who are like ourselves, and the implications for organizations, see H. Ibarra, "Homophily and Differential Returns: Sex Differences in Network Structure and Access in an Advertising Firm," *Administrative Science Quarterly* 37, no. 3 (1994): 422–447.

CHAPTER 2

1. For more detailed results from this surgical study, see J. H. Gittell, *High Performance Healthcare: Using the Power of Relationships to Achieve Quality, Efficiency and Resilience* (New York: McGraw-Hill, 2009). See also J. H. Gittell, K. Fairfield, B. Bierbaum, R. Jackson, M. Kelly, R. Laskin, S. Lipson, J. Siliski, T. Thornhill, and J. Zuckerman, "Impact of Relational Coordination on Quality of Care, Post-Operative Pain and Functioning, and Length of Stay: A Nine-Hospital Study of Surgical Patients," *Medical Care* 38, no. 8 (2000): 807–819.

2. M. Weber, *Economy and Society: An Outline of Interpretive Sociology* (New York: Bedminster, 1968); M. Weber, "Bureaucracy," in *Critical Studies in Organization and Bureaucracy*, ed. F. Fischer and C. Sirianni (1920; repr. Philadelphia: Temple University Press, 1984), 24–39.

3. M. P. Follett, *Freedom and Co-ordination: Lectures in Business Organization* (London: Management Publications Trust, 1949), 198.

4. See M. Piore, "The Social Embeddedness of Labor Markets and Cognitive Processes," *Labour* 7, no. 3 (1993): 3–18.

5. Follett, *Freedom and Co-ordination*, 214.

6. J. March and H. Simon, *Organizations* (New York: Wiley, 1958). See also J. P. Thompson, *Organizations in Action: Social Science Bases of Administrative Theory* (New York: McGraw-Hill, 1968).

7. J. Womack, D. Jones, and D. Roos, *The Machine That Changed the World: The Story of Lean Production* (Cambridge, MA: MIT Press, 1990).

8. J. Galbraith, "Organization Design: An Information Processing View," in *Organization Planning: Cases and Concepts*, ed. P. Lawrence and J. Lorsch (Homewood, IL: Irwin, 1972), 49–74; M. Tushman and D. Nadler, "Information Processing as an Integrating Concept in Organizational Design," *Academy of Management Review* 3, no. 3 (1978): 613–624; and L. Argote, "Input Uncertainty and Organizational Coordination in Hospital Emergency Units," *Administrative Science Quarterly* 27, no. 3 (1982): 420–434.

9. D. Gordon, R. Edwards, and M. Reich, *Segmented Work, Divided Workers: The Historical Transformation of Labor in the United States* (New York: Cambridge University Press, 1982).

10. For a review of these findings and full citations, see J. H. Gittell and C. K. Logan, "The Impact of Relational Coordination on Performance, and How Organizations Support Its Development" (working paper, Heller School, Brandeis University, 2016).

11. Ibid.

12. Ibid.

13. Ibid.

14. J. M. Cramm, M. Hoeljmakers, and A. P. Nieboer, "Relational Coordination Between Community Health Nurses and Other Professionals in Delivering Care to Community-Dwelling Frail People," *Journal of Nursing Management* 22, no. 2 (2014):170–176.

15. For a review of these findings and the sources, see Gittell and Logan, "Impact of Relational Coordination."

16. M. P. Follett, "Relating: The Circular Response," in *The Creative Experience* (New York: Longmans and Green, 1924).

17. M. Buber, *I and Thou* (New York: Simon and Schuster, 1937).

18. S. Freud, *Civilization and Its Discontents: The Standard Edition*, trans. James Strachey (1930; repr. New York: Norton, 1961), 46.

19. J. B. Miller, *Toward a New Psychology of Women* (Boston: Beacon, 1976).

20. W. Kahn, "Relational Systems at Work," in *Research in Organizational Behavior*, vol. 20, ed. B. M. Staw and L. I. Cummings (Greenwich, CT: JAI Press, 1998), 39–76; M. Williams and J. E. Dutton, "Corrosive Political Climates: The Heavy Toll of Negative Political Behavior in Organizations," in *The Pressing Problems of Modern Organizations: Transforming the Agenda for Research and Practice*, ed. R. E. Quinn, R. M. O'Neill, and L. St. Clair (New York:

American Management Association, 1999), 3–30; R. Lewin and B. Regine, *The Soul at Work* (New York: Simon and Schuster, 2000); J. E. Dutton, *Energize Your Workplace: How to Create and Sustain High-Quality Connections at Work* (San Francisco: Jossey-Bass, 2003); J. E. Dutton and E. D. Heaphy, "Coming to Life: The Power of High Quality Connections at Work," in *Positive Organizational Scholarship: Foundations of a New Discipline*, ed. K. S. Cameron, J. E. Dutton, and R. E. Quinn (San Francisco: Berrett-Koehler, 2003); and J. E. Dutton and B. R. Ragins, *Exploring Positive Relationships at Work: Building a Theoretical and Research Foundation* (Mahwah, NJ: Lawrence Erlbaum, 2007).

21. A. Smith, *The Wealth of Nations* (1776; repr., ed. E. Cannan, New York: Modern Library, 2000); K. Marx, "The German Ideology," in *Marx and Engels: Basic Writings on Politics and Philosophy*, ed. L. Feuer (1845; New York: Anchor, 1959); Freud, *Civilization and Its Discontents*; E. Durkheim, *The Division of Labor in Society* (New York: Macmillan, 1933).

22. J. Fletcher, *Disappearing Acts: Gender, Power and Relational Practice at Work* (Cambridge, MA: MIT Press, 2001).

23. B. M. Staw, L. E. Sandelands, and J. E. Dutton, "Threat Rigidity Effects in Organizational Behavior: A Multilevel Analysis," *Administrative Science Quarterly* 26, no. 4 (1981): 501–524.

CHAPTER 3

1. J. L. Brudney and R. E. England, "Toward a Definition of the Coproduction Concept," *Public Administration Review* 43, no. 1 (1983): 59–65; C. Needham and S. Carr, *Co-Production: An Emerging Evidence Base for Adult Social Transformation* (London: Social Care Institute for Excellence, 2009).

2. R. T. Chappell, "Can TQM in Public Education Survive Without Coproduction?" *Quality Progress* 27, no. 7 (1994): 41–45; M. Marschall, "Citizen Participation and the Neighborhood Context: A New Look at the Coproduction of Local Public Goods," *Political Research Quarterly* 57, no. 2 (2004): 231–245; R. Bifulco and H. F. Ladd, "Institutional Change and Coproduction of Public Services: The Effect of Charter Schools on Parental Involvement," *Journal of Public Administration Research and Theory* 16, no. 4 (2006): 553–577.

3. M. J. Bitner, W. T. Faranda, A. R. Hubbert, and V. A. Zeithaml, "Customer Contributions and Roles in Service Delivery," *International Journal of Service Industry Management* 8, no. 3 (1997): 193–205.

4. V. Ramaswamy and K. Ozcan, *The Co-Creation Paradigm* (Stanford, CA: Stanford University Press, 2014).

5. B. A. Gutek, *The Dynamics of Service: Reflections on the Changing Nature of Provider/ Customer Interactions* (San Francisco: Jossey-Bass, 1995).

6. A. Douglass and J. H. Gittell, "Transforming Professionalism: Relational Bureaucracy and Parent-Teacher Partnerships in Child Care Settings," *Journal of Early Childhood Research* 10, no. 3 (2012): 267–281.

7. Elizabeth Nolan, pers. comm.

8. A. Douglass and L. Klerman, "The Strengthening Families Initiative and Child Care Quality Improvement: How Strengthening Families Influenced Change in Child Care Programs in One State," *Early Education and Development* 23, no. 3 (2012): 373–392.

9. M. E. Warfield, G. Chiri, W. N. Leutz, and M. Timberlake, "Family Well-Being in a Participant-Directed Autism Waiver Program: The Role of Relational Coordination," *Journal of Intellectual Disability Research* 58, no. 12 (2014): 1091–1104; J. M. Cramm and A. P. Nieboer, "The Importance of Productive Patient-Professional Interaction for the Well-Being of Chronically Ill Patients," *Quality of Life Research* 24, no. 4 (2015): 897–903; J. M. Cramm and A. P. Nieboer, "A Longitudinal Study to Identify the Influence of Quality of Chronic Care Delivery on Productive Interactions Between Patients and (Teams of) Healthcare Professionals Within Disease Management Programs," *BMJ Open* 4, no. 9 (2014): e005914.

10. D. B. Weinberg, W. Lusenhop, J. H. Gittell, and C. Kautz, "Coordination Between Formal Providers and Informal Caregivers," *Health Care Management Review* 32, no. 2 (2007): 140–150.

11. J. H. Gittell and F. Hagigi, "Modularity and the Coordination of Complex Work: The Case of Patient Care" (working paper, Brandeis University, 2014).

12. L. Plé, "How Does the Customer Fit in Relational Coordination? An Empirical Study in Multichannel Retail Banking," *M@n@gement* 16, no. 1 (2013): 1–30.

13. Ibid.

14. Ibid.

15. Ibid.

16. J. Skakon, "Relational and Course Coordination at the University: Can the Principles of Relational Coordination Incorporated Into the Course Coordinator Role Strengthen Constructive Alignment?" in *Proceedings of the 11th International Symposium on Human Factors in Organizational Design and Management (ODAM), and 46th Annual Nordic Ergonomics Society Conference (NES)*, ed. O. Broberg, N. Fallentin, P. Hasle, P. L. Jensen, A. Kabel, M. E. Larsen, and T. Weller (Santa Monica, CA: IEA Press 2014), 625–630.

17. C. Simon, "Informal Carers and the Primary Care Team," *British Journal of General Practice* 51 (2001): 920–923; N. Y. Glazer, "The Home as Workshop: Women as Amateur Nurses and Medical Care Providers," *Gender and Society* 4, no. 4 (1990): 479–499.

18. Douglass and Gittell, "Transforming Professionalism."

19. M. Weber, *Economy and Society: An Outline of Interpretive Sociology* (New York: Bedminster, 1968).

20. Douglass and Gittell, "Transforming Professionalism."

21. H. Hwang and W. W. Powell, "The Rationalization of Charity: The Influences of Professionalism in the Non-Profit Sector," *Administrative Science Quarterly* 54, no. 2 (2009): 268–298; J. Sachs, *The Activist Teaching Profession* (Philadelphia: Open University Press, 2003).

22. P. S. Adler, S. Kwon, and C. Heckscher, "Professional Work: The Emergence of Collaborative Community," *Organization Science* 19, no. 2 (2008): 359–376.

23. Sachs, *Activist Teaching Profession*; J. K. Fletcher, "Leadership, Power, and Positive Relationships," in *Exploring Positive Relationships at Work: Building a Theoretical and Research Foundation*, ed. J. E. Dutton and B. R. Ragins (Mahwah, NJ: Lawrence Erlbaum Associates, 2007), 347–371, esp. 356; W. Kahn, *Holding Fast: The Struggle to Create Resilient Caregiving Organizations* (Hove, UK: Brunner-Routledge, 2005).

24. S. Barle and G. Kunda, "Bringing Work Back In," *Organization Science* 12, no. 1 (2001): 76–95.

25. A. M. O'Connor, H. A. Llewellyn-Thomas, and A. B. Flood, "Modifying Unwarranted Variations in Health Care: Shared Decision Making Using Patient Decision Aids," *Health Affairs*, October 7, 2004.

26. W. T. Branch and T. K. Malik, "Using 'Windows of Opportunity' in Brief Interactions to Understand Patients' Concerns," *Journal of the American Medical Association* 269, no. 13 (1993): 1667–1668.

27. B. A. Gutek, B. Cherry, A. D. Bhappu, S. Schneider, and L. Woolf, "Features of Service Relationships and Encounters," *Work and Occupations* 27, no. 3 (2000): 321.

28. V. A. Parker, "Connecting Relational Work and Workgroup Context in Caregiving Organizations," *Journal of Applied Behavioral Science* 38, no. 3 (2002): 276–297; S. J. Potter and J. B. McKinlay, "From a Relationship to Encounter: An Examination of Longitudinal and Lateral Dimensions in the Doctor-Patient Relationship," *Social Science and Medicine* 61, no. 2 (2005): 465–479; D. B. Weinberg, J. H. Gittell, R. W. Lusenhop, C. Kautz, and J. Wright, "Beyond Our Walls: Impact of Patient and Provider Coordination Across the Continuum on Surgical Outcomes," *Health Services Research* 42, no. 1 (2007): 7–24.

CHAPTER 4

1. N. Turner, "Collective Leadership: If Everyone Leads, Who Follows?" (panel discussion, Wagner School of Public Service, New York University, May 1, 2014).

2. J. H. Gittell and A. Douglass, "Relational Bureaucracy: Structuring Reciprocal Relationships Into Roles," *Academy of Management Review* 37, no. 4 (2012): 709–754.

3. G. Loveman, *Committing to Leadership: American Airlines* (Boston: Harvard Business Publishing, 1993); R. Hackman and G. Oldham, *Work Redesign* (New York: Addison-Wesley, 1980).

4. This section draws from J. H. Gittell, "Supervisory Span, Relational Coordination and Flight Departure Performance: A Reassessment of Post-Bureaucracy Theory," *Organization Science* 12, no. 4 (2001): 467–482.

5. Gittell, "Supervisory Span, Relational Coordination and Flight Departure Performance."

6. D. McGregor, *The Human Side of Enterprise* (New York: McGraw-Hill, 1960), 76.

7. F. W. Taylor, *The Principles of Scientific Management* (Toronto, Canada: Dover Publications, 1911).

8. R. G. Hunt, "Technology and Organization," *Academy of Management Journal* 13, no. 3 (1970): 235–252; B. Blau, "Interdependence and Hierarchy in Organizations," *Social Science Research* 1 (1972): 1–24; A. Van de Ven, A. Delbecq, and R. Koenig, "Determinants of Coordination Modes Within Organizations," *American Sociological Review* 41 (1976): 322–338.

9. J. Woodward, *Industrial Organization: Theory and Practice* (New York: Oxford University Press, 1965); R. G. Lord and M. Rouzee, "Task Interdependence, Temporal Phase and Cognitive Heterogeneity as Determinants of Leadership Behavior and Behavior-Performance Relations," *Organizational Behavior and Human Performance* 23 (1979): 182–200; L. W. Fry, S. Kerr, and C. Lee, "Effects of Different Leader Behaviors Under Different Levels of Task Interdependence," *Human Relations* 39 (1986): 1067–1082; D. G. Ancona, "Outward Bound: Strategies for Team Survival in an Organization," *Academy of Management Journal* 33, no. 2 (1990): 334–365; K. Eisenhardt and B. N. Tabrizi, "Accelerating Adaptive Processes:

Product Innovation in the Global Computer Industry," *Administrative Science Quarterly* 40, no. 1 (1995): 84–110.

10. This section draws from Gittell and Douglass, "Relational Bureaucracy."

11. See M. Weber, "Bureaucracy," in *Critical Studies in Organization and Bureaucracy*, ed. F. Fischer and C. Sirianni (1920; repr. Philadelphia: Temple University Press, 1984). See also M. Lipsky, *Street-Level Bureaucracy: Dilemmas of the Individual in Public Service* (New York: Russell Sage Foundation, 1980); A. Wrzesniewski and J. E. Dutton, "Crafting a Job: Revisioning Employees as Active Crafters of Their Work," *Academy of Management Review* 26, no. 2 (2001): 179–201.

12. C. Heckscher, "The Post-Bureaucratic Organizational Type," in *The Post-Bureaucratic Organization*, ed. C. Heckscher and A. Donnellon (Thousand Oaks, CA: Sage, 1994).

13. M. P. Follett, *Freedom and Co-ordination: Lectures in Business Organization* (London: Management Publications Trust, 1949), 183, 226.

14. D. McGregor, *The Human Side of Enterprise* (New York: McGraw-Hill, 1960).

15. Gittell and Douglass, "Relational Bureaucracy."

16. D. Ancona and H. Bresman, *X-Teams: How To Build Teams That Lead, Innovate and Succeed* (Boston, MA: Harvard Business School Press, 2007).

17. J. B. Carson, P. E. Tesluk, and J. A. Marrone, "Shared Leadership in Teams: An Investigation of Antecedent Conditions and Performance," *Academy of Management Journal* 50, no. 5 (2007): 1217–1234.

18. J. Lipman-Blumen, "Connective Leadership: Female Leadership Styles in the 21st Century Workplace," *Sociological Perspectives* 35, no. 1 (1992): 183–203.

19. J. K. Fletcher, "Leadership, Power and Positive Relationships," in *Exploring Positive Relationships at Work: Building a Theoretical and Research Foundation*, ed. J. E. Dutton and B. R. Ragins (Mahwah, NJ: Lawrence Erlbaum, 2007), 356.

20. E. H. Schein, *Humble Inquiry: The Gentle Art of Asking Rather Than Telling* (San Francisco, CA: Jossey-Bass, 2013); E. H. Schein, *Helping: How to Offer, Give and Receive Help* (San Francisco: Berrett-Koehler, 2009); M. Uhl-Bien, "Relational Leadership Theory: Exploring the Social Processes of Leadership and Organizing," *Leadership Quarterly* 17, no. 6 (2006): 654–676.

21. Gittell and Douglass, "Relational Bureaucracy."

22. This case was published in J. H. Gittell and A. Suchman, "Connecting and Leading with Others," in *Wisdom Leadership*, ed. M. Plews-Ogan and G. Beyt (London: Radcliffe, 2013).

23. C. Hornstrup and M. Johansen, *Strategisk Relationel Ledelse* (Copenhagen: Danish Psychological Press, 2013).

24. These final sections draw on the panel discussion "Collective Leadership: If Everyone Leads, Who Follows?" NYU Wagner School of Public Service, May 1, 2014, led by Professors Sonia Ospina and Erica Foldy.

CHAPTER 5

1. M. Piore, "The Social Embeddedness of Labor Markets and Cognitive Processes," *Labour* 7, no. 3 (1993): 20.

2. Ibid.

3. C. Heckscher, "Defining the Post-Bureaucratic Type," in *The Post-Bureaucratic Organization*, ed. C. Heckscher and A. Donnellon (Thousand Oaks, CA: Sage, 1994), 14–62; D. Krackhardt and D. Brass, "Intraorganizational Networks: The Micro Side," in *Advances in Social Network Analysis: Research in the Social and Behavioral Sciences*, ed. S. Wasserman and J. Galaskawiecz (Beverly Hills, CA: Sage, 1994), 207–229.

4. This theoretical argument is made at length in J. H. Gittell and A. Douglass, "Relational Bureaucracy: Embedding Reciprocal Relationships Into Roles," *Academy of Management Review* 37, no. 4 (2012): 709–733, and was previewed in J. H. Gittell, R. B. Seidner, and J. Wimbush, "A Relational Model of How High-Performance Work Systems Work," *Organization Science* 21, no. 2 (2010): 490–506.

5. H. Ibarra, "Homophily and Differential Returns: Sex Differences in Network Structure and Access in an Advertising Firm," *Administrative Science Quarterly* 37, no. 3 (1992): 422–447.

6. G. A. Bigley and K. Roberts, "The Incident Command System: High Reliability Organizing for Complex and Volatile Task Environments," *Academy of Management Journal* 44, no. 6 (2001): 1281–1299; J. R. Carlson and R. W. Zmud, "Channel Expansion Theory and the Experiential Nature of Media Richness Perceptions," *Academy of Management Journal* 42, no. 2 (1999): 153–170.

7. E. H. Schein, *Organizational Culture and Leadership*, 4th ed. (San Francisco: Jossey-Bass, 2010).

8. M. Williams, "Perspective Taking," in *Oxford Handbook of Positive Organizational Scholarship*, ed. K. Cameron and G. Spreitzer (Oxford: Oxford University Press, 2011), 462–473.

9. J. Fletcher, "Leadership, Power, and Positive Relationships," in *Exploring Positive Relationships at Work: Building a Theoretical and Research Foundation*, ed. J. E. Dutton and B. R. Ragins (New York: Psychology Press, 2007), 347–372.

10. A. Douglass, "Improving Family Engagement: The Organizational Context and Its Influence on Partnering with Parents in Formal Child Care Settings," *Early Childhood Research and Practice* 13, no. 2 (2011), http://ecrp.uiuc.edu/v13n2/douglass.; S. C. Eaton, "Beyond 'Unloving Care': Linking Human Resource Management and Patient Care Quality on Nursing Homes," *International Journal of Human Resource Management* 11, no. 3 (2000): 591–616.

11. J. H. Gittell, "Organizing Work to Support Relational Coordination," *International Journal of Human Resource Management* 11, no. 3 (2000): 517–539.

12. For the original analysis of subgoal optimization, see J. March and H. Simon, *Organizations* (New York: Wiley, 1958). See also R. H. Chenhall, "Integrative Strategic Performance Measurement Systems: Strategic Alignment of Manufacturing, Learning and Strategic Outcomes," *Accounting Organization and Society* 30 (2005): 395–422; W. E. Deming, *Out of the Crisis* (Cambridge, MA: MIT Press, 1986); E. Locke and G. Latham, *A Theory of Goal-Setting and Task Performance* (Englewood Cliffs, NJ: Prentice Hall, 1990).

13. Gittell, Seidner, and Wimbush, "Relational Model"; J. H. Gittell, "Paradox of Coordination and Control," *California Management Review* 42, no. 3 (2000): 177–183; R. Austin and J. H. Gittell, "When It Should Not Work but Does: Anomalies of High Performance," in *Business Performance Measurement: Theory and Practice*, ed. A. Neely (Cambridge: Cambridge University Press, 2002).

14. For more about these legal structures of accountability and how they constrain organizational innovation, see Chapter 21 of J. H. Gittell, *High Performance Healthcare: Using the Power of Relationships to Achieve Quality, Efficiency and Resilience* (New York: McGraw-Hill, 2009).

15. "Southwest Airlines Employees to Split Record-Setting Profit Sharing Amount in 40th Consecutive Payment," Southwest Airlines news release, April 14, 2014, http://southwest.investorroom.com/index.php?s=43&item=1882.

16. J. Niclas and S. Carey, "Once Brassy Southwest Suffers Grown-Up Woes," *Wall Street Journal,* April 2, 2014.

17. Ibid.

18. S. Warren, "Southwest Airlines' CEO Plans New Growth," *Wall Street Journal,* December 19, 2005.

19. F. Heller and G. Yukl, "Participation, Managerial Decision-Making and Situational Variables," *Organizational Behavior and Human Performance* 4 (1969): 227–241; B. E. Goodstadt and D. Kipnis, "Situational Influences on the Use of Power," *Journal of Applied Psychology* 54 (1970): 201–207; J. D. Ford, "Department Context and Formal Structure as Constraints on Leader Behavior," *Academy of Management Journal* 24, no. 2 (1981): 274–288; L. Porter and E. Lawler, "The Effects of 'Tall' Versus 'Flat' Organization Structures on Managerial Job Satisfaction," *Personnel Psychology* 17, no. 2 (1964): 135–148; P. Blau, "The Hierarchy of Authority in Organizations," *American Journal of Sociology* 73 (1968): 453–467.

20. J. H. Gittell, "Supervisory Span, Relational Coordination and Flight Departure Performance: A Reassessment of Post-Bureaucracy Theory," *Organization Science* 12, no. 4 (2001): 467–482.

21. S. A. Mohrman, "Integrating Roles and Structures in the Lateral Organization," in *Organizing for the Future,* ed. J. R. Galbraith and E. E. Lawler (San Francisco: Jossey-Bass, 1993).

22. Gittell, "Paradox of Coordination and Control"; Gittell, Seidner, and Wimbush, "Relational Model."

23. Gittell, "Organizing Work"; J. H. Gittell, "Coordinating Mechanisms in Care Provider Groups: Relational Coordination as a Mediator and Input Uncertainty as a Moderator of Performance Effects," *Management Science* 48, no. 11 (2002): 1408–1426.

24. March and Simon, *Organizations.*

25. M. P. Follett, "Constructive Conflict," in *Dynamic Administration: The Collected Papers of Mary Parker Follett,* ed. H. C. Metcalf and L. Urwick (1926; repr. New York: Harper and Brothers, 1942), 30–49; K. Jehn, "A Multi-Method Examination of the Benefits and Detriments of Intra-Group Conflict," *Administrative Science Quarterly* 40, no. 2 (1995): 256–282.

26. P. M. Mareschal, "Solving Problems and Transforming Relationships: The Bifocal Approach to Mediation," *American Review of Public Administration* 33 (2003): 423–449.

27. T. Simon and R. Peterson, "Task Conflict and Relationship Conflict in Top Management Teams: The Pivotal Role of Intragroup Trust," *Journal of Applied Psychology* 85 (2000): 102–111; A. Edmondson and D. M. Smith, "Too Hot to Handle: How to Manage Relationship Conflict," *California Management Review* 49, no. 1 (2006): 6–31; Gittell, "Organizing Work."

28. E. Goffman, *Encounters* (Indianapolis, IN: Bobbs Merrill, 1961); N. Nohria and R. Eccles, "Face-to-Face: Making Network Organizations Work," in *Networks and Organizations:*

Structure, Form and Action, ed. R. Eccles and N. Nohria (Boston: Harvard Business School Press, 1992), 288–308.

29. L. Argote, "Input Uncertainty and Organizational Coordination in Hospital Emergency Units," *Administrative Science Quarterly* 27, no. 3 (1982): 420–434; S. Faraj and Y. Xiao, "Coordination in Fast Response Organizations," *Management Science* 52, no. 8 (2006): 1155–1169.

30. Gittell, "Coordinating Mechanisms."

31. P. S. Adler and B. Borys, "Two Types of Bureaucracy: Enabling and Coercive," *Administrative Science Quarterly* 41, no. 1 (1996): 61–89.

32. M. S. Feldman and A. Rafaeli, "Organizational Routines as Sources of Connections and Understandings," *Journal of Management Studies* 39, no. 3 (2002): 309–331.

33. Faraj and Xiao, "Coordination in Fast Response Organizations."

34. Gittell, "Coordinating Mechanisms."

35. C. Davies, "Competence Versus Care? Gender and Caring Work Revisited," *Acta Sociologica* 38 (1995): 17–31; M. Noordegraaf, "From 'Pure' to 'Hybrid' Professionalism: Present-Day Professionalism in Ambiguous Public Domains," *Administration and Society* 39 (2007): 761–785.

36. R. S. Selladurai, "Mass Customization in Operations Management: Oxymoron or Reality?" *Omega* 32, no. 4 (2004): 295–300.

37. A. Douglass, "Improving Family Engagement"; Eaton, "Beyond 'Unloving Care.'"

38. R. Wachter, *The Digital Doctor: Hope, Hype and Harm at the Dawn of Medicine's Computer Age* (New York: McGraw-Hill, 2015).

39. E. Brynjolfsson and L. Hitt, "Paradox Lost? Firm-Level Evidence on Returns to Information Technology Spending," *Management Science* 42, no. 4 (1996): 541–558.

40. S. Zuboff, *In the Age of the Smart Machine* (Cambridge, MA: Harvard University Press, 1988).

41. M. Hansen, "The Search-Transfer Paradox: The Role of Weak Ties in Integrating Knowledge Across Organizational Subunits," *Administrative Science Quarterly* 44, no. 1 (1999): 82–111.

42. G. Loveman, "An Assessment of the Productivity Impact of Information Technologies," in *Information Technology and the Corporation of the 1990s: Research Studies*, ed. T. Allen and M. S. Morton (New York: Oxford University Press, 1994), 84–110.

43. Gittell, "Organizing Work."

44. Gittell, Seidner, and Wimbush, "Relational Model."

45. R. Gibbons and R. Henderson, "Relational Contracts and Organizational Capabilities," *Organization Science* 23, no. 5 (2012): 1350–1364.

PART II

1. J. H. Gittell, J. Beswick, and K. McDonald, "Interventional Uses of Relational Coordination: Early Evidence from Four Countries" (working paper, Brandeis University, 2015).

CHAPTER 6

1. E. H. Schein, *Helping: How to Offer, Give and Receive Help* (San Francisco: Berrett-Koehler, 2011).

2. J. Hoffer, "The Socially Embedded Human Subject: A Moral Standpoint for Achieving Social Justice" (thesis, Reed College, 1985).

3. E. H. Schein, *The Corporate Culture Survival Guide* (San Francisco: Jossey-Bass, 2009); E. H. Schein, *Humble Inquiry: The Gentle Art of Asking Rather Than Telling* (San Francisco: Jossey-Bass, 2013); A. Edmondson, *Teaming: How Organizations Learn, Innovate and Compete in the Knowledge Economy* (San Francisco: Jossey-Bass, 2012); A. Suchman, *Leading Change in Healthcare: Transforming Organizations Using Complexity, Positive Psychology and Relationship-Centered Care* (London: Radcliffe, 2011); R. A. Heifetz, M. Grinsky, and A. Grashow, *The Practice of Adaptive Leadership: Tools and Tactics for Changing Your Organization and the World* (Boston: Harvard Business School Press, 2009); J. B. Miller, *Toward a New Psychology of Women* (Boston: Beacon, 1987); J. Jordan and C. Dooley, *Relational Practice in Action: A Group Manual* (Wellesley, MA: Stone Center / Wellesley College, 2000); J. Fletcher, *Disappearing Acts: Gender, Power and Relational Practice at Work* (Cambridge, MA: MIT Press, 2001).

4. J. H. Gittell, "Relational Coordination Between Service Providers and Its Impact on Customers," *Journal of Service Research* 4, no. 4 (2002): 299–311.

5. W. E. Deming, *Out of the Crisis* (Cambridge, MA: MIT Press, 1986); J. P. Womack, D. T. Jones, and D. Roos, *The Machine That Changed the World: The Story of Lean Production* (Cambridge, MA: MIT Press, 1990); J. P. MacDuffie and J. Krafcik, "Integrating Technology and Human Resources for High Performance Manufacturing: Evidence from the International Auto Industry," in *Transforming Organizations*, ed. T. A. Kochan and M. Useem (New York: Oxford University Press, 1992), 209–226; M. Hammer, and J. Champy, *Reengineering the Corporation: A Manifesto for Business Revolution* (New York: Harper Business, 1993).

6. Deming, *Out of the Crisis*.

7. S. Covey, quoted in Shingo Institute training materials.

8. J. H. Gittell, *High Performance Healthcare: Using the Power of Relationships to Achieve Quality, Efficiency and Resilience* (New York: McGraw-Hill, 2009).

9. R. Ackoff, "Beyond Continual Improvement: Systems-Based Improvement," 2010, https://www.youtube.com/watch?v=OqEeIG8aPPk.

10. P. Batalden, E. Nelson, M. Godfrey, and J. S. Lazar, *Value by Design: Developing Clinical Microsystems to Achieve Organizational Excellence* (San Francisco: Jossey-Bass, 2011). See also E. Nelson, P. Batalden, and M. Godfrey, *Quality by Design: A Clinical Microsystems Approach* (San Francisco: Jossey-Bass, 2007).

11. For more about this story, see J. H. Gittell, *The Southwest Airlines Way: Using the Power of Relationships to Achieve High Performance* (New York: McGraw-Hill, 2003).

12. Evaluation studies of patient-centered medical home efforts document the challenges of implementation. See, for example, A. Bitton, G. R. Schwartz, E. E. Stewart, D. E. Henderson, C. A. Keohane, D. W. Bates, and G. D. Schiff, "Off the Hamster Wheel? Qualitative Evaluation of a Payment-Linked Patient-Centered Medical Home Pilot," *Milbank Quarterly* 90, no. 3 (2012): 484–515; M. W. Friedberg, E. C. Schneider, M. B. Rosenthal, K. G. Volpp, and R. M. Werner, "Association Between Participation in a Multipayer Medical Home Intervention and Changes in Quality, Utilization and Costs of Care," *Journal of the American Medical Association* 311, no. 8 (2014): 815–825.

13. Schein, *Corporate Culture Survival Guide*.

14. J. H. Gittell, A. Edmondson, and E. H. Schein, "Learning to Coordinate: A Relational Model of Organizational Change" (paper presented at the Annual Meeting of the Academy of Management, San Antonio, 2011).

CHAPTER 7

1. J. H. Gittell, R. Seidner, and J. Wimbush, "A Relational Model of How High Performance Work Systems Work," *Organization Science* 21, no. 2 (2010): 490–506; J. H. Gittell, "Organizing Work to Support Relational Coordination," *International Journal of Human Resource Management* 11, no. 3 (2000): 517–539; J. H. Gittell, "Paradox of Coordination and Control," *California Management Review* 42, no. 3 (2000): 177–183.

2. There was a fair amount of stability in the top management team. Scott Armstrong, the president and CEO, had been in his current role since 2005 and with Group Health since 1986, in positions ranging from assistant hospital administrator to chief operating officer. As Group Health's top leadership focused on navigating the organization through a new environment, they seemed less focused on the innovations underway at the frontline. When asked about top leadership, one frontline leader noted, "We are fairly autonomous."

3. R. J. Reid, K. Coleman, E. A. Johnson, P. A. Fishman, C. Hsu, M. P. Soman, et al., "The Group Health Medical Home at Year Two: Cost Savings, Higher Patient Satisfaction, and Less Burnout for Providers," *Health Affairs* 29, no. 5 (2010): 835–843; R. J. Reid, E. A. Johnson, C. Hsu, K. Ehrlich, K. Coleman, C. Trescott, M. Erikson, T. R. Ross, D. Liss, and P. A. Fishman, "Spreading a Medical Home Redesign: Effects on Emergency Department Use and Hospital Admissions," *Annals of Family Medicine* 11, no. S1 (2013): S19–S26.

4. R. J. Reid, P. A. Fishman, O. Yu, T. R. Ross, J. T. Tufano, M. P. Soman, and E. B. Larson, "Patient-Centered Medical Home Demonstration: A Prospective, Quasi-Experimental, Before and After Evaluation," *American Journal of Managed Care* 15, no. 9 (2009): e71–e87.

5. P. Noel, H. Lanham, R. Palmer, L. Leykhum, and M. Sieve, "The Importance of Relational Coordination and Reciprocal Learning for Chronic Illness Care in Primary Care Teams," *Health Care Management Review* 38, no. 1 (2013): 20–28.

6. Once the relational coordination initiative was up and running, the long-time medical director for primary care, Claire Trescott, who had helped to inspire the initiative, stepped down from her leadership role and retired from Group Health.

7. For more about the relational coordination intervention workshop, "Improving Work Processes with Relational Coordination," visit http://www.rchcweb.com/Our-Programs/RC-Workshop.

8. B. L. Fredrickson, "The Broaden-and-Build Theory of Positive Emotions," *Philosophical Transactions Royal Society London Biological Sciences* 359, no. 1449 (2004): 1367–1378.

9. Group Health uses a secure messaging platform for electronic patient-provider messaging that is sometimes referred to by staff and patients colloquially as "email."

10. For more about the Lencioni framework, see P. Lencioni, *Overcoming the Five Dysfunctions of a Team: A Field Guide for Leaders, Managers, and Facilitators* (San Francisco: Jossey-Bass, 2005). For more about the Myers-Briggs assessment tool, see I. B. Myers, M. H. McCaulley, and R. Most, *Manual: A Guide to the Development and Use of the Myers-Briggs Type Indicator* (Palo Alto, CA: Consulting Psychologists Press, 1985).

11. For more on selecting and deselecting based on teamwork capabilities, see J. H. Gittell, *The Southwest Airlines Way: Using the Power of Relationships to Achieve High Performance* (New York: McGraw-Hill, 2003), chap. 6.

12. For a review of this research over several decades, see J. H. Gittell, "Supervisory Span, Relational Coordination and Flight Departure Performance: A Reassessment of Post-Bureaucracy Theory," *Organization Science* 12, no. 4 (2001): 467–482.

13. Group Health was a lead user of the Epic electronic health record and an innovative user of its patient portal. See J. D. Ralston, D. P. Martin, M. L. Anderson, P. A. Fishman, D. A. Conrad, E. B. Larson, and D. Grembowski, "Group Health Cooperative's Transformation Toward Patient-Centered Access," *Medical Care Research and Review* 66, no. 6 (2009): 703–724. See also J. D. Ralston, K. Coleman, R. J. Reid, M. R. Handley, and E. B. Larson, "Patient Experience Should Be Part of Meaningful-Use Criteria," *Health Affairs* 29, no. 4 (2010): 607–613.

14. D. Arterburn, R. Wellman, E. Westbrook, C. Rutter, T. Ross, D. McCulloch, and C. Jung, "Introducing Decision Aids at Group Health Was Linked to Sharply Lower Hip and Knee Surgery Rates and Costs," *Health Affairs* 31, no. 9 (2012): 2094–2104.

15. J. H. Gittell, J. Resnick, E. Temkin, and S. Lax, "Building Relational Coordination Across Work Groups at Kaiser-Permanente," in *The Evolving Healthcare Landscape: How Employees, Organizations, and Institutions Adapt and Innovate*, ed. A. Avgar and T. J. Vogus (Champaign, IL: Labor and Employment Relations Association Press, 2016).

16. The McColl Center for Health Care Innovation within the Group Health Research Institute was engaged in an evaluation of the relational coordination primary care change initiative, with support from Relational Coordination Analytics and the Relational Coordination Research Collaborative at Brandeis University.

CHAPTER 8

1. B. A. Gutek, *The Dynamics of Service: Reflections on the Changing Nature of Provider/ Customer Interactions* (San Francisco: Jossey-Bass, 1995); M. J. Bitner, W. T. Faranda, A. R. Hubbert, and V. A. Zeithaml, "Customer Contributions and Roles in Service Delivery," *International Journal of Service Industry Management* 8, no. 3 (1997): 193–205; C. Needham and S. Carr, *Co-Production: An Emerging Evidence Base for Adult Social Transformation* (London: Social Care Institute for Excellence, 2009); V. Ramaswamy and K. Ozcan, *The Co-Creation Paradigm* (Stanford, CA: Stanford University Press, 2014).

CHAPTER 9

1. J. H. Gittell and A. Douglass, "Relational Bureaucracy: Structuring Reciprocal Relationships Into Roles," *Academy of Management Review* 37, no. 4 (2012): 709–754.

2. Dartmouth-Hitchcock Medical Center was formed in 1973 by the joining of three institutions—Dartmouth-Hitchcock Clinic, Mary Hitchcock Memorial Hospital, and the Dartmouth Medical School.

3. http://tdi.dartmouth.edu/.

4. The shared decision-making movement in the United States and beyond was supported by the Informed Medical Decisions Foundation, founded by Jack Wennberg and Al Mulley, and by the first-in-the-nation Center for Shared Decision Making, founded by now-CEO James Weinstein and surgical leader Dale Collins Vidal. Both organizations helped to lay the foundation for a key element of relational coproduction—engaging patients and families in the decision-making process regarding options for treatment and providing them with the tools to engage knowledgeably in choosing among these options. See Chapter 3 for a deeper dive into relational coproduction.

5. In 2013, Dartmouth and fifteen other healthcare systems in the High Value Healthcare Collaborative won a $26 million grant from the US Center for Medicare and Medicaid Innovation. Together, these systems planned to implement a program to engage patients and implement shared decision making for patients facing hip, knee, or spine surgery and for patients with diabetes or congestive heart failure. The members of the High Value Healthcare Collaborative collectively served 50 million patients per year in health systems across the United States.

6. These perceptions were born out by the data. Dartmouth-Hitchcock was rated in the bottom 10 percent of academic health centers for the promotion of women into faculty and leadership positions. See *Women in Academic Medicine Statistics and Medical School Benchmarking, 2011–2012* (report by the Association of Academic Medical Centers, Washington, DC, 2012).

7. The team coaching approach was developed by M. M. Godfrey, *Improvement Capability at the Front Lines of Healthcare: Helping through Leading and Coaching* (PhD diss., Jönköping University, School of Health Science, Quality Improvement and Leadership in Health and Welfare, 2013). For more about the program, see http://www.clinicalmicro system.org/.

8. Several key publications summarize the microsystem research and theory. See, for example, E. C. Nelson, P. B. Batalden, and M. M. Godfrey, *Quality by Design: A Clinical Microsystems Approach* (San Francisco: Jossey-Bass, 2007); E. C. Nelson, P. B. Batalden, M. M. Godfrey, and J. C. Lazar, *Value by Design: Developing Clinical Microsystems to Achieve Organizational Excellence* (San Francisco: Jossey-Bass, 2011). For the Microsystem Academy at the Dartmouth Institute, see http://www.clinicalmicrosystem.org/.

9. R. Kegan and L. L. Lahey, *How the Way We Talk Can Change the Way We Work: Seven Languages for Transformation* (San Francisco: Jossey-Bass, 2002).

10. B. L. Fredrickson, "The Broaden-and-Build Theory of Positive Emotions," *Philosophical Transactions Royal Society London Biological Sciences* 359, no. 1449 (2004): 1367–1378. See also A. Suchman, *Leading Change in Healthcare: Transforming Organizations Using Complexity, Positive Psychology and Relationship Centered Care* (London: Radcliffe, 2011).

CHAPTER 10

1. Magnet designation given by the American Nurses Credentialing Center.

2. For the relevance of relational coordination across organizations, see T. G. Rundall, F. M. Wu, V. A. Lewis, K. E. Schoenherr, and S. M. Shortell. "Contributions of Relational Coordination to Care Management in Accountable Care Organizations: Views of Managerial

and Clinical Leaders," *Health Care Management Review* (forthcoming). For bundled payment reforms, see P. S. Hussey, M. S. Ridgely, and M. B. Rosenthal, "The PROMETHEUS Bundled Payment Experiment: Slow Start Shows Problems in Implementing New Payment Models," *Health Affairs* 30, no. 11 (2011): 2116–2124; and R. Mechanic and C. Tompkins, "Lessons Learned Preparing for Medicare Bundled Payments," *New England Journal of Medicine* 367, no. 20 (2012): 1873–1875.

3. C. Lindberg and M. Schneider, "Combating Infections at Maine Medical Center: Insights Into Complexity Informed Leadership from Positive Deviance," *Leadership* 9, no. 2 (2013): 229–253. See also M. Uhl-Bien, M. Marion, and B. McKelvey, "Complexity Leadership Theory: Shifting Leadership from the Industrial Age to the Knowledge Era," *Leadership Quarterly* 18, no. 4 (2007): 298–318.

4. http://www.positivedeviance.org/; J. H. Gittell, J. Beswick, D. Goldmann, and S. Wallack, "Teamwork Methodologies for Accountable Care: Relational Coordination and Team-STEPPS," *Health Care Management Review* 40, no. 2 (2015): 116–125.

5. MRSA refers to methicillin-resistant *Staphylococcus aureus.*

6. A. Singhal and B. Buscell, *Learning to See and Stop MRSA at Billings Clinic* (Bordentown, NJ: Plexus Institute, 2012).

7. J. K. Fletcher, *Disappearing Acts: Gender, Power and Relational Practice at Work* (Cambridge, MA: MIT Press, 1999).

8. For findings that hospitalists achieve better quality and efficiency outcomes through relational coordination with the other disciplines, see J. H. Gittell, D. Weinberg, A. Bennett, J. A. Miller, "Is the Doctor In? A Relational Approach to Job Design and the Coordination of Work," *Human Resource Management* 47, no. 4 (2008): 729–755. See also C. McAllister, L. K. Leykum, H. Lanham, H. S. Reisinger, J. L. Kohn, R. Palmer, C. Pezzia, M. Agar, M. Parchman, J. Pugh, and R. R. McDaniel Jr., "Relationships Within Inpatient Physician Housestaff Teams and Their Association with Hospitalized Patient Outcomes," *Journal of Hospital Medicine* 9 (2014): 764–771.

CHAPTER 11

1. E. H. Schein, *Organizational Culture and Leadership*, 4th ed. (San Francisco: Jossey-Bass, 2010); A. Edmondson, *Teaming: How Teams Learn, Innovate and Compete in the Knowledge Economy* (San Francisco: Jossey-Bass, 2013); E. C. Nelson, P. B. Batalden, and M. M. Godfrey, *Quality by Design: A Clinical Microsystems Approach* (San Francisco: Jossey-Bass, 2007); E. C. Nelson, P. B. Batalden, M. M. Godfrey, and J. C. Lazar, *Value by Design: Developing Clinical Microsystems to Achieve Organizational Excellence* (San Francisco: Jossey-Bass, 2011); A. Suchman, *Leading Change in Healthcare: Transforming Organizations Using Complexity, Positive Psychology and Relationship-Centered Care* (London: Radcliffe, 2011); B. Zimmerman, C. Lindberg, and P. Plsek, *Edgeware: Lessons from Complexity Science for Healthcare Leaders* (Irving, TX: VHA, 1998).

2. T. Suchman, pers. comm.

3. E. Schein, *The Corporate Culture Survival Guide* (San Francisco: Jossey-Bass, 2009).

4. E. H. Schein, *Humble Inquiry: The Gentle Art of Asking Rather Than Telling* (San Francisco: Jossey-Bass, 2013).

5. Similar relational mapping exercises have since been developed by Curt Lindberg for Liberating Structures, Marjorie Godfrey for the Microsystems Academy, and Debbie Friedman and her colleagues for the Service Employee International Union (SEIU) 1199 Labor Management Project.

6. G. J. Langley, R. Moen, K. M. Nolan, T. W. Nolan, C. L. Norman, and L. P. Provost, *The Improvement Guide: A Practical Approach to Enhancing Organizational Performance* (San Francisco: Jossey-Bass, 2009); D. Otley, "Performance Management: A Framework for Management Control Systems Research," *Management Accounting Research* 10, no. 4 (1999): 363–382.

7. W. E. Deming, *Out of the Crisis* (Cambridge, MA: MIT Press, 1986).

8. See M. Valentine, I. Nembhard, and A. Edmondson, "Measuring Teamwork in Health Care Settings: A Review of Survey Instruments," *Medical Care* 53, no. 4 (2015): e16–e30; see also J. H. Gittell, J. Beswick, D. Goldmann, and S. Wallack, "Teamwork Methods for Accountable Care: Relational Coordination and TeamSTEPPS," *Health Care Management Review* 40, no. 2 (2015): 116–125. Of the thirty-nine measures considered by Valentine et al., only 10 met all four criteria for psychometric validation: internal consistency, interrater reliability, structural validity, and content validity. Of the ten fully validated measures, only two were designed for unbounded teams and therefore amenable to measuring teamwork at multiple levels, whether cross-professional, cross-unit, cross-organization, or between patients and providers. These two measures were the Relational Coordination Survey and the Nursing Teamwork Survey. While the Nursing Teamwork Survey can measure teamwork across multiple levels, it is designed to consider the perspective of only one discipline.

9. For access to the Relational Coordination Survey, assistance in customizing it to your particular needs, and help with interpreting results, contact Relational Coordination Analytics at http://rcanalytic.com.

10. J. H. Gittell and C. K. Logan, "The Impact of Relational Coordination on Performance, and How Organizations Support Its Development" (working paper, Brandeis University, 2014).

11. http://rcrc.brandeis.edu/survey/using-survey-for-change.html.

12. H. Lipmanowicz and K. McCandless, *The Surprising Power of Liberating Structures: Simple Rules to Unleash a Culture of Innovation* (Seattle: Liberating Structures Press, 2014).

13. A. Suchman, "When Teammates Don't Connect: Learning to Manage Interdependence," January 30, 2013, http://www.rchcweb.com/Portals/0/Documents/Learning%20to%20Manage%20Interdependence.pdf?ver=2015-10-27-164728-133.

14. M. Williams, "Perspective Taking: Building Positive Interpersonal Connections and Trustworthiness One Interaction at a Time," in *The Oxford Handbook of Positive Organizational Scholarship*, ed. K. S. Cameron and G. M. Spreitzer (New York: Oxford University Press, 2012), 462–473.

15. For information about the Relational Coordination Intervention Workshop, "Improving Work Processes with Relational Coordination," visit http://www.rchcweb.com/Our-Programs/RC-Workshop.

16. M. M. Godfrey, *Improvement Capability at the Front Lines of Healthcare: Helping Through Leading and Coaching* (PhD diss., Jönköping University, 2013).

17. J. M. Cramm and A. Nieboer, "Disease Management: The Need for a Focus on Broader Self-Management Abilities and Quality of Life," *Population Health Management* 18, no. 4 (2014): 246–255.

18. B. L. Fredrickson, "The Broaden-and-Build Theory of Positive Emotions," *Philosophical Transactions Royal Society London Biological Sciences* 359, no. 1449 (2004): 1367–1378.

19. E. H. Schein, pers. comm., 2013.

CHAPTER 12

1. Y. Wadsworth, "Shared Inquiry Capabilities and Differing Inquiry Preferences: Navigating 'Full Cycle' Iterations of Action Research," in *Handbook of Action Research*, ed. Hilary Bradbury, 3rd ed. (London: Sage, 2015), 751–761. See also Y. Wadsworth, "Systemic Human Relations in Dynamic Equilibrium," *Systemic Practice Action Research* 21 (2008): 15–34.

2. J. H. Gittell, J. Beswick, and K. M. McDonald, "Interventional Uses of Relational Coordination: Early Evidence from Four Countries" (working paper, Brandeis University, 2015).

3. L. U. De Sitter, "A System Theoretical Paradigm of Social Interaction: Towards a New Approach to Qualitative System Dynamics," *Annals of System Research* 3, no. 3 (1973): 109–140; E. L. Trist, *The Evolution of Socio-Technical Systems: A Conceptual Framework and an Action Research Program*, Issues in the Quality of Working Life (Toronto: Ontario Quality of Working Life Centre, 1981); J. Achterbergh and D. Vriens, *Organizations: Social Systems Conducting Experiments* (Dordrecht: Springer, 2009).

4. C. Kenney and D. Berwick, *Transforming Health Care: Virginia Mason Medical Center's Pursuit of the Perfect Patient Experience* (Boca Raton, FL: CRC Press, 2010); P. Plsek, *Accelerating Health Care Transformation with Lean and Innovation: The Virginia Mason Experience* (New York: Productivity Press, 2013).

5. M. M. Godfrey, "Improvement Capability at the Front Lines of Healthcare: Helping Through Leading and Coaching" (PhD diss., Jönköping University, 2013).

6. A. Chandrasekaran, C. Senot, and K. K. Boyer, "Process Management Impact on Clinical and Experiential Quality: Managing Tensions Between Safe and Patient-Centered Healthcare," *Manufacturing and Service Operations Management* 14, no. 4 (2012): 548–566.

7. E. C. Nelson, P. B. Batalden, and M. M. Godfrey, *Quality by Design: A Clinical Microsystems Approach* (San Francisco: Jossey-Bass, 2007).

8. B. Zimmerman, C. Lindberg, and P. E. Plsek, *Edgeware: Insights from Complexity Science for Health Care Leaders* (Irving, TX: VHA, 1998), as cited in Nelson, Batalden, and Godfrey, *Quality by Design*.

9. R. Ackoff, "Beyond Continual Improvement: Systems-Based Improvement," 2010, https://www.youtube.com/watch?v=OqEeIG8aPPk.

10. J. Dammand, M. Hørlyck, T. L. Jacobsen, R. Lueg, and R. L. Röck, "Lean Management in Hospitals: Evidence from Denmark," *Revista "Administratie si Management Public" (RAMP)* 23 (2014): 19–35.

11. C. Lindberg and M. Schneider, "Combating Infections at Maine Medical Center: Insights Into Complexity-Informed Leadership from Positive Deviance," *Leadership* 9, no. 2 (2013): 229–253.

12. I. C. Chadwick and J. L. Raver, "Continuously Improving in Tough Times: Overcoming Resource Constraints with Psychological Capital," *Academy of Management Proceedings* (New York: Academy of Management, 2013).

13. These insights into the A3 tool were shared by Kim Demacedo of Group Health. For further references on the A3 and other lean tools, see J. Shook and J. P. Womack, *Managing to Learn: Using the A3 Management Process to Solve Problems, Gain Agreement, Mentor and Lead* (Cambridge, MA: Lean Enterprises Institute, 2008); D. Sobek and A. Smalley, *Understanding A3 Thinking: A Critical Component of Toyota's PDCA Management System* (New York: Productivity Press, 2008); J. Liker and J. Meier, *The Toyota Way Fieldbook* (New York: McGraw-Hill, 2005).

14. Gittell, Beswick, and McDonald, "Interventional Uses of Relational Coordination."

15. J. H. Gittell, *The Southwest Airlines Way: Using the Power of Relationships to Achieve High Performance* (New York: McGraw-Hill, 2003).

16. A. Byrne and J. P. Womack, *The Lean Turnaround: How Business Leaders Use Lean Principles to Create Value and Transform Their Company* (New York: McGraw-Hill, 2012).

CHAPTER 13

1. W. Brandel, "Addressing Population Health Management through Team-Based Care at Partners" (working paper, Brandeis University, 2014).

2. J. H. Gittell and C. K. Logan, "The Impact of Relational Coordination for Performance, and How Organizations Support Its Development" (working paper, Brandeis University, 2016).

3. For evidence that shared protocols support high levels of relational coordination, see J. H. Gittell, "Coordinating Mechanisms in Care Provider Groups: Relational Coordination as a Mediator and Input Uncertainty as a Moderator of Performance Effects," *Management Science* 48, no. 11 (2002): 1408–1426. For contrasting evidence, see S. Deneckere, M. Euwema, P. Van Herck, C. Lodewijckx, M. Panella, W. Sermeus, and K. Vanhaecht, "Care Pathways Lead to Better Teamwork: Results of a Systematic Review," *Social Science and Medicine* 75 (2012): 264–268.

4. I. M. Sebastian, "The Influence of Information Systems Affordances on Work Practices in High Velocity, High Reliability Organizations: A Relational Coordination Approach" (PhD diss., University of Hawaii, 2014). For evidence that information systems sometimes support the communication elements of relational coordination but not the relational elements, see D. S. Romanow, "The Impact of IT-Enabled and Team Relational Coordination on Patient Satisfaction" (PhD diss., Georgia State University, 2013).

5. L. Garvin, "A Healthy Connection: Modeling, Prioritizing and Piloting Veterans' My HealtheVet Patient Portal Meaningful Use Measures" (PhD diss., Brandeis University, 2014); T. Otte-Trojel and T. Rundall, "Relational Coordination and Inter-Organizational Patient Portals (working paper, Berkeley School of Public Health, University of California, 2014).

6. S. Ranson, B. Hinings, and R. Greenwood, "The Structuring of Organizational Structures," *Administrative Science Quarterly* 25, no. 1 (1980): 1–17; A. Giddens, *The Constitution of Society* (Berkeley: University of California Press, 1984); W. Orlikowski and J. Yates,

"Genre Repertoire: The Structuring of Communicative Practices in Organizations," *Administrative Science Quarterly* 39, no. 4 (1994): 541–574; S. R. Barley and P. S. Tolbert, "Institutionalization and Structuration: Studying the Links between Action and Institution," *Organization Studies* 18, no. 1 (1997): 93–117; M. S. Feldman, "A Performative Perspective on Stability and Change in Organizational Routines," *Industrial and Corporate Change* 12, no. 4 (2003): 727–752; L. Perlow, J. H. Gittell, and N. Katz, "Contextualizing Patterns of Work Group Interaction: Toward a Nested Theory of Structuration," *Organization Science* 15, no. 5 (2004): 520–536.

CHAPTER 14

1. A relational/structural approach to change is described in K. Kellogg, "Operating Room: Relational Space and Micro-Institutional Changes in Surgery," *American Journal of Sociology* 115 (2009): 657–711; and in J. K. Fletcher, L. Bailyn, and S. Blake-Beard, "Practical Pushing: Creating Discursive Space in Organizational Narratives," in *Critical Management Studies at Work: Negotiating Tensions Between Theory and Practice*, ed. J. W. Cox, T. G. LeTrent-Jones, M. Voronov, and D. Weir (Northampton, MA: Edward Elgar, 2009), 82–93.

2. Student essay written as part of the application process for membership in the National Honor Society.

3. J. H. Gittell, K. Cameron, S. Lim, and V. Rivas, "Relationships, Layoffs and Organizational Resilience: Airline Industry Responses to September 11th," *Journal of Applied Behavioral Science* 42, no. 3 (2006): 300–329.

4. J. H. Gittell, *The Southwest Airlines Way: Using the Power of Relationships to Achieve High Performance* (New York: McGraw-Hill, 2003).

5. M. Buber, *I and Thou* (New York: Simon and Schuster, 1937).

6. J. Hoffer, "The Socially Embedded Human Subject: A Moral Standpoint for Achieving Social Justice" (thesis, Reed College, 1985).

7. B. E. Wexler, *Brain and Culture: Neurobiology, Ideology and Social Change* (Cambridge, MA: MIT Press, 2006).

8. K. S. Cameron, J. E. Dutton, and R. E. Quinn, *Positive Organizational Scholarship: Foundations of a New Discipline* (San Francisco: Jossey-Bass, 2003); J. Dutton and B. Ragins, *Exploring Positive Relationships at Work: Building a Theoretical and Research Foundation* (Mahwah, NJ: Lawrence Erlbaum, 2006).

9. C. D. Ryff and B. H. Singer, *Emotion, Social Relationships and Health* (New York: Oxford University Press, 2001); T. F. Seeman, "Social Ties and Health: The Benefits of Social Integration," *Annals of Epidemiology* 6 (1996): 442–451.

10. E. D. Heaphy and J. E. Dutton, "Positive Social Interactions and the Human Body at Work: Linking Organizations and Physiology," *Academy of Management Review* 33, no. 1 (2008): 137–162.

11. R. J. Gittell and A. Vidal, *Community Organizing: Building Social Capital as a Development Strategy* (Thousand Oaks, CA: Sage, 1999); R. Putnam, *Bowling Alone: The Collapse and Revival of American Community* (New York: Simon and Schuster, 2001); W. Baker, *Achieving Success Through Social Capital* (San Francisco: Jossey-Bass, 2000).

12. A. Smith, *The Wealth of Nations* (1776; repr. New York: Bantam Classics, 2003).

13. E. Saez, "Striking It Richer: The Evolution of Top Incomes in the United States" (working paper, University of California, Berkeley, September 3, 2012).

14. Reich, R. *Inequality for All*, directed by J. Kornbluth (Los Angeles: 72 Productions, 2013), DVD.

15. J. P. Shonkoff and D. A. Phillips, eds. *From Neurons to Neighborhoods: The Science of Early Childhood Development* (Washington, DC: National Academy Press, 2000).

16. B. E. Wexler, *Brain and Culture: Neurobiology, Ideology and Social Change* (Cambridge, MA: MIT Press, 2006).

17. D. S. Wilson, S. Hayes, A. Biglan, and D. Embry, "Evolving the Future: Toward a Science of Intentional Change," *Brain and Behavioral Sciences* 37, no. 4 (2014): 395–416.

18. R. Gittell and A. Vidal, *Community Organizing: Building Social Capital as a Development Strategy* (Thousand Oaks, CA: Sage, 1998).

19. E. Ostrom, *Governing the Commons: The Evolution of Institutions for Collective Action* (Cambridge: Cambridge University Press, 1990).

20. R. Kanso, M. Hewstone, E. Hawkins, M. Waszcuk, and A. C. Nobre, "Power Corrupts Co-Operation: Cognitive and Motivational Effects in a Double EEG Paradigm," *Social Affective and Cognitive Neuroscience* 9 (2014): 218–224.

INDEX